INDIAN LIBRARY AND INFORMATION SCIENCE LITERATURE
(1990-1991)

CONCEPTS IN COMMUNICATION
INFORMATICS & LIBRARIANSHIP
(CICIL)

For a list of titles in this series,
see pp. 393 at the end of the book

Concepts in Communication
Informatics & Librarianship-59

General Editor : **S.P. Agrawal**

INDIAN LIBRARY AND INFORMATION SCIENCE LITERATURE (1990-1991)

SEWA SINGH
Reader
Department of Library and Information Science
Guru Nanak Dev University
Amritsar

CONCEPT PUBLISHING COMPANY, NEW DELHI 110059

ISBN 81-7022-523-X

First Published 1994

Published and Printed by
Ashok Kumar Mittal
Concept Publishing Company
A/15-16, Commercial Block, Mohan Garden
NEW DELHI-110059 (India)

Lasertypeset by
Printing Express
H-13, Bali Nagar
NEW DELHI-110015

GENERAL EDITOR'S INTRODUCTION

During the past two decades there has been a phenomenal development in the field of Library and Information Science (LIS) in India. Government involvement in improving the library and information services has been mainly responsible for this changed scenario. University Grants Commission's efforts, in particular, have brought about revolutionary change in the University and College libraries. Based on Commission's generous grants and favourable attitude towards libraries, some of the University libraries have made spectacular development, quantitatively and qualitatively. With the quantum jump in the university libraries, a large number of schools of education (LISE) Library and Information Science has come up for providing education and training to ever increasing aspirants of library profession. LISE Schools are also engaged in research work on LIS and are producing professional literature on different aspects of LIS through their journals and other means. Besides these, specialised libraries information bureaus which have been set up by industries and government departments have also made their presence felt in the domain of LIS Services. The special libraries and information bureaus are also bringing out journals and occasional monographs relating to their specialised jobs. All together these have been responsible for the appreciable growth of the LIS literature in India.

Importance of professional literature cannot be over emphasised. It helps the librarians and information scientists to keep abreast of the new trends and developments in their profession and to enhance their skill in performance of their professional duties. It is a matter of great concern that much of the professional writings as reported in our journals and seminars and conferences is not properly recorded for study and citation and whatever is reported is not rated very high. Some of these writings, none-the-less are of high grade quality and display depth and imagination. Moreover, it may not be irrelevant to mention in their connection that even in developed countries which are for ahead of us in LIS matters and which have enormous resources at their command, there is a general feeling that the professional literature produced by their libraries, information centres and schools of education hardly stands comparison with the literature brought out in other disciplines. There is also valid criticism that the research work done by the LIS schools there is meagre.

To bring this literature, which is scattered in various forms, under Bibliographical Control is a difficult task indeed. So far as periodical contents are concerned the problem can be sorted out, but the difficulty arises when it comes to collect the proceedings of the seminars and conferences and the reports brought out on LIS by the Central or State Government – in fact even those by professional bodies. To obtain reports or information from the Government departments is the most exasperating job, as the Government officials, are always reluctant to furnish the same to those who need them. And the offices of professional bodies do not care less.

Dr. Sewa Singh has done commendable job by publishing two such listing on the subject covering the period from 1981 to 1989.

The present publication in CICIL series covers the period of 1990 and 1991. Barring LIS dissertation and grey literature, the annotated bibliography attempts to include articles (in English language only) published in Indian LIS journals, books, monographs, proceedings of the seminars and conferences and reports of the government and non-government agencies, as also articles by Indian authors in foreign journals, books, etc. This publication is a penetrating task for providing the latest developments in the field and will prove very useful for LIS profession – Administrators, Educationists, Researchers and Students alike. It is hoped to issue 1992-93 update and keep it current.

S.P. AGRAWAL

PREFACE

There is greater awareness now than before on the importance of library services in learning, scholarship, knowledge advancement, problems solving, etc. It is being increasingly recognised that information is an essential input to development process, and libraries as storehouses of knowledge and information provide vital support. Informations now is regarded as resource of resources. This application of the importance of information will make far better informed users, and their level of expectation will be much higher. This introduces elements of change and the role of library and information centres has already changed in the Western society. Due to this favourable environment the role of libraries and information centres has been undergoing a change also in India during the last more than a decade or so.

On looking at the library scene in India, we find all round development in all types of libraries and documentation/information centres. The development of public libraries has been greatly helped by the Raja Rammohun Roy Library Foundation ever since its establishment. Although the exact figures about the census of public libraries are not available, yet it can be concluded that they constitute the largest library system in the country.

At present there are about 200 universities and about 8,000 colleges in the country. The number of various types of schools is in thousands. Almost all the universities and colleges have set up libraries of various sizes, but unfortunately a large number of schools do not have their libraries.

A large number of special libraries and information centres have been set up in the country in the areas of sciences and technology, agriculture, defence, medicine, social science, arts and humanities. These are developing a sound and balanced collection equipped with gadgets of modern technology.

All these libraries have become agents of change and active force in the programmes of institutions, society and nation. They make a significant contribution to the educational advancement, cultural enrichment, scientific and technological development, economic progress. Correspondingly, the libraries of today have not only to organise the variety of documentary and non-documentary sources of information but also to make available the specific information to the users. For performing these functions, they, today and tomorrow, need essentially to know new publications, their sources, and the forms in which they are available.

There has also been development in the LIS education in the country. The number of LIS schools at the university level alone has grown tremendously, taking their strength to more than 78 in which are working about 300 teachers. Together these schools produce about 2,700 first degree holders, 400 to 450 with M L I Sc degrees, about 30 to 35 M Phil degree holders, and between 5-10 with Ph D degrees every year.

This all round growth has resulted in the growth of professional literature published in about 25 active English language journals; some regional language journals; while some publish abroad. LIS literature is also reported in the proceedings of seminars/conferences organised by the various national level associations, state level associations, and specialised associations, etc.

Besides, the professional literature is also publishing in book form by many Indian authors now. It is estimated that about 25-30 books are published in India every year. These also include the various festschrift volumes brought out in honour of the library professionals, books edited for other purposes from time to time, and so on.

Some literature is also brought out in report form by various government and non-government agencies, such as the University Grants Commission, Planning Commission, Raja Rammohun Roy Library Foundation, etc.

This plethora of literature being published in Indian sources is increasing every year since the last few years, and has now reached the annual average of about 700 items. It, therefore, requires bibliographical control to have easy access to all the items of published literature. Efforts are being made at the national level, particularly by IASLIC by publishing *Indian Library Science Abstract,* which unfortunately has not been up-to-date.

Besides, various bibliographies on LIS literature published in India have been compiled from time to time. The earliest being the one by Prof P N Kaula in 1956; and the latest bibliography has been compiled by Dr Sewa Singh in 1991 for the period 1986-89. Another bibliography has been compiled by B M Gupta for the 1970-90 period, but there are hardly any items published in 1990 in it. Moreover, it is largely duplication of earlier bibliographies of this authors.

Some specialised bibliographies in classification and cataloguing, library education, Colon Classification, etc have also been compiled from time to time. For some LIS journals in India cumulative indexes have been brought out recently, e.g, for Annals of Library Science and Documentation, Herald of Library Science, Library Science with a slant to Documentation and Information Studies. Some bibliographies for Ph D theses and MLISc dissertations are also available. This provides, in brief, an overview of the various bibliographical control efforts made from time to time. However, these remain dated, and even the *Indian Library Science Abstracts* is not up-to-date, nor is it fully comprehensive in its coverage because it does not include articles published in books edited for various purposes.

The present work is an attempt at bibliographic control of the publications pertaining to the Indian librarians, library and information science teachers, and other scholars, of different aspects of library and information science. It cover the following :

- Articles published in LIS journals in English language only;
- Literature published in the form of books, monographs, reports, edited books, conference/seminar proceedings, etc;
- Articles by Indian LIS authors in foreign journals, books, etc;
- Contribution of foreign authors published in Indian LIS journals, books, etc.

It does not include in its scope the Ph D theses and M L I Sc dissertations. It also excludes 'grey literature', book reviews, notes and news, and the like. This bibliographical work covers the published literature for the first two years of the 1990s, i.e., 1990 and 1991 only.

Thus besides being a useful guide for librarians, this annotated bibliography is equally important, rather a *sine qua non*, for researchers, students and teachers who want to conduct survey in any branch of Indian library and information science literature.

It avoids any duplicate effort already attempted in other bibliographical sources, and includes only that professional literature published during the two years of 1990 and 1991.

Although no effort has been spared to scan all the possible sources available in different university libraries at Amritsar, Chandigarh,

Kurukshetra, Patiala, Delhi, etc yet a few of these might have eluded me due to a variety of reasons. One notable reason has been the time lag in publication of journals, so much so that till now some of them have not published their complete volumes for 1991. A comprehensive coverage for the years 1990-1991 is, therefore, not claimed, though that has been the cherished goal.

Despite this the total number of contributions has gone up during the last two years when compared with any other two years of the 1980s. The total citations included in Sewa Singh's two bibliographies for 1980s is about 4,650 for the period 1981-89, with an yearly average of 516 items. However, the yearly average for 1986-89 is about 665 items which is close to the annual average for 1990-91.

The present volume includes a total of 1412 citations, including 90 citations for 1989 which remained uncovered in the bibliography for 1986-89. Thus it brings the actual citations for 1990-91 to 1322, but at the same time about 100 contributions for 1991 still remain uncovered in the present volume. It shows a remarkable increase in the Indian contribution to the body of LIS literature in recent years. This increase speaks volumes of the maturity of Indian librarianship and greater awareness among the library and information professionals, a step in the right direction.

For the compilation of this volume well recognised national and international practices of bibliographies have closely been followed. Standard abbreviations with minor variations are used for the periodicals covered. To meet the needs of the complexities of LIS literature published in these years, the citations are arranged in classified order according to the 20th Edition of Dewey Decimal Classification system with extended schedules at various places depending on the requirements of literature. Both the subject headings and their notational representation in DDC numbers are given for the convenience of the professional users. The citations are arranged alphabetically by author/s under each subject heading. For the quick and relevant retrieval, all the references are serially numbered. The full bibliographical information with regard to an item is in this order : Citation number, Author/s, Title of article, Name of the journal (in abbreviated form), Volume number, issue number/s, month/s, year/s, particular pages, and annotation or abstract. All the citations included in this bibliographical guide are fully annotated. The abstracts/annotations are informative in nature in most of the cases so as to provide useful and required information to the needy users.

This work is divided into four parts. Part I includes citations on subjects like general knowledge, computers, bibliographies, etc (000-019); Part II covers citations on different aspects of library and information science (020-029); while Part III includes citations on other related subjects including library legislation (030-999). Part IV includes two indexes : Subject Index and Author Index which refer to the citation number/s included in Parts I-III.

The hours of overwork, effort, and sweat involved in the preparation of this volume will mean a time well invested if it is of any help and use to the librarians, LIS teachers, researchers, foreign scholars interested in Indian librarianship, and students surveying literature and gathering necessary information on various facets of library and information science.

I would like to express my thanks to the personnel of various libraries who allowed me free access to their holdings. Thanks are due to friends in the profession who helped me in ways more than one. However, I would like to record my sincere thanks to Prof P B Mangla, Krishan Kumar, and J L Sardana of the University of Delhi; Ms Rekha Mittal of INSDOC, New Delhi; Dr Jasmer Singh of Punjabi University, Patiala; Dr P S G Kumar of University of Nagpur; Dr B B Shukla, Editor, Indian Journal of Information, Library & Society; Sh D R Kalia, Editor, CLIS Observer; Sh G S Dhillon of CSIO, Chandigarh; the Editor, *Granthana*; the Editor, *College Librarian*; the Editor, *Annals of Library Literature*; and others. My wife, Narinder Kaur, and children deserve my appreciation for their patience and cooperation in completing the work in time. For mistakes, if any, the responsibility is entirely mine. I am finally obliged to M/s Concept Publishing Company, New Delhi for undertaking the publishing of this volume.

SEWA SINGH

CONTENTS

ABBREVIATIONS AND THEIR EXPLANATIONS

ALIS	**Sharma, C D** and **Ojha, D C,** *eds* Advances in library and information science, 2v, Jaipur : RBSA Publishers, 1988-89.
CALNE	**Vashishth, C P,** *ed* Computerization and library networks : Seminar papers, thirty-sixth All India Library Conference, University of Jodhpur, Dec 26-29, 1990, Delhi : ILA, 1990. viii, 345 p.
CPT	**Khan, H A** and **Ijari, S R,** *eds* Current problems and trends in library and information services : Prof K S Deshpande festschrift volume, Varanasi : Indian Bibliographical Centre, 1990. iii, 370 p.
DLIS	**Venkatappaiah,** V, et al, *eds* Dimensions of library and information science : Kaula festschrift, New Delhi : Concept Publishing Company, 1990. 690 p.
DRTC 1989	**DRTC, Bangalore** Annual Seminar, 23, 1989 : Computer software for information work and services, edited by I K Ravichandra Rao, Bangalore : DRTC, 1989. various pagings.
HLAICI	Handbook of libraries, archives and information centres in India, edited by B M Gupta, New Delhi: Aditya Prakashan, vol 7-10, 1990-91.
IASLIC	Indian Association of Special Libraries and Information Centres, Calcutta.
ILA	Indian Library Association, Delhi.
IM	**Chatterjee, Amitabha** and **Sen, Subir,** *eds* Information management in library and information centres in India, Papers, Calcutta: IASLIC, 1991. iv, 75p.

ISL **Dhyani, Pushpa**
Information science and libraries, New Delhi : Atlantic Publishers and Distributors, 1990. viii, 288 p.

LISE **Tejomurty, A**, *ed*
Library and information science education and teaching methods (Papers of Ujjain and Gulbarga Seminars), Jaipur : RBSA Publishers, 1991. 251 p.

MLC National Seminar on Modernisation of library catalogue, 5-7 March 1990: Reading material, Waltair : Dept of Library and Information Science, Andhra University, 1990. various pagings.

MLSUL National seminar on Modernisation of library services in university libraries, Sept 22-23, 1989 : Papers and proceedings, Mysore University Library, 1989. x, 166 p.

NIPP National information policies and programmes : Seminar papers, 37th All India Library Conference, IIT Madras, Dec 4-7, 1991, Delhi : ILA, 1991. iv, 463 p.

OPMC **Nagarajan, S** and **Jain, H C,** *eds*
Online information processing through mini and micro computers, New Delhi : Batra Book Service, 1989. 237 p.

OSUL **Sood, S P** and **Sharma, C L,** *eds*
Outstanding studies in university librarianship, Jaipur: RBSA Publishers, 1991 x, 278 p.

PL **Devarajan, G, Gopalakrishanan, Nair, P** and **Rajan, A C,** *eds*
Professional librarianship : C A Augustine festschrift, New Delhi : Ess Ess Publications, 1991. xiv, 121 p.

PLSI **Augustine, C A** and **Devarajan, G,** *eds*
Public library system in India, New Delhi : Ess Ess Publications, 1990. xii, 135 p.

PLSP **Punjab Library Association, Patiala**
Seminar on public library system in Punjab, held at Punjabi University, Patiala, Nov 22-23, 1991, Seminar Papers, Patiala: Punjab Library Association, 1991. vi, 184 p.

SALP	**IASLIC, Calcutta** Status and authority of library profession in library management, *Papers* presented at the 14th National Seminar, Mysore, 14-17 Nov 1990; edited by Amitabha Chatterjee, Subir Sen, S K Kapoor and M N Nagaraj, Calcutta : IASLIC, 1990. 97 p.
SSI	**Binwal, J C, Chandel, A S** and **Saraf, Veena** Social science information : Problems and prospects, New Delhi: Har-Anand Publications, in association with Vikas Publishing House, 1990. xvi, 494 p.
ULI	**Prasher, R G,** *ed* University libraries in India ; 1980s and beyond : Essays in honour of Prof T P Saxena, New Delhi : Medallion Press, 1991. viii, 290 p.

LIST OF JOURNALS INDEXED

AGLIS Jl	AGLIS Journal
Ann Lib Lit	Annals of Library Literature
Ann Lib Sc & Doc	Annals of Library Science and Documentation
CLIS Observer	CLIS Observer
College Libn	College Librarian – a Forum
DESIDOC Bull	DESIDOC Bull
Granthana	Granthana; Indian Journal of Library Studies
Her Lib Sci	Herald of Library Science
IASLIC Bull	IASLIC Bulletin
Ind Exp	Indian Express
Ind Jl Inf Lib & Society	Indian Journal of Information Library and Society
ILA Bull	ILA Bulletin
INICAE	International Information Communication and Education
Int Forum Inf & Doc	International Forum of Information and Documentation
Int Lib Move	International Library Movement
Jl Lib & Inf Sci	Journal of Library and Information Science
Lib Her	Library Herald
Lib Progress (Int)	Library Progress (International)
Lib Sci slant Doc & Inf Std	Library Science slant to Documentation and Information Studies
Lib Today	Library Today
Luck Libn	Lucknow Librarian
NISSAT Newsletter	NISSAT Newsletter
RILISAR Bull	RILISAR Bulletin
SISCOM	SISCOM
Univ News	University News

PART-I

KNOWLEDGE, COMPUTER SCIENCE, BIBLIOGRAPHIES, ETC

001 KNOWLEDGE

Chattopadhyaya, D P 1

World of words, *Granthana* 1(1) Jan 1990 : 10-18.

Explains and discovers the world of words through philosophical expression. Answers many associated and interesting questions regarding the power of words.

Khanna, J K 2

Communicating knowledge, vol 1: Gateway to knowledge, Kurukshetra : Research Publications, 1990, 418 p.

Divided into five chapters. Highlights the techniques being used by the librarians to face the intellectual challenges being thrown by the knowledge explosion and proliferation of literature.

001.2 Scholarship and Learning

Taher, Mohamed 3

American studies in India, *HLAICI,* v 8, 230-240.

Provides importance of American studies. Traces development of American studies in India. Discusses individual contributions from Indian Americanists, on American literature, American politics. Describes institutional contributions in our dimensions such as teaching and research agencies, funding agencies, document resource centres, and other agencies and bodies. Also lists documentary contributions.

002 THE BOOK

Ghatak, Arun Kumar 4

Books-libraries in ancient India : A brief historical survey, *College Libn* 6 (1-4) 1990: 21-24.

Traces origin of writing in general and in India. Mentions some monasteries where reading and writing of Manuscripts was done. Discusses some important monasteries where libraries were also set up such as Nalanda, Vikramsila, Odantapuri, Vallabhi, etc.

Kunze, H C Horst 5

My attitude towards the book and its illustrations, *DLIS*, 375-380.

Deals with book promotion activities particularly with illustrated works. Describes the development of illustrations and illustrated works in Germany stating also significance and advantages. This paper is based on the "Kaula Endowment Lecture" delivered in Berlin in Nov 1986, and published in *Herald of Lib Sc* 28 (1-2) Jan-Apr 1989 : 75-79.

Venugopal, M V and Kanakachary, M 6

Books for common man : Proceedings of the seminar, *Her Lib Sc* 30 (3-4) July-Oct 1991 : 254-255.

Reports about a seminar to discuss the problem of books and information paticularly to serve the common man, held in March 1991 at the City Central Libraray, Hyderabad. Directed by A K Dasgupta. D B Eswara Reddy gave the introductory remarks. About a dozen papers on different aspects of the topic were presented.

003 SYSTEMS

Curras, Emilia 7

Dialectic interaction in science, *INICAE* 9(1) Mar 1990 : 5-17.

Gives a background of system dialectics referring to the "dialectics systems". Explains science as a system, presenting mental outline of science system split into primary and secondary modes with real and conceptual components. Attempts to classify the system using taxonomy of system theory. Examines variable elements. Discusses informations recearch leading to dicoveries and inventions in science system.

004 COMPUTER SCIENCE

Mohan Krishna, P 8

Introducing computers, *DLIS,* 171-197.

Defines computer. Describes computer generations from I to IV. Discusses types of computers, categories of computers, hardware, software, output devices etc.

004.16 MICROCOMPUTERS

Devadason, F J 9

Microcomputers and MS DOS, *MLC*, 1-24.

Explains the necessity and support microcomputers give in using its potentialities in aplication to library operations. Describes computers, microcomputer, memory, external storage, I/O devices, communication interface, LAN, software, OS, DBMS, MS-DOS and its commands.

004.69(1) HYPERTEXT

Bedi, D S 10

Hypertext-an aid to information seeking, *DESIDOC Bull* 10 (3) May 1990 : 3-10.

Gives an introduction to the world of hypertext. Discusses features of an ideal hypertext system focussing on machine-supported links as its essential features. Surveys some of the important design issues. Outlines major application areas of hypretext technology. Highlights advantages and disadvantages of the hypertext systems.

005.3 SOFTWARE, PROGRAMS

Saha, Sharmila 11

WIPRO SIM Plus : A general purpose simulation software, *DRTC 1989*, G 1-11

Discusses merits and demerits of simulation as an OR technique an some of the well known simulation software. Focusses on general purpose simulation package developed by WIPRO. Gives its features, philosophy and structure.

005.71 DATA COMMUNICATION

Agrawal, I K 12

Data communication facilities in India, *NIPP*, 355-370.

Describes the salient features, functioning of and access to Gateway Packet Switching System (GPSS) of the Videsh Sanchar Nigam. Gives main features of various networks in operation in India. Explains other specialised informantion networks as BTISNET, CALIBNET, DELNET, SIRNET, ERNET, etc.

005.8 DATA SECURITY

Tejomurty, A and **Bose, Kaushik** 13

Security and privacy in a network enviroment, *NIPP*, 344-349.

Discusses the concept of secruity and privacy in a network environment. Stresses the need to take precautionary measures to check the unauthorised access and routing the information illegally. Highlights various preventive measures. Discusses cryptography and concludes that in near future various specific systems will be developed to deal with the problem.

011.38 TALKING BOOKS

Clyke, Frank Kurt 14

Long term planning for talking book programme, *Her Lib Sc* (1-2) Jan-Apr 1990 : 68-69.

Narrates the programme and services of the National Library Service for the Blind and Physically Handicapped (NLS), Library of Congress, Washington, DC. Explains the study launched to improve services and finds out alternatives.

PART-II

LIBRARY AND INFORMATION SCIENCE

002 LIBRARY AND INFORMATION SCIENCE

Amudhavalli, A 15

Librarianship in transition, *PL,* 25-28.

Considers some of the challenges of library profession that lie ahead in the future. Discusses various factors that break from the traditional look and take to enter into modern information society so as to convert it into information science.

Bankapur, M B and **Kalpana, K** 16

Knowledge and skills needs for various types of services in library and information sector, *Lib Her* 29 (1-2) Apr-Sept 1990 : 72-82.

States that present day informaion system is mostly of evolutionary kind caused by technology, social pressures and growth of recorded knowledge. Highlights basic characteristics such as good administration, reasoning power, commonsense, motivation, value judgement, conceptual framework etc among library professionals to know the user problems.

Bhattacharyya, G 17

Library and information service as a profession, *SALP*, 1-11.

Explains the term profession. Describes self-consciousness of a profession and its significant features. Discusses fundamental nature of foundation discipline. Describes the commonality in the approach for professional manpower development. Explains the current status of library an information service. Concludes that persons engaged in rendering library and information service are definitely library professionals as they have to acquire specialised knowldge.

Deogan, M S 18

Is librarianship a dying profession? *SALP*, 21-24.

Discusses the basic function of librarianship, i.e., supplying books and related material. States that the persent scene is changing because of onslaught of IT and user has become more demanding. Explains the disparity between means and ends which causes threat to librarianship. Suggests for self-perceptions and catch with the times.

Dhyani, Pushpa 19

Information science and libraries, New Delhi : Atlantic Publishers and Distributors, 1990. viii, 288p.

Includes twelve articles contributed by eminent scholars from abroad and India who have extensive theoretical and practical experience. Deals with the different aspects of information science.

Gopalakrishnan, S 20

Need for a new breed of information professionals, *NIPP*, 403-407.

States that development of technology is changing the role of information and its management necessitating information professionals to be exposed to new technologies. Analyses the need for new breed of information professionals.

Gopinath, M A 21

Librarianship in library management, *Lib Sc slant Doc & Inf Std* 26 (4) Dec 1989 : 273-284.

Defines library and librarianship. Gives areas of activity of librarianship centreing around collection development, collection organisation and users' services. Proposes structural changes in the library profession.

Gopinath, M A 22

A plan for librarian's adaptation to changing information environment, *Lib Sc slant Doc & Inf Std* 27 (2) June 1990 : 90- 103.

Discusses impact of IT on changing information environment in society. Identifies role of information professionals as to provide access to information. Calls for change in knowledge and skill. Provides a module for a course in IT for information professionals.

Gopinath, M A 23

Librarianship in library management : Keynote address, *IASLIC Bull* 35 (4) Dec 1990 : 135-142.

Delivered as the Keynote address, explains the purpose of a library. Discusses areas of activities of librarianship centreing round collection development, collection organisation and users' service. Proposes structural changes in the profession, and the role of librarian and communicator.

Kalia, D R 24

From the Editor; an appeal, *CLIS Observer* 7 (3-4) July- Dec 1990: 67-68.

Makes a fervent appeal to the librarians, heads of teaching department to subscribe to the professional journal *CLIS Observer* as otherwise it will stop publication from Jan 1992.

Kalia D R 25

Libraries and the Eighth Five Year Plan (1990-95), *CLIS Observer* 7(1-2) Jan-June 1990: 1-4.

Describes in this Editorial the appointment of the Working Group on libraries and informatics by the Planning Commission, Government of India, for the Eighth Five Year Plan period. Gives the financial outlay as recommended by the Working Group for different components of libraries and information services.

Kaula, P N 26

Elucidation of major issues in library science, *Her Lib Sc* 29 (1-2) Jan-Apr 1990: 76-87.

Records a brief account of Prof P N Kaula's lectures, etc. delivered throughout the country at places like Allahabad, Agra, Pune, Jaipur, Varanasi, Aurangabad, Calcutta, Imphal, Gwalior, Aligarh, Hyderabad and Lucknow from Dec 1989 to April 1990.

Kaula, P N 27

Rethinking on engima infested profession, *Her Lib Sc* 29 (1-2) Jan-Apr 1990: 50-62.

Explains the team work followed in the profession in early days and praiseworthy task of IASLIC. As a result of dynamics of change, information deluge, etc., there comes the use of IT. States its impact on libraries including INFLIBNET, VIDYANET, etc for modernisation of library services. Explains the present paradoxical situation. Discusses need for planning the manpower in view of new demands.

Kaula, P N 28

Women studies with specific reference to their role in librarianship and networking, *Her Lib Sc* 29 (3-4) July-Oct 1990 : 193-200.

States the concept of area studies. Points out place of women studies in it. Discusses status of women in Indian society. Examines role of women in librarianship in US, UK, etc., including India. Suggests need for a database on women studies.

Mahajan, S G 29

Local studies librarianship : National seminar, *Her Lib Sc* 29 (1-2) Jan-Apr 1990 : 94-95.

Describes the inauguration, papers discussed, concluding session, and Resolutions adopted at the National Seminar on Local Studies Librarianship held at University of Poona, Dept of LIS from 19-21 March 1989.

Manorama Srinath 30

Entropy of librarianship, *PL*, 94-97.

Explores causes of entropy of the profession. Analyses such factors as technological innovation, lack of recognition of library staff, role of authorities in university libraries in South India. States that these are responsible for the prevailing status of librarianship.

Matsumoto, Hisao 31

Japan-US Conference on libraries and information science in higher education, *Her Lib Sc* (1-2) Jan-Apr 1990 : 101-102.

Discusses the theme of the fourth Japan-US Conference of Libraries and Information Science in Higher Education held in Racone, Wis, 3-6 October 1988, organised by the International Relations Committee of the ALA.

Mittra, Anubha 32

New challenges and library profession, *SALP*, 93.

Describes that in the information-intensive society library and information professionals must be acquainted with sophisticated user friendly packages, need-based databases, enhanced ES, etc. Mentions that they must be given facility to refresh and up to date his/her experience.

Mukhopadhyay, Kabita 33

Why library science in Generalia class? *College Libn* 6 (1-4) 1990 : 13-14.

Discusses the inclusion of 'Library Science' as a subject in 'Generalia Class' in DDC even after many revisions and editions. States that Ranganathan has dealt with it as independent subject.

Considers various options of including 'Library Science, in 'Arts', 'Social Science', 'Applied Science'.

Ochai, Adakole 34

Librarianship : A self-hating profession, *Int Lib Move* 12 (1) Mar 1990 : 12-18.

Remarks that ours is a self-hating profession. Examines the remark in relation to our actions and inactions in the course of professional practice. Describes the personality of the librarian. Mentions how the poor public image can be improved. Concludes that librarians should recognise themselves as equals to others.

Prins, Hans 35

Status, image and reputation of librarianship : Results of an empirical study, *Jl Lib & Inf Sc* 16 (1) June 1991 :11-24.

Observes that the status, image and reputation of librarianship is considered low. Examines the reasons given by an empirical study conducted by RTMLA. Follows survey research method and analysis is done using statistical techniques including rank method.

Rajan, A C 36

New dimensions of librarianship, *PL*, 44-58.

Mentions that librarianship is changing with social, economic changes. Deals with onward march of profession to information industry today. Explains the challenges of computers, paperless society, shrinking resources. Gives new vistas in librarianship. Describes such services as CAS, clipping, SDI, etc. which constitute new dimensions.

Ramakrishnan, M N 37

Antiprofessional activities of librarians, *PL*, 110-114.

Defines a profession. Describes some anti-professional activities of the senior librarians and the leaders of the profession in order to help new entrants to resist such activities.

Samyuktha, R and **Raghavan, K S** 38

Professional image of library and information workers: An assessment, *SALP*, 27-32.

Studies, on the basis of questionnaire, the self-image of librarians's perception of their role and importance, and identifies any perceptible difference in their self-image on the basis of sex, types of library, income level, experience, age and qualification. Concludes that there is no perceptible difference between different groups.

Sethi, A R 39

Sustainable librarianship, *Lib Her* 30 (2-4) July 1991-Jan 1992 : 216-225.

Explains the concept of sustainable. Traces its history from Adam Smith to Brundtland Reprot. Discusses its relevance in librarianship. Relates sustainable librarianship to the continued growth of stock, staff and services in libraries. Dwells on challenges facing librarianship today. Suggests a framework of premises for its sustainability. Explains how five laws of library science can provide for sustainable librarianship.

Sewa Singh 40

Library profession and modernisation of libraries in India, *PL*, 29-33.

Portraits the picture of library profession by indicating functions of library which are changing for the last three decades or so. Deals with growth of literature and its relation with new media of new technology. Stresses need for modernization of libraries in view of the new IT and computers. Discusses other storage media. Describes need of new breed of librarians and new LIS education in view of the IT applications.

Sharify, Nasser 41

Thoughts on a changing profession : Kaula Endowment Lecture, *Her Lib Sc* 29 (1-2) Jan-Apr 1990 : 70-75.

Through personal reminiscences explains how the author entered library profession. Expresses gratitude to the profession which has honoured him several times. Discusses the role of profession since 1950s and changes that took place in the sixties and took the concept beyond national frontiers to the global role and third world countries. Gives new definition of librarianship with international aspect in view.

Sharma, Prabha 42

Changing information scenario and new roles of the librarians and information professionals, *SALP*, 88.

States that technological development has made tremendous impact on information processing. Discusses that librarians need to develop new roles to meet users needs. Suggests some roles such as that of educator, guide, information consultant, intermediator, and counsellor.

Time to brace up, *NISSAT Newsletter* 9(3) July-Sept 1990. 43

Calls upon the professional associations to extend their activities beyond the organization of annual conferences, and put up a good show in ventures like IFLA General Conference.

Verma, L N 44

Is library and information science a profession? *SALP*, 80-81.

Gives the professional attributes in theoretical perspectives. States that librarianship fulfills these attributes of a profession, but it has to gain the desired recognition.

020(1) LIS – National Policy

Baradol, A K 45

The national policy on information for India, *NIPP*, 18-21.

Describes the need for a national policy on information and its objectives. Explains the areas to be included in the policy on information, viz., computerized databases, CD-ROM, online infomation networks, information technology, etc. Suggests the linkage of the existing computerized databases and online information networks with the international databases.

Barua, B P 46

Towards a national policy on library and information systems, *NIPP*, 5-14.

Makes a brief survey of writings, reports and programmes relating to national library policy from 1944 to 1986. Discusses in detail ideas of Ranganathan. Points out recommendation of Library Advisory Committee, steps taken by Govt. of India, international developments, establishment of CONPOLIS and its report submitted in 1986.

National Policy on Library and Information System - a presentation, *Granthana* 1 (1) Jan 1990 : 62-72. 47

Based on the RRRLF's National Policy on Library and Information System and that of the ILA. This is the final draft on the National Policy. Discusses objectives, public library system, academic library system, special library and information system, national library system and bibliographical services, manpower development and professional status, modernisation of library and information systems, etc.

Paez-Urdaneta, Iraset 48

National information policy and modernization of development : A redefinition of the information professional in the Third World from the point of view of education and social action, *INICAE* 10(2) Sept 1991 : 153-164.

Price, Douglas 49

Future of federal information policies : A summary of FLICC meeting proceedings, *INICAE* 9 (2) Sept 1990 : 206-210.

Mentions about 200th anniversary of the Congress and FLICC joined in celebration. Gives historical perspective of Federal information policies of the Congress. Points out inaccessible government information. Describes the impact of electornic age on government publishing and how government supports the new technology. Mentions the role of ALA in documenting government information. Discusses impact of IT on research, industry, university, and government.

Raja Rammohan Roy Library foundation, Calcutta 50

National Policy on Library and Information System: A draft policy statement, *Granthana* 1(1) Jan 1990 : 55-61.

Reports the National Policy on Library and Information System drafted by the RRRLF for consideration. Considers all aspects of the library development.

Rajeshwari, D 51

National information policy for India, *NIPP*, 15-17.

Mentions need for national information policy. Lists objectives of information policy. Gives functions of national information system and policy for India with factors governing the national information policy. Gives need for international cooperation, and need for standardization.

Swaroop Rani, B S 52

National information policy for data communication facilities, *NIPP,* 380-383.

Gives objectives of a national information policy for data communication with methods to be adopted in India. Explains a protocol model of data communication at various levels for implementation covering all subjects in view of rapidly growing IT. Highlights that India must strive towards having a strong and efficient data communication infrastructure.

Vijayalakshmi, K 53

National information policy for India: Analysis, *NIPP,* 22-27.

Emphasises need for the union and state governments to formulate a policy which ensures the optimum provision for information services to the different sections of society. Covers some of the key elements of this policy, the emerging Indian information scene and manpower development. Demands the need for some urgent areas of action.

020.14 Terminology

Galinski, Christian 54

Terminology work and application, *INICAE* 9(2) Sept 1990: 218-222.

Mentions foundations of terminology by defining it. Gives approaches to terminology work. Discusses structure of terminology science and terminography. Provides applications of terminology. Stresses on the need for cooperation and networking in termino-logy. Describes the responsibility of the subject specialist in this regard.

020.16 LIS – Bibliographies

Sewa Singh 55

Indian library and information science literature (1986-89), New Delhi : Ess Ess Publications, 1991. xxxiv, 612 p.

Includes more than 2,700 citations for 1986-1989 collected from published Indian sources such as books, periodicals. Also includes citations of Indian authors published in foreign sources. Provides informative annotations to all the citations for use by the scholars and researchers. Provides subject and author indexes.

020.18 LIS – Standards

Gupta, Shamsher and **Yadav, Rashmi** 56

Standardisation in library and information work and services, *Int Lib Move* 13(2) June 1991 : 98-101.

Defines standardization. Gives need for standardization. Describes norms and standards for library and information services in India with regard to library building, reading material, and library staff.

Satija, M P 57

Indian standards in information and documentation : Their formulation and sources, *CLIS Observer* 8 (3-4) July-Dec 1991 : 26-32.

Describes the activities of the Bureau of Indian Standards and the formulation of standards for library operations. Lists the standards already issued by the BIS.

Schwaraz, Helga 58

Sharing information by means of standardization, *Jl Lib and Inf Sc* 16(1) June 1991 : 25-33.

Explains the situation of standardization twenty years ago. Describes the seven layers of standardization for a union catalogue. Discusses OSI as standard between system tries to meet requirements of world wide data exchange and processing especially in the field of interlibraty loans, bibliographic search, retrieval and update.

Sewa Singh and **Sukhbir Singh** 59

Library and information science periodicals in India : A study towards standardization, *Her Lib Sc* 29 (3-4) July-Oct 1990 : 200-212.

Defines standards and their kinds. Discusses need for standardization in periodicals. Traces briefly development of LIS journals. Studies in detail various parameters regarding the layout of LIS journals on the basis of standards prepared by ISI (now BSI). Emphasizes need to revise existing standards in view of change in requirements. Offers suggestions.

Vij, Ved P 60

Keep informed about world standards in the competitive market place, *HLAICI* v 7, 219-224.

Explains need for standards informations and the Bureau of Indian Standards, New Delhi. Describes its holdings, technical services, reference enquiry service, bibliographical services, information bulletin, translation service, GATT enquiry point, ISONET, etc.

Vishwa Mohan, V and **Ramakrishna, D** 61

Developing performance standards in library and information system in India, *ILA Bull* 27 (3) Oct-Dec 1991 : 102-106.

Discusses need for performance standards in library and information systems. Outlines model performance standards. Lists various aspects essential for formulation and implementation of performance standards. Suggests that national library associations may have to conduct detailed study to develop precise standards for collecting data relating to performance of professionals.

Viswanathan, T 62

Emerging standards for library networks, *Ann Lib Sc & Dec* 38 (3) Sept 1991 : 79-84.

Discusses the emerging standards for both the bibliographic and network based library services. Illustrates the role of CCF. Explains service definitions and protocol specifications of the standards for interlibrary loan and search and retrieval of databases.

020.15 LIS – Directories

Kar, Rabindranath 63

Directory of librarians and libraries of colleges in West Bengal, *College Libn* 6 (1-4) 1990 : 35-41.

Publishes directory of the Librarians and Asstt Librarians of some of the non-government colleges in West Bengal. States that the directory of government college librarians and libraries will be published later on.

020.3 LIS – Dictionaries/Encyclopaedias

Chopra, R N 64

Dictionary of library science, New Delhi : Anmol Publications, 1990. v, 375 p.

Covers all the concepts and terms about library and information science which help the users to understand the meaning of each of them.

Sharma, Pandey S K 65

Concise encyclopaedia of library and information science, New Delhi : Ess Ess Publications, 1991. 171 p.

Aims at acquainting a librarian with the common technical terms, concepts and activities of computer work and computerized activities in libraries.' Explains 444 major terms culled out of 69 books published since 1950s giving in simple language all relevant aspects of computing from its history to its use in libraries.

Sharma, S K and **Vinod Kumar** 66

World acronyms dictionary of library and information science, Delhi : Sarita Book House, 1991. vii, 184 p.

Includes acronyms in LIS arranged in alphabetical order, and explained for the use of students practising librarians, documentalists and all those who are engaged in the field of information storage and retrieval. Also gives, at the end, currency symbols, abstracting and indexing services.

020.5 LIS – Periodicals

Granthana; Indian Journal of Library Studies 67

Editor : D P Chattopadhyaya

Executive Editor : B P Barua

Address : Raja Rammohun Roy Library Foundation, Calcutta 700064

Vol 1-, 1990-

Half-Yearly

Rs. 175.00

Publishes original contributions, survey reports, reviews, short communications, pertaining to library studies and allied subjects with a slant towards public library.

Ijari, S R and **Kannappanavar, B U** 68

Growth of periodicals in the field of library and information science since 1876, *IASLIC Bull* 35(3) Sept 1990 : 97-103.

Examines growth of periodicals in LIS. Shows that 86.57% of the world output of LIS periodicals started publication during 1950-87, and three-fourth of publishing periodicals are from USA, UK, India, Canada, Australia, West Germany. Also gives recent trends and role of associations.

Journel of Information Sciences 69

Editor : Anil Sharma

Address : Arun Publishing House, SCO 49-51, Sector 17-C, Chandigarh 160017. Vol 1 -, 1990-

Quarterly

Rs. 300.00

Accepts original contributions on new developments in, and thinking about information sciences and related fields, particularly as they affect and support research communication, technology transfer, and innovation.

Society for Information Science, New Delhi 70

Library and information science periodicals in India : A critical study, *Her Lib Sc* 29 (1-2) Jan-Apr 1990 : 102-104.

Studies the number of LIS journals currently published in India, how many regular and on schedule, what kind of topics discussed, their relevance in new context. Covers the period 1983-88. Gives findings and recommendations.

020.621 International Organizations

Dhyani, Pushpa 71

International organisations – in pursuit of informationa services, *ISL*, 187.

Attempts to focus on the role and contributions of four international organisations, namely, FID, IFLA, UNESCO, and VINITI.

020.621 (1) ASTINFO

ASTINFO activities in India, *NISSAT Newsletter,* 10 (4) Oct-Dec 1991 : 19-22. 72

Describes the ASTINFO-UNESCO activities for 1990-91 including CDS/ISIS, marketing of information products and services, teaching aids, oceanographic information, APINMAP, etc.

020.621 (1) FID

Harrison, Colin 73

FID/ET seminer and FID conference, *INICAE* 10 (1) Mar 1991 : 89-94.

Reports about the FID/ET seminar held in Havana, Cuba, giving the theme, areas of research, etc. Also gives reporting of the 45th Congress and Conference.

Ramaiah, L S 74

45th FID Conference and Congress, *Her Lib Sc* 30 (1-2) Jan-Apr 1991 : 80-83.

Reports about the theme and topics for discussion at the 45th FID Conference held at Havana, 19-22 Sept 1990. Describes about its inauguaration, various sessions, papers contributed, pre-Congress seminars, Expo-FID 90 Exhibition, post Congress course, etc.

020.621 IASL

Malahan, I V 75

18th Annual Conference of International Association of School Librarianship: Conference report, *Her Lib Sc* 30 (1-2) Jan-Apr 1991 : 84-85.

Reports about the Conference, its inauguration, sessions and themes of papers, discussions held, business meeting, and book exhibition. The Conference was held at Kuala Lumper, 22-26 July 1989.

020.621 (1) IFLA

Bergdahl, Birgita 76

Advancement of librarianship in the Thirld World : ALP – a proposal for the future, *Jl Lib and Inf Sc* 15 (1) June 1990 : 1-27.

Gives membership, programmes of IFLA and its relation with the Third World. States that the IFLA-ALP Core Programme was launched in Aug 1990 conference of IFLA at Stockholm. Describes various aspects of this Programme, including its need, usefulness, structure and activities.

Mangla, P B 77

IFLA and PAC, *Jl Lib and Inf Sc* 16 (1) June 1919: 1-10.

Gives details about IFLA. Describes activities and programmes of Preservation and Conservation (PAC) Core Programme of IFLA. Deals with such areas as publications, audiovisual programmes, conference, seminar and training. Describes in brief activities of the Regional Centre.

Mobley, Emly R 78

Libraries-information for knowledge: 56th IFLA General Conference, 1990, *Her Lib Sc* 30 (3-4) July-Oct 1991 : 244-247.

Reports about the 56th IFLA General Conference held at Stockholm, Sweden during Aug 18-24, 1990, with a total of 5,000 persons present from 120 countries. His Majesty King Carl XVI Gustaf opened the Conference. The topics debated included impact of new technology, rising prices, censorship, educating public, etc.

020.621(1) UNESCO

Lahiri, A 79

UNESCO information activities in India, *NISSAT Newsletter* 10(2) April-June 1991 : 9-11.

Attempts to assess the impact and contribution of ASTINFO/PGI activities in the overall development of library and information service in India. Lists some supported events in India during 1985-90.

Montviloff, V 80

UNESCO concept and experience in the formulation of national STI policies, *NIPP,* 1-4.

States that formulation and implementation of national information policies and plans is an important aspect of the activities of UNESCO (PGI). Explains the utility of national information policies for the development and management of efficient information systems and services. Describes the role of PGI in encouraging member states in formulating national information polcies. Also identifies some problems.

020.62254 National Library Associations – India

Krishan Kumar 81

Library professional associations and adult education, *ILA Bull* 27 (3) Oct-Dec 1991 :135-141.

Underlines the significance of literacy for the well being of nation. Discusses the role of library associations in developing standards of library services. Makes out a case for strong and effective public library network.

Pulla Reddy, V 82

Academic librarians and library associations, *CLIS Observer* 8 (3-4) July-Dec 1991 : 18-22.

Identifies extent of membership of library associations held by college and university librarians of Delhi. Gives classification of associations as well as that of membership. Surveys the extent of involvement of academic librarians of Delhi in library associations of the country.

020.62254 (1) Academy of Library Science

Academy of Library of Information Sciences, *HLAICI,* v 10, 146-147. 83

Deals with the management, membership, finances, and activities of the Academy established in 1975 with office in Trivandrum.

020.62254(1) Academy of Library Science and Documentation

Ramaiah, L S 84

Academy of Library Science and Documentation, *HLAICI,* v 10, 148-154.

Gives origin and aims and objectives of the Academy. Mentions about its membership, management and finances. Explains in details its activities such as conferences, seminars, lectures, education and training programmes. Gives other activities also.

020.62254(1) AIPLA

Narayana Rao, Kodati, Ramchandra Rao, T and **Venkatappaiah, V** 85

All India Public Library Association (AIPLA), 1919-1979, *HLAICI,* v 10, 7-13.

Mentions public library movement as a product of national

awakening. Traces history from 1918 when Government Conference of Librarians was held at Lahore. Discusses about the various all-India public library conferences held since 1919 and their achievement. Gives account of the *Indian Library Journal* started in 1924, efforts towards library legislation, library education, etc.

020.62254(1) AALDI

Moitra, S 86

The Association of Agricultural Librarians and Documentalists of India (AALDI), *HLAICI,* v 10, 14-17.

Traces origin of AALDI. Gives its aims and objectives, structure and membership. Explains various activities such as seminars/ conferences, publications, awards, and other activities.

020.62254(1) AGLIS

Rangra, V K 87

Association of Government Librarians and Information Specialists (AGLIS), *HLAICI,* v 10, 18-27.

States the need of government libraries association. Gives origin. Discusses constitution and objectives. Describes the activities of the Association. Mentions its publications. States how AGLIS has been active in improvement of career prospects and status of government librarians. Gives more information in Appendices.

020.62254(1) IASLIC

Fourteenth National Seminar of IASLIC, Mysore, 14-17 Nov 1990: Summary of proceedings, *IASLIC Bull* 35(40 Dec 1990 : 133.

88

Gives brief about the inauguration of the 14th National Seminar of IASLIC held at Mysore University. Keynote address was given by Dr. M A Gopinath, and Dr (Ms) P Selvie Das, Vice Chancellor, presided. The thematic sessions started in the CFTRI. Subhash Biswas was the Director of the three thematic sessions. Dr N K Sharma acted as Rapporteur General, and Ms Khaisar J Beghum acted as Rapporteur.

Fourteenth National Seminar of IASLIC, Mysore, 14-17 Nov 1990 : Technical sessions: Summary of proceedings, *IASLIC Bull* 35(4) Dec 1990 : 143-152. 89

Gives the summary of the proceedings of the 14th IASLIC National Seminar, held at Mysore University in Nov 1990, which was directed by Subhash Biswas, President ILA, with Dr. N K Sharma as Rapporteur General. There were 48 papers and 45 papers were included in the Conference volume. 16 papers have been published in full, and the remaining 29 are given in abstract form. Covers recommendations and SIG sessions.

Gupta, B M 90

Indian Association of Special Libraries and Information Centres (IASLIC), *HLAICI,* v 10, 80-91.

Traces origin of IASLIC. Gives aims and objectives, structure, membership, finances, infrastructure. Discusses its activities such as education programme, national seminars/conferences, lectures, information service, special projects. Gives its various types of publications. Mentions about professional status and hopes and expectations.

Iaslic, Calcutta 91

Annual report and audited statement of accounts, 1990, Calcutta : IASLIC, 1991. 12 p.

Contains the report of the Executive and Finance Committee from Oct 1990 to Sep 1991. Also gives information about the 14th IASLIC Seminar held at Mysore in Nov 1990, total membership upto 1991, publications, study circle meetings, and other activities.

Iaslic, Calcutta 92

List of members, as on 30 Septemebr, 1991, Calcutta : IASLIC, 1991, 50 p.

Includes list of 4 Honorary members, 552 Life members, 12 members abroad, 230 Ordinary members, 361 Institutional members (N P), 46 Institutional members (PM).

020.62254(1) 18th IASLIC Conference

Eighteenth All India conference of IASLIC, Kurukshetra, 26-29 Dec 1991: Summary of proceedings, *IASLIC .Bull* 36(4) Dec 1991: 137-138. 93

Describes the inauguration and thematic sessions of the 18th All

India Conference of IASLIC held at Kurukshetra during 26-29 Dec 1991.

Eighteenth All India Conference of IASLIC, Technical sessions : Summary of proceedings, *IASLIC Bull* 36 (4) Dec 1991 : 145-152. 94

Describes various Technical Sessions of the 18th IASLIC Conference. Gives Summary of proceedings of all the technical sessions as well as the Special Interest Groups (SIGs).

020.62254 (1) 32nd Annual General Meeting of IASLIC

Iaslic, Calcutta 95

32nd Annual General Meeting of the IASLIC : Proceedings, *IASLIC Bull* 35(4) Dec 1990 : 153-154.

Gives the proceedings of the AGM held an 15 Nov 1990 at CFTRI, Mysore with Ms P G Joshi, Vice President, IASLIC, in the chair. Includes various suggestions given in the meeting.

020.62254(1) 33rd Annual General Meeting of IASLIC

Iaslic, Calcutta 96

33rd Annual General Meeting of IASLIC, *IASLIC Bull* 36(4) Dec 1991 : 153-156.

Relates the 33rd AGM of the IASLIC held at Kurukshetra on 27 December 1991 during the 18th All India IASLIC Conference.

020.62254(1) IATLIS

Asundi, A Y 97

Specialisation in library and information science education : IATLIS National Seminar (Bangalore) : 1991, *Her Lib Sc* 30 (3-4) July-Oct 1991 : 249-251.

Reports about the VIII IATLIS National Seminar held during 31 Jan-2 Feb 1991 at Bangalore University, and was inaugurated by the Vice Chancellor. Papers were read on the Technical sessions on Need for Specialisation (Session I), Areas of Specialisation (Sessions II-IV), and Specialists (Sessions V-VI).

Kumar, P S G 98

Indian Association of Teachers of Library and Information Science (IATLIS), *HLAICI,* v 10, 92-95.

Traces origin of IATLIS. Gives its aims and objectives, structure, membership. Describes activities including seminars/conferences, publications. Mentions nature of professional issues taken up with the Government bodies. Gives other activities also.

020.62254(1) Indian Library Association (ILA)

Vashishth, C P 99

Indian Library Association (ILA), *HLAICI,* v 10, 96-108.

Gives the beginning of the ILA. Mentions its original objectives. Discusses organisational structure, office, growth in terms of membership and finance. Describes activities of ILA such as conference, publications, continuing education programmes, consultancy projects. Discussas relations with other bodies. Mentions about Awards being given. Gives future programmes. Gives a list of available publications.

Vashishth, C P 100

Indian Library Association : A historical perspective, *ILA Bull* 26 (1) Apr-June 1990 : 1-13.

Traces history of the ILA since 1933. Describes its organisational structure. Discusses growth in membership. Presents a resume of numerous activities, conference themes, venues, dates. Mentions official organ and other important publications, different ongoing consultancy projects in hand. Lists the Awards and Prizes instituted. Discusses relations with other bodies. Mentions future programmes.

020.62254(1) 36th ILA Conference

Indian Library Association, Delhi 101

Computerization & library network : Seminar papers, Thirty-sixth All India Library Conference, University of Jodhpur, December 26-29, 1990, edited by C P Vashishth; associate editors R K Dave and M L Saini, Delhi : ILA, 1990. viii, 345 p.

Includes 43 papers divided into 16 sections presented at the 36th All India Library Conference, held at Jodhpur University during

Dec 26-29, 1990. Describes information retrieval systems, library management systems, local IRS/LIM systems, creation and conversion of bibliographic records, databases, manpower requirements, general data network, etc.

020.62254(1) 37th ILA Conference

Indian Library Association, Delhi 102

National information policies and programmes : Seminar papers of 37th All India Library Conference, held at IIT, Madras, December 4-7, 1991, Delhi: ILA, 1991. 463 p.

Editorial committee:S Parthasarthy, K S Raghavan, A Amudhavalli, M N Seetharaman, and I R N Goudar. Contains 63 papers divided into 7 sections. Section 1: Information Policy (1-6); Section 2 : Information Resources and Services (7-17); Section 3: Information Systems (18-40); Section 4: Information Networks (41-50); Section 6 : Manpower Development (54-58); Section 7 : Impact of Information Technology (59-63).

020.62254(1) INDAAL

Gupta, B M 103

Indian Association of Academic Librarians, *HLAICI,* v 10. 76-79.

Gives need, aims and objectives, structure, membership of the INDAAL. Describes its activities such as conferences, seminars, publications, study circles, etc. Discusses nature of professional issues taken up. States that presently it is in dormant state.

020.62254(1) Computer Society of India

Computer Society of India 104

25 years of fruitful growth, *HLAICI* v 10, 36-56.

Traces advent of computers in India and the idea of a User Group which culminated into Society in 1964. Gives objectives, growth and problems of the CSI. Discusses management structure with region, divisions, chapters, etc. Describes international activities, publications, CSI Award. Gives its role vis-a-vis government.

020.62254(1) The Library Council

The Library Council, *HLAICI*, v 10, 234-235. 105

Mentions aims and objectives, management, membership. Discusses about the activities of the Council since its formation particluarly the training at the level of Certificate Course in Library Science. Mentions its publications.

020.62254(1) Medical Library Association of India

Medical Library Association of India (MLAI); an overview, *HLAICI*, v 10, 122-125. 106

Lists the aims and objectives. Discusses various activities of MLAI such as seminars, national information policy and network, continuing education programmes, and other proposed activities. Gives a list of publications.

020.62254(1) MCI

Micrographic Congress (India), *HLAICI*, v 10, 126-129. 107

Explains the need for forming a professional body for promotion of micrographics in India. Gives aims and objectives. Discusses structure and membership. Explains various activities of the Congress.

020.62254(1) Society for Documentation & Inf Science

Society for Documentation and Information Science, *HLAICI*, v 10, 265-266. 108

Lists aims and objectives of the Society. Gives its membership and finances. Discusses activities of the Society such as education and training, seminars and workshops.

020.62254(1) Society for Information Science

Gupta, B M 109

Society for Information Science (SIS), *HLAICI*, v 10 136-145.

Gives genesis. Mentions aims and objectives. Describes structure, membership, activities, seminars of the SIS. Explains the annual conference and conventions from the first held in 1981 to the 10th held in 1991. Gives a list of publications and awards given to different individuals.

Society for Information Science 110

Directory of SIS members, 1990, New Delhi.: SIS, 1990.

Includes the biodata in brief of 126 members of the SIS, giving their photographs in most of the cases, arranged in alphabetical order. Also lists 49 more members whose biodata had not been received.

Society for Information Science 111

Siscom : Special Number, Jan 1990, New Delhi: SIS, 1990.

Brings out, in this Special Number of the SIS information about the IX Annual Convention and Conference held at NIO, Goa during 18-20 Jan 1990 on the theme of 'Local Area Network: Its significance in Information Systems'. Includes Secretary's report, Fellowhisp Awards, abstracts of the papers and membership list for 1988-89.

020.62254(1) 10th SIS Conference

Society for Information Science 112

Tenth annual convention and conference of SIS, Trivandrum, 17-19 January, 1991, *SISCOM* 11 (2-3) Feb-Mar 1991 : 1-3.

Reports about the X Conference held on the theme of 'Information Systems'. About two dozen technical papers were presented in the 5 technical sessions devoted to various facets of information generation, handling, storage and retrieval.

Tenth SIS Convention, Trivandrum, *NISSAT Newsletter,* 10(1) Jan-Mar 1991: 13-18. 113

Reports about the Tenth Annual Convention of the SIS held at RRL, Trivandrum during 17-18 Jan 1991. Mentions the inauguration, awards of Fellowships, preliminary session, technical sessions. Gives recommendations adopted at the Convention. Reported by Ram D Taneja and R N Sharma.

020.6225492 Library Associations-East Pakistan

Ahmad, Nasiruddin 114

Professional associations: A study of the East Pakistan Library Association, 1956-1970, *Lib Her* 29 (1-2) Apr-Sept 1990: 83-91.

Traces origin and growth of East Pakistan Library Association. Describes efforts of a few people towards growth of library services and library education in the new born province of East Pakistan (now Bangladesh), 1947-70.

020.62354(1) ADLFWA

Venkatappaiah, V 115

Andhra Desa Library Field Workers Association, *HLAICI*, v 10, 155-158.

Deals with the activities of the Association such as organisation of conferences, training programme, granthalaya yatras, etc. Mentions its present position.

020.62354(1) APLA

Raju, AAN 116

Andhra Pradesh Library Association (APLA), *HLAICI*, v 10, 159-167.

Gives origin and genesis, objectives, contribution, membership. Describes activities of APLA such as organisation of village libraries, library conferences, library pilgrimages, mobile library services, spring festivals, adult education, library legislation, library science education, publications, etc.

020.62354(1) APPLA

Majeed Khan, M A 117

Andhra Pradesh Public Library Association, *HLAICI*, v 10, 168-172.

Gives main aims and objectives of APPLA. Discusses about its management, membership, and activities including education and training, conferences/seminars/workshops, lectures. Gives a list of publications. Discusses nature of professional issues taken up. Maintains a public library also.

020.62354 (1) BLA

Banerjee, S B 118

Bengal Library Association, *HLAIÇI*, v 10, 173-190.

Gives the social background of Bengal and organisation of Bengal library conference. Mentions change of name to BLA and gives its constitution and Memorandum with objectives. Discusses about membership, management, finance and infrastructure. Describes various activities such as education and training, publications, library day, lectures, conferences, etc. Discusses about its achievements and future programmes.

020.62354(1) BILSA

Rab, S F 119

Bihar Library Service Association (BILSA), *HLAICI*, v 10, 191-192.

Deals with BILSA, its origin, development, aims and objectives, and activities including seminars, etc.

020.62354(1) BRPS

Bihar Rajya Pustakalaya Sangh, *HLAICI*, v 10, 193-196. 120

Gives its origir, aim and objectives. Discusses its branches, membership, finances. Describes its activities such as education and training, conference, seminars, lectures, publications, nature of professional issues, and relation with government.

020.62354(1) BOSLA

Mishra, V N 121

Bombay Science Libraries Association, *HLAICI*, v 10, 197-200.

Mentions formation of BOSLA. Gives its aims and objectives, management and membership. Discusses its activities. Describes its role in resource sharing, education and training. Gives a list of its publications and mentions other activities.

020.62354(1) DLA

Chopra, H R 122

Delhi Library Association : A living monument of P N Kaula, *DLIS*, 437-446.

Describes the foundation, structure, activities and achievements of the Delhi Library Association which was founded and nursed for several years by Porf P. N. Kaula. Also refers to the Address presented to Kaula by the Association.

Rajwant Singh 123

Delhi Library Association; an appraisal, *HLAICI* v 10, 201-206.

Points out genesis. Lists aims and objectives. Discusses its contribution, finance. Gives publications brought out and membership. Describes educational activities such as Certificate Course, Diploma Course. Points out its role in library cooperation and in improvement of service conditions of librarians.

020.62354(1) Goa Library Association

Navelkar, V R and **Pissurlekar, Vivek** 124

Gomantak Granthalaya Sangh (Goa Library Association), *HLAICI*, v 10, 207-212.

Gives importance of library in society and genesis of Goa Library Association. Mentions its aims, objectives and constitution. Describes its activities to make people of Goa aware of the library power and involve them in library movement.

020.62354(1) Gujarat Granthalaya Sangh

Shah, P C 125

Gujarat Granthalaya Sangh *HLAICI*, v 10, 213-215.

States the aims and objectives. Discusses structure and membership, activities, education and training, conferences and lectures organised, publications brought out, and professional issues taken up.

020.62354(1) Gujarat Pustakalaya Mandal

Pathak, Pragnaya J 126

Gujarat Pustakalya Mandal, *HLAICI*, v 10, 216-218.

Gives the structure and membership of the Association. Discusses its activities, education and training, state conferences it organised. Provides a list of publications of the Mandal. Mentions professioanl issues taken up and its relation with the government.

020.62354(1) HLA

Janak Raj 127
Haryana Library Association, *HLAICI*, v 10, 219-222.
Gives formation of HLA. Mentions its aims and objectives. Discusses management and membership. Describes activities of HLA particularly the seminars/conferences/workshops, publications, and the professional issues taken up.

020.62354(1) Kerala Granthasala Sanghom

Kerala Granthasala Sanghom, *HLAICI*, v 10, 227-230. 128
Explains the aims and objectives, the constitution, finance, growth of Sanghom. Describes its various activities such as education and training, projects, and publications. Gives the present position.

020.62354(1) Karanataka Library Association

129
Karnataka Library Association (KALA), *HLAICI*, v 10, 223-226.
States the main objectives as listed in constitution of KALA. Gives its structures, and membership. Describes its activities such as seminars, lectures, study circles, library week, education and training, consultancy, and publications.

020.62354(1) KLA

Devarajan, G 130
Kerala Library Association (KLA), *HLAICI*, v 10, 231-233.
Outlines aims and objectives of KLA. Mentions its membership. Discusses the management and activities which include seminars, Gold Medal, study circle, etc. Gives a list of its publications.

020.62354(1) MALA

Kumar, Suseela 131

Madras Library Association (MALA) *HLAICI*, v 10, 236-245.

Gives origin of MALA. Lists aims and objectives. Discusses its growth since 1928 in phases wherein it has played role in library awareness, rural library service, adult education, school library development, library science education, publications, efforts towards library legislation. Discusses the years of its consolidation after 1953. Describes the impact of sociological and technological development. Explains the current activities of MALA. Mentions the future role.

Impact of informatics – MALA seminar, *NISSAT Newsletter* 10(3) July-Sept 1991: 18-19. 132

Reports about the one day seminar on 'Trends in and impact of informatics' organised by MALA on 23 August 1991, and Inaugurated by Dr M S Swaminathan.

020.62354(1) MFCLA

Baheti, S R 133

Maharashtra Federation of College Library Association (MFCLA), *HLAICI*, v 10, 246-252.

Explains the genesis of MFCLA. Gives its objectives. Discusses its activities such as conferences etc and the professional issues it has taken up with the government bodies. Lists its publications. Gives the future plans of MFCLA.

020.62354(1) Punjab Library Association (PLA)

Gupta, B M 134

Punjab Library Association, *HLAICI*, v 10, 253-259.

Traces origin and history. Discusses its main objectives as defined in byelaws. Discusses its activities and developments in pre-partition and post-independence period. Mentions some of the seminars it organised. Reports only upto 1976.

Sukhdev Singh 135

Punjab Library Association and the library legislation, *PLSP*, 117-126.

Discusses historical perspective of the PLA from its inception upto partition of Punjab. States role of the PLA to further library movement in the state. Describes efforts made by the PLA in the direction of library legislation in the state.

Verma, Rama 136

PLA : Objectives, *PLSP*, 181-184.

Discusses need for restructuring PLA's objectives. Describes achievements of the Association vis-a-vis its objectives. Makes some suggestions.

020.62354(1) Rajasthan Library Association (RLA)

Gupta, B L 137

Rajasthan Library Association (RLA), *HLAICI*, v 10, 260-264.

Traces its origin. Gives aims and objectives of RLA. Mentions its membership and organisational structure. Discusses activities of this Association. Explains its programmes to achieve its objectives.

020.62354(1) UP Library Association (UPLA)

Shukl, R K and **Srivastava, R K** 138

Uttar Pradesh Library Association (UPLA), *HLAICI*, v 10, 267-272.

Deals with the origin and development of UPLA. Discusses its activities such as conferences and seminars it organised. Details out its library services. Mentions its publications. Gives its cooperation with other associations, and professional issues it took up.

020.688 Library Marketing

Chadha, Ravinder Kumar and **Arora, Jagdish** 139

Creating corporate identity: A visual apporach to marketing library services, *DLIS*, 369-373.

Mentions the concept of corporate identity and library identity. Deals with specific issues pertaining to marketing phenomena as applied to library services.

Chadha, Ravinder Kumar and **Arora, Jagdish** 140

Inspiring a marketing behaviour in social science information services, *SSI*, 458-463.

Explains the concept of marketing. Describes marketing communication. Describes developing the marketing programme in view of the needs of people which will help in attaining and maintaining people's support for library as an indispensible agency.

Chakrabarty, Bipul Kumar 141

Marketing information management with reference to agricultural marketing : Strategic thoughts, *IM*, 19-24.

Describes role of information management in agricultural marketing pointing out regional information centres, centre for agricultural marketing, marketing management, etc. Discusses marketing research and marketing information system giving its functions and features. Points out marketing strategies of marketing information management.

Janak Raj 142

Library marketing, *DLIS,* 347-368.

Discusses library marketing. Evaluates all aspects of marketing strategy and alternative marketing strategy. Presents the marketing promotion programmes.

Marketing of information products – IPE study, *NISSAT Newsletter* 10 (1) Jan-Mar 1991 : 11. 143

Reports the study by the Institute of Public Enterprise, Hyderabad conducted on marketing of information products and services by libraries and information centres, commissioned by NISSAT. Lists main recommendations.

Pulla Ready, V 144

Marketing research for information services, *Int Lib Move* 13(3) Sept 1991: 123-131.

Identifies information environment. Defines marketing research. States when information firm should take marketing research. Mentions kinds of marketing research. Lists steps in marketing research process such as formulation of hypotheses, data gathering methods, sampling, etc. States that after this data is to be analysed and interpreted and findings to be reported. Concludes that in India marketing research of information services is scant.

Ramanna, B and **Ranganath, K A** 145

Marketing of information products and services of the National Information Centre for Food Science and Technology (NICFOS) – a case study, *Lib Sc slant Doc & Inf Std* 26(2) June 1989 : 114-126.

Explains the efforts made by the NICFOS and experience gained in rendering information services and generating various information products to meet the specific needs of users in R and D institutions, industry, government departments, etc in the area of food science and technology. Gives marketing trends also.

020.7 Library and Information Science (LIS) Education

Chandran, D 146

Practice oriented library education, *LISE,* 215-219.

Deals with LIS education in relation with the curriculum content vs national development, knowledge, skills and methods to move to the new concept of information society. States that the ultimate objective is to train appropriate manpower for information work and service.

Gopinath, M A 147

Creative methods and evaluation in LIS education, *LISE*, 73-81.

Mentions aims of higher education in LIS. Mentions knowledge and skills to be developed in students. Discusses some of the techniques which help in triggering creative abilities such as brainstorming, synectics, systems analyses, and case study method.

Gopinath, M A 148

Information technology on teaching and learning process in library and information science, *LISE*, 62-72.

Gives the impact of IT on education, teaching and learning methods. Discusses such technologies as TV, videotex, teleconferencing, audiographics, CAL, etc. These would help in the basic objectives of information acquisition.

Lundu, Maurice C 149

Teaching of information science in the Southern African Development Coordination Conference (SADCC) sub-region: Conformity or diversity?, *DLIS*, 107-120.

Describes the SADCC sub-region and its information environment, development objectives. Discusses information science and information science programme, University of Zambia, Dept of Library Studies set up with assistance of UNESCO and University of Botswana, Dept of Library Studies.

Neelameghan, A 150

Learning about and practice of designing local databases as a harmonizing factor, *In* Johnson, Ian M, Neil, J Richard and Terry, Martha B (Eds), *Harmonization of education and training programmes for library, information and archival personnel*, Proceedings of an international colloquium. London, August 9-15, 1987, IFLA, v 2, 1989, pp 213-224.

Deals with the designing of local databases as a harmonizing factor in library and information science education.

Simon, H R 151

Needs and gaps in the training of specialists for information : A status report, *ULI*, 256-284.

Investigates into the offer and demand for further educational measures reveal obvious discrepancies. Notes about training at universities and colleges. Highlights job situation and good job prospects with specialised knowledge including EDP and new media.

Yadav, Rashmi and **Gupta, Shamsher** 152

Education for special library and information work, *Int Lib Move* 12(1) Mar 1990 : 31-39.

Describes scientific information explosion. Identifies various problems such as political situation, economics of information, IT, etc. Lists basic functions of information. Mentions programmes in schools of library/information science to train the information workers so as to meet the new situations.

020.7(1) LIS Education Through Distance Education

Dhyani, Pushpa 153

Library science through distance education: IGNOU experiment, *Her Lib Sc* 29 (1-2) Jan-Apr 1990 : 37-42.

Discusses infrastructure of BLSc programme of IGNOU. Records a desperate situation as expressed by the candidates. Examines medium of instruction used in teaching against the background education of candidates. Evaluates content of papers prescribed and limitations in teaching process. Expresses predicament of BLSc counsellors associated with teaching programme. Refers to the objections raised when course was initially started from Open University of Hyderabad.

Sathyanarayana, R 154

Library and information science education through distance education, *Lib Sci slant Doc and Inf Std* 27(3) Sept 1990 : 151-172.

States that the concept of 'Distance Education ' is a relatively new one aimed at the expansion of education through the use of modern communication technology. Describes the imparting of LIS education through distance education in India.

020.7094 LIS Education – Western Europe

Karivalo, Merja 155

West European Round Table on Information and Documentation (WERTID), *Her Lib Sc* 30(3-4) July-Oct 1990 : 247-249.

Reports about the Meeting of the WERTID held on 10 June 1990 in Paris on the state of the art in education and training of library and information professionals in Western European countries and scope for international cooperation. Gives significant decisions taken at the symposium.

020.7095 LIS Education – Developing Countries

Kaula, P N 156

Education for information manpower development in developing countries, *INICAE* 10(1) Mar 1991 : 59-60.

Gives the role of information workers and need for reorientation of LIS education to produce target groups. Suggests main areas of study for education programme. Evaluates diverse education programme in Asia. Advocates revolutionary innovations in curricula and in continuing education programmes.

020.70954 LIS Education - India

Gopalakrishnan, N K 157

Management education and library administration, *Lib Sc slant Doc and Inf Std* 27(2) June 1990 : 112-122.

Gives objectives of the course for training librarians and library administrators conducted by the Institute of Public Enterprise, Hyderabad. Mentions its coverage, range of topics, MBO, costing, pricing, marketing, etc.

Jagtar Singh 158

Accreditation of library and information science programmes in India, *LISE,* 220-226.

Gives meaning of accreditation. Traces its history. Gives standards which should relate to curriculum, faculty, students, etc. Describes position of accreditation in India.

Jagtar Singh 159

Accreditation of LIS programmes in India, *ULI,* 241-247.

Gives meaning and types of accreditation. Mentions need for accreditation on the basis of various seminars recommendations. Gives facets for formulating standards for accreditation. Pleads for setting up of a follow up committee to prevail upon the UGC for the establishment of a special agency for accreditation of LIS education in India.

Kumar, P S G 160

National policy perspective for library and information science education *NIPP*, 384-392.

Describes the contribution of UGC and IATLIS in evolving policy perspective towards LIS education. Discusses efforts of RRRLF and ILA. States that draft policy towards LIS education highlights the formation of a Standing Committee on LIS Education and Training; ICLIS; and National Institute for LIS, with National Information Centre for LIS.

Kumar, P S G 161

Some issues in education for librarianship in India, *LISE*, 108-117.

States the importance of IT. Gives its impact on library education. Discusses status of the departments with faculty position. Describes teachers and their contribution in research and teaching. Gives supply and demand position, distance education, 2-year MLISc course, etc. Gives some suggestions to prepare suitable manpower.

Mangla, P B 162

Library and information science education in India: Trends and issues, *Granthana* 1(2) July 1990 : 29-44.

Gives historical development of LIS education in India at the post-graduate level. Assesses the library/information infrastructure in the country. Discusses such major areas as levels of education, course contents, research, teaching faculty, accreditation, etc. Gives outline of courses suggested by the UGC Panel on LIS.

Mangla, P B 163

Library and information science education in India: Trends and issues, *Univ News* 28(24) June 11, 1990 : 7-15.

Traces background of librarianship. Gives library and information service infrastructure in India. Identifies major areas of discussion in LIS education. Describes various levels of training, course contents, conventional v/s information science courses. Discusses teaching faculty, research activity, student characteristics. Discusses some problems of LIS education and the issues that need attention.

Mitra, A 164

Remodelling of education for academic librarianship in India, *LISE*, 191-196.

Deals with the need for modernisation of LIS education. Describes basic requirements for academic librarianship education, role of library science educators, factors in relation to Indian situation

Navjot Kaur 165

Impact of environmental changes on library education in India, *LISE*, 118-125.

Identifies need of special library and introduction of special library as a paper at MLISc level. States that in view of the development in technology such as computers, telecommunication, CD-ROM, new sources of information, etc. Gives impact of new environment on present curriculum in Indian library schools.

Sahay, S S 166

Library and information science teaching in India : Need for restructuring curriculum, *LISE,* 1-8.

Mentions the role of library, librarian and library scientists. Gives the aim of library schools. Defines curriculum and gives its aims. Discusses lecture method of imparting education and group teaching, education by observation, seminar method. Concludes that a blending of conventional and non-conventional methods is the right solution.

Srivastava, S N 167

Qualitative improvement in LIS education, *ULI*, 248-255.

Traces history of LIS education in India. Shows that India has adequate LIS manpower development facilities. Mentions that LIS schools have wide variations in their resources. States that there in need to improve the quality of LIS education. Offers suggestions on levels of education, admission requirements, teaching faculty, curriculum development, teaching methods, etc.

Tejomurty, A, *Ed* 168

Library and information science education and teaching methods (Papers of Ujjain and Gulbarga seminars), Jaipur: RBSA Publishers, 1991.251 p.

Contains 28 papers presented at two UGC-sponsored seminars held at Vikram University, Ujjain and Gulbarga University, Gulbarga on the latest ideas of LIS education in India and other subjects such as college library, university library, user education, IT, etc.

Verma, S C 169

Library and information science education in India, *LISE*, 22-30.

Gives historical perspective of LIS education in India. Mentions recommendations made by various committees and conferences on LIS education. Makes a critical appraisal about syllabi, teaching methods, calibre of teachers, physical facilities, etc. Offers various suggestions on syllabus, accreditation, teaching methods, and evaluation method.

020.7095413 LIS Education – Orissa

Rath, P K, *Comp* 170

Dissertations submitted in partial fulfilment of Master's degree in Library and Information Science at the Utkal University (Orissa) from 1983-84 to 1987-88, *CLIS Observer* 7(1-2) Jan-June 1990 :30-35.

Lists 67 MLISc dissertations arranged alphabetically by the name of the candidate under the headings : (a) Name of the Awardee, (b) year, (c) subject, and (d) Guide/Supervisor.

Rath, P K, *Comp* 171

Dissertations submitted in partial fulfilment of Master's degree in Library and Information Science at the Sambalpur University (Orissa) from 1983-84 to 1987-88, *CLIS Observer* 7(1-2) Jan-June 1990 : 36-38.

Lists 21 items under the legend (a) name of the awardee, (b) year, (c) subject, and (d) Guide/Supervisor. These are arranged alphabetically by the name of the awardee.

020.7095483 LIS Education – Kerala

Varghese, P V 172

Library manpower development in Kerala with special reference to the experiments in the training of semi-professionals, *PL*, 75-84.

States that professional manpower in Kerala in the past got education from outside state. Mentions random courses organised by Kerala Grandhasala Sanghom. Describes Certificate course of University of Kerala, admission procedure of Certificate course by Trivandrum Public Library (SCL). Suggests changes for the better. Gives a review of the course with suggestions for improvement.

020.7095484 LIS Education – AP

Ramaiah, L S and **Kankachary, M** 173

Library automation vis-a-vis the manpower production: A case study of library and information science education in Andhra Pradesh, *CALNE*, 192-200.

Considers information as a major resource for a country's progress and development. Discusses importance of computers in new environs even in India. Discusses important requirements of automation and library networking. Examines in view of the deficiency of manpower, the LIS education at BLISc and MLISc levels in universities in AP. Makes suggestions.

020.7095492 LIS Education – Bangladesh

Ahmad, Nasiruddin 174

Problems and prospects of library education in Bangladesh, *Her Lib Sc* 30(1-2) Jan-Apr 1991 : 46-50.

Stresses the need for proper training of library personnel. Examines the present courses of studies in Bangladesh. Discusses various problems of LIS education such as lack of adequate objectives, scanty programme, dearth of competent teachers, dearth of reading material, lack of cooperation, etc. Presents overview prospects of LIS education. Makes suggestions.

020.709667 LIS Education – Ghana

Alemna, A A 175

Education for librarianship and information science in Ghana, *Int Lib Move* 12 (4) Dec 1990 : 191-197.

Traces the library training programme in West Africa. Describes LIS education in Ghana. Discusses various programmes of University of Ghana, its facilities, courses. Compares these with other library schools in English-speaking West Africa. Offers various recommendations.

Alemna A A 176

Education of librarianship and information science in Ghana. *Ann Lib Sc and Doc* 36(4) Dec 1989 : 148-152.

Focusses on historical development of library school in Ghana, its programmes, admission requirements, areas of specialisation and training facilities. Makes recommendation for changes in the curriculum.

020.709669 LIS Education – Nigeria

Ochogwu, Michael G 177

Producing the basic competencies in information science education in Nigeria, *Jl Lib and Inf Sc* 14(2) Dec 1989 : 157-165.

Gives a theoretical overview of the information science as a discipline. Analyses problems of teaching and producing information science professionals in Nigeria. Suggests various measures to overcome various shortcomings.

Onadiran, R W 178

The curriculum of library science programmes in Nigeria, *Int Lib Move* 13(1) Mar 1991 : 50-60.

Describes courses of study in LIS organised by universities and polytechnics that lead to the award of either Diploma in Library Science, B Lib Sc, M Lib Sc or Doctor of Philosophy in Library Science in Nigeria. Examines development of curriculum and library schools, literature review, implementation of curriculum and staff.

020.71 Library and Information Science Schools

Sharma, Devender K 179

Library schools in India as on 1 August 1990, *CLIS Observer* 7(1-2) Jan-June 1990: 44-53.

Lists 115 institutions imparting LIS education in India at various levels. These include universities, colleges, polytechnics, library associations, academies, open universities, etc.

020.711 LIS Education-Courses and Curriculum

Bhattacharyya, G 180

Curriculum for development of professional manpower for secondary information work and service, *Lib Sc slant Doc and Inf Std* 27(1) Mar 1990 : 30-51.

Discusses need for adaptation of knowledge and skills of information professionals to the changing information environs. Identifies secondary information work and service as the main domain of information professionals. Mentions variety of knowledge and services needed for utilising IT. Provides a curriculum for IT for library and information professionals.

Gopalakrishnan, N K 181

Curriculum for marketing management for information professionals, *Lib Sc slant Doc and Inf Std* 27(3) Sept 1990 : 129-134.

Discusses value of marketing approach to information systems and services. Identifies objectives for a Marketing Management course for information professionals. Delineates a module of course contents for such a programme. Calls for a short and long term programmes in Marketing Management.

Gopinath, M A 182

Curriculum for knowledge base retrieval system : A case for inclusion in information science, *Lib Sc slant Doc and Inf Std* 28(4) Dec 1991 : 131-136.

Delineates the developments in various processing stages of information systems and ES. Discusses the knowledge and skills needed in developing an ES as an information system and vice-versa. Presents a curriculum for a course on Intelligent Knowledge Base System.

Karisiddappa, C R and **Sangam, S L** 183

Standards for designing of library and information science syllabus, *Ind Jl Inf Lib and Society* 3(1-2) Mar-June 1990 : 49-57.

Discusses the concept of standard in LIS education. Mentions need for standard syllabus. Suggests guiding principles to design standard syllabus including the factors for designing. Considers that standard syllabus should be realistic and not idealistic.

Krishnamurthy, R 184

Micrographics education for library and information professionals, *Lib Sc slant Doc and Inf Std* 27 (3) Sept 1990 : 136-150.

Discusses developments in micrographics. Identifies value of micrographics in information storage, retrieval and dissemination. Presents a curriculum for micrographics for specialisation by the library and information professionals.

Mishra, Bhawanath 185

Evaluation of library and information science courses in India, *DLIS,* 121-134.

Traces history of LIS education in India since 1911 with Baroda school, Punjab school, Madras school, etc upto independence. Gives details of post-independent period including INSDOC and DRTC courses. Gives evaluation of training programmes with observations on various aspects.

Parthasarathy, S and **Neelameghan, A** 186

Curriculum development in information studies with special reference to information technology, *Lib Sc slant Doc and Inf Std* 27 (1) Mar 1990 : 1-29.

Discusses variety of innovations developing in IT sector. Delineates areas in which IT has impact on library/information systems and services, consequent need for reformulation of modules for courses in information science with particular reference to Indian context. Presents a status report on curriculum development at international and national levels. Presents a model curriculum.

Pathak, Hasmukh and **Shukla, K H** 187

MLIS syllabus and admission criteria in Gujarat : A comparative study, *LISE*, 227-232.

Traces brief history of LIS education in Gujarat. Describes BLIS programme and objectives of MLIS programme by various universities in the state. Gives faculty strength. Examines the various patterns of syllabi in four universities with MLIS programme. Describes the admission criteria to MLIS.

Prasher, R G 188

Post-graduate library course for special libraries, *LISE*, 9-21.

Describes the inadequacy and limitations of existing library training particularly for agricultural libraries and libraries of allied disciplines. Discusses manpower requirements for managing agro-biological libraries. Emphasises need for a post-graduate library course in agricultural veterinary sciences giving objectives of the course, admission, duration, staff, finance, physical facilities, outlines and contents of MLIS course.

Rajan, T N and **Satyanarayana, R** 189

Guidelines for curriculum for library and information science education and training in India in the nineties, *Lib Sc slant Doc and Inf Std* 27(2) June 1990 : 81-89.

States a few premises. Identifies a few parameters for professionals preparation. Mentions few ideas in drafting a course modules which should include a learning and teaching package. Outlines course contents for LIS courses at Bachelors and Masters levels.

Rangra, V K 190

Curriculum development for training in information technology, *Lib Sc slant Doc and Inf Std* 27(1) Mar 1990 : 52-67.

Explains briefly concept of curriculum development and its application to training programme in IT at DESIDOC. Gives details of course/contents as modules with allocation of training hours to each topic.

Seetharama, S 191

Management of information systems and services: A course module, *Lib Sc slant doc and Inf Std* 27(2) June 1990 :104-111.

Discusses inputs from management science, IT and economics into development of information systems and services. Delineates objectives in providing education in these fields to library/ information professionals. Gives a course module for management education.

Sen, B K 192

Information technology – curriculum for library and information science course at INSDOC, New Delhi, *LIB Sc slant Doc and Inf Std* 27(2) June 1990 : 69-80.

Discusses various IT emerging during last 30 years. Identifies their role in the design and development of information products and services. Provides a guideline on selecting the appropriate aspects of IT in LIS curriculum. Provides curriculum structure adopted for IT course in INSDOC.

020.715 LIS Education – Continuing Education

Gursharanjit Singh 193

Continuing education of library personnel in the public libraries of Punjab, *PLSP*, 155-164.

Defines continuing education and gives its factors. Stresses need of continuing education for professional staff in public libraries. Suggests the agencies which should take up this work. Discusses the present image of public libraries in Punjab.

Harikumar, S 194

Training and continuing education for the professional development among librarians, *PL*, 85-93.

Mentions that library personnel now require a thorough

knowledge of contemporary issues. States the need of continuing education for professional development. Describes that training and CE can help improve the talent of library staff. Discusses problems and gives recommendations.

Konnur, P V and **Biradar, B S** 195

Continuing education for teachers in library and information science, *LISE*, 126-132.

Defines continuing education (CE). Gives its importance to library/information workers. Mentions need for CE. Gives its aims. Describes the types of CE programmes such as formal methods and informal methods. Concludes that existing programme of CE is quite encouraging.

Kumar, S and **Kumar, Abha** 196

Teachers orientation programme : Its application for teachers in library and information science, *LISE*, 233-243.

Traces genesis and historical background of teachers orientation programme in India. Discusses Academic Staff College and gives its objectives. Discuses the programme components, organisation, formal evaluation, course content, component for LIS teachers and librarians.

Rajasekharan, K 197

Continuing education for working librarians, *ILA Bull* 26(1) Apr-June 1990 : 26-30.

Discusses factors necessitating continuing education (CE) programmes and their current status in India. Makes a proposal for a nation-wide CE programme and the priority areas for CE in India. Also gives curriculum for short-term courses on CE.

Raju, A A N 198

Planning for professional advancement programmes in library and information science, *Her Lib Sc* 30(3-4) July-Oct 1991: 167-174.

Refers to the UGC scheme for orientation/refresher course for academic staff and the Academic Staff College in the universities. Estimates that there are 3,528 professionals in the lecturer's grade working in the catchment area, and ASC of Osmania University has to conduct 87 Refresher courses with an intake of 40 participants per course. Suggests two more ASCs in the Southern and Eastern

India. Refers to the first Refresher course conducted by the Academic Staff College of Osmania University.

020.716 LIS Education – Methods of Teaching

Agrawal, S S 199

Techniques in library science teaching programme, *LISE*, 43-51.

Gives need of teaching techniques. Describes in detail various teaching techniques such as lecture method, tutorial method, discussion method, seminar method, AV method, learning by doing method, observation method, etc.

Asundi, A Y 200

LEARNDOC-a simulated CAT software on teaching DDC, *DRTC 1989,* MI-16.

Discusses a package for simulation of CAI on teaching DDC. The menu driven programmes are written in BASIC and it can be installed on IBM compatible PCs or PC/XTs.

Bhattacharyya, G 201

On teaching of library and information science, *Lib Sc Slant Doc and Inf Std* 28 (2) June 1991 : 68-81.

Discusses contents of LIS as an intellectual analysis of information for specific purpose of use. Identifies a variety of methods of teaching the professional aspect of LIS. Demonstrates the approach of information analysis and consolidation as summum bonum of teaching an learning.

Chatterjee, S K and **Barua, P** 202

Use of teaching methods and instructional material in library and information science education, *LISE,* 52-61.

Defines professional education, and method to be used in LIS education. Lists criteria of a good method. Describes various effective teaching methods. Provides a chart for teaching individual papers through different methods. Gives suitability of different AV instructional materials.

Navalani, K 203

Simulation method of teaching in library and information science education, *LISE*, 37-42.

Defines LIS education. Mentions its aim. Enumerates various

teaching methods. Discusses in detail the simulation method in which role playing is important aspect. Gives its aim, advantages, applications, criticism, etc.

Tejomurty, A and **Chopra, H R** 204

Teaching methods in library and information education in India : Some considerations, *LISE*, 31-36.

Suggests and describes various teaching methods for BLISc and MLISc courses. These include class room lectures, seminars and class discussion, use of AVs, assignments, tutorials, internship, consultancy, visit, etc.

Varma, A K 205

Methods of teaching and evaluation in library cataloguing practice, *LISE*, 88-93.

Lays emphasis on the practical training of library cataloguing. Reviews the methods of teaching and evaluation in cataloguing practice in various schools of LIS in India. Studies on the basis of the experience of the author at Ravishankar University.

020.72 Library and Information Science Research

Humayoon Kabir, S 206

Historical and survey method of research in library and information science : A comparative study, *Int Lib Move* 13(3) Sept 1991 : 140-148.

Defines research and historical research. Mentions purpose and steps of historical research. Gives sources of data and tools employed. Identifies types and areas of study, requisites of historical research, merits, demerits and problems with examples.

Humayoon, Kabir S. 207

Historical and survey method of research in library and information science: A comparative study, *ILA Bull* 26(1) Apr-June 1990 : 38-44.

Defines research and history. Makes a comparative study of historical research and survey research as applicable to the field of library and information science.

Ijari, S R and **Savanur, S K** 208

Research in library and information science : Some problems, *CPT*, 155-159.

Defines research. Identifies problems of research in library and information science in India, such as administrative, financial, thematic, and problems concerning facilities, recognition and application, and others.

Rajyalakshmi, D 209

Practicing librarian and the need for creative research, *Lib Her* 29 (3-4) Oct 1990-Jan 1991 : 177-182.

Defines concept of research in LIS. Points out need for practicing librarian for publication work and creative research. Describes present role of librarians for assisting faculty research services, need for involving himself in creative research to enhance assertive services and face challenges of information age.

Sapre, S B 210

Quality improvement programmes for working librarians, *DLIS*, 135-140.

States the importance of research. Gives meaning of research and library research. Discusses quality improvement programmes and that learning resource centres be set up in India also.

Sharma, Dev Raj, *Comp*

Doctoral theses in library and information science accepted by Indian universities (1985-1989), *CLIS Observer* 7 (1-2) Jan-June 1990 : 39-43. 211

Includes 56 Ph D theses awarded during 1985-89 arranged alphabetically under the name of the awardee with more information on year of award of degree, title of the thesis, university to which thesis submitted, name of the Guide, and present address of the awardee.

Vyasmoorthy, P 212

Research ideas in library science, *CLIS Observer* 7(3-4) July-Dec 1990 : 79-83.

Suggests ideas and areas on which Indian library and information scientists could work on for their research degrees or otherwise.

020.76 LIS Education – Evaluation

Krishan Kumar 213

Evaluation of MLISc students using method of evaluations by stage at which performed, *LISE*, 82-87.

Mentions importance of evaluation. Discusses four stages of evaluation, namely precourse evaluation, ongoing evaluation, technical evaluation, and follow up evaluation.

Patel, Jashu 214

Evaluation techniques and methods in library science: A selected review of the literature and a proposed study of the effects of students performance evaluation in library education in UK and USA, *Her Lib Sc* 30(3-4) July-Oct, 1991: 159-167.

Examines development of testing methods used in the evaluation of LIS education in UK and USA. Discusses various evaluating methods, reason for more failures and need for accurate assessment techniques. Identifies relevant problems. States difficulties of students in obtaining LIS qualifications.

Tejomurty, A and **Kumar, S** 215

Librametric study of MLIS results of Vikram University, 1971-87, *LISE*, 94-107.

Evaluates the performance of MLIS students of Vikram University during 1971-87. Calculates coefficient of association, standard deviation, mean, standard error of mean and mode of all the papers, etc.

020.78 LIS Education – Teaching Aids

Chopra, H R 216

Use of audio-visual aids in library and information science teaching in India, *Int Lib Move* 13(4) Dec 1991 : 201-203.

Mentions the development of AV aids. Describes the use of AV aids in LIS teaching in the West and in India. Gives their advantages. Mentions cost factor, and need for training of teachers in this respect.

Nedosa, P S 217

Formatting instructional package for use in the university library : Suggested course outline for schools, *Int Lib Move* 13(3) Sept 1991 : 149-155, 162.

Explains purpose of university education framing of international package and goals and objectives to be achieved. Stresses on the use of the audio-visuals, choice of instructional method, etc.

020.79 LIS – Awards

Ranganathan-Kaula Award for 1986 conferred on Dr Indra Narayan Sengupta, *Ind Jl Inf Lib and Society* 4(3-4) Sept-Dec 1991: i-iv. 218

Reproduces citation of this Award conferred on Dr I N Sengupta of Indian Institute of Chemical Biology, Calcutta in recognition of his outstanding contribution in Bibliometrics, and information science.

Venkatappaiah, V 219

Dr. Nasser Sharify receives Kaula Award : Presentation ceremony in New York *Her Lib Sc* 29(1-2) Jan-Apr 1990 : 87-93.

Describes the programme when on 13 June 1989 Dr Nasser Sharify, Dean Emeritus and Distinguished Professor, School of Computer, Information and Library Sciences, Pratt Institute, Brooklyn, New York (USA) received Prof Kaula Gold Medal and Citation.

Venkatappaiah, V 220

Ranganathan-Kaula Award to Dr Mohanrajan, *Her Lib Sc* 30 (3-4) July-Oct 1990 : 283.

States that Dr. P N Mohanrajan, Librarian, University of Madras has been awarded Ranganathan-Kaula Award for 1990 by the National Award Committee of Prof Kaula Endowment for Library and Information Science. Reproduces the press report.

020.8 LIS – Anthologies

Devarajan, G, Gopalakrishnan Nair, P and **Rajan, A C,** *Eds* 221

Professional librarianship (C A Augustine festschrift), New Delhi : Ess Ess Publications, 1991. xiv, 121 p.

Covers 15 papers in this volume, the fourth by the Kerala Library

Association, dealing with the specific facet of the broader subjects. Includes papers on library profession in India, professional development, manpower resources, continuing education, ethics of librarianship, etc.

Handbook of libraries, archives and information centres in India, volume 7 : Science and technology information systems and centres, edited by B M Gupta and S S Nathan, Delhi: Aditya Prakashan, 1990. ix, 289 p. 222

Includes 36 papers written by various authors on different information systems, networks, centres in science and technology in India.

Handbook of libraries, archives and information centres in India, volume 8: Social sciences information systems and centres, edited by B M Gupta and V K Jain, Delhi: Aditya Prakashan, 1990. ix, 276 p. 223

Incorporates 32 articles on the state of art on current information systems and centres in different areas of social sciences being operated at the national level and sectoral level in the country.

Handbook of libraries, archives and information centres in India, volume 9, Part 1: Humanities information systems and centres, edited by B M Gupta, Delhi : Aditya Prakashan, 1991. vii, 238+9 unnumbered p. 224

Covers 31 essays on the humanities information systems and centres in Part 1 of vol 9 of this Handbook.

Handbook of libraries, archives and information centres in India, volume 9, Part 2: Humanities – information systems and services, edited by B M Gupta, Delhi: Aditya Prakashan, 1991. viii, 239-489p. 225

As a continuation of Part 1 of Volume 9, this Part 2 includes articles 32-67 on various information systems and centres in the area of humanities.

Handbook of libraries, archives and information centres in India, volume 10 : Professional organisations and association, edited by B M Gupta, P S G Kumar and L S Ramaiah, New Delhi : Aditya Prakashan, 1990. viii, 279 p. 226

Deals with various professional organisations and associations of national, regional and state level. Includes 44 such organisation giving vast amount of information about many of them.

Handbook of libraries, archives and information centres in India, volume 11 : Libraries, archives and information technology : An annotated bibliography, 1970-1990, Part 1, edited by B M Gupta, Delhi : Aditya Prakashan, 1991. xxviii, 454 p. 227

Includes 2, 957 entries arranged alphabetically under 16 subject headings from 'Acquisition' to 'Library & Information Management'. Gives author index, publisher index, corporate subject index, subject index, list of publishers, distributors and exporters, list of LIS serials published from India, list of books and reports published in 1980-90.

Khan, H A and **Ijari, S R,** *Eds* 228

Current problems and trend in library and information services : Prof K S Deshpande festschrift volume, Varanasi : Indian Bibliographical Centre, 1990. iii, 370 p.

Includes 36 essays written by library and information scientists on various aspects divided into three broad groups : Section A : Library Development (21 articles); Section B: Information Systems, Information Networks and Services (12 articles); Section C : User Studies (3 articles). Gives a couple of biographical notes in the beginning.

Venkatappaiah, V et al, *Eds* 229

Dimensions of library and information science: Kaula festschrift : Papers contributed in honour of Prof P N Kaula on his sixty-first birthday, Associate Editors S R Gupta, Sister M Esperanza and S R Rab, New Delhi : Concept Publishing Company, 1990. 629 p.

Divided into 21 themes includes 53 articles in all on various aspects of librarianship such as academic libraries, research and technical libraries, indological libraries, LIS education, library automation, IT, information systems, comparative and international librarianship, library marketing, subject analysis, union catalogues, library associations, and Prof Kaula's contribution, etc.

020.9 Comparative Librarianship

Sami, Lalita K 230

Comparative librarianship, *CLIS Observer* 8(3-4) July-Dec 1991 : 3-6.

Defines comparative librarianship. Brings out distinction between comparative librarianship and international librarianship. Discusses comparative librarianship as a method of study, as well as a subject. Enumerates the facets and purpose of comparative librarianship.

020.92 Biography of Librarians, LIS Teachers, etc

Girja Kumar 231

Ranganathan, Dewey and C V Raman : A study in the arrogance of intellectual power, New Delhi : Har-Anand Publications, 1991. 147p.

Divided in 6 chapters and a Supplement, makes a comparative biography of Raman – a great physicist and Noble Laureate, Ranganathan and Dewey – the great of library science. Describes them in terms of accumulating, assimilating and retaining power for purpose of intellectual pursuit and ego satisfaction. Traces their life histories, achievements, etc.

Kumar, P S G 232

Kaula and Ranganathan: A perspective, *DLIS*,, 523-533.

Presents an analysis of the work of Kaula and that of S R Ranganathan pointing out latter's impact on Kaula as librarian, teacher, editor, project designer. Refers to the work that Kaula did for Ranganathan in popularising his ideas. Also records views of Ranganathan on Kaula.

Venkatappaiah, V 233

Iyyanki, Ranganathan and Kaula, *Her Lib Sc* 30(1-2) Jan-Apr 1991 : 3-8.

Mentions pioneering work of Ranganathan, Ramanayya and Kaula. Describes the work of Iyyanki and his contact with Ranganathan. Refers to the observations of Ranganathan about A P library movement causing adverse reaction from IVR and subsequent withdrawal of the statement. States also the observation of IVR on the work of Kaula and his association with library movement in Andhra Pradesh.

020.92 A Augustine, C A

Isaac, K A 234

Shri C A Augustine, *PL*, ix-xi.

Describes his birth, childhood, education, his joining the profession in the library, and then as teacher of LIS until his pre-mature retirement. Discusses his other activities and contribution to the profession.

020.92 D Deshpande, K S

Murthy, L Sridhara 235

Prof K S Deshpande : A biographical tribute, *CPT*, 3-5.

Relates author's first meeting with Prof K S Deshpande in Mysore University Library. Discusses his work, his publication, his experience, his beliefs, and recognition in the profession through the quotes of the giants.

Raghavendra Rao, K 236

A good guy among bad guys, *CPT*.

A poem written as a friend's tribute to Prof K S Deshpande, Librarian Extraordinary of Karnataka.

020.92 DE Dewey, Melvil

Comaromi, John P and **Satija, M P** 237

Melvil Dewey : And the Dewey Decimal classification; a chronology, *Int Lib Move* 12(2) June 1990 : 54-63.

Provides a chronology of Melvil Dewey and his DDC since 1851 upto the publication of the 20th Edition of the DDC in 1989.

020.92 G Gangadhar Rao, P

Ramesh Babu, B 238

Report on the condolence meeting organised by the RILISAR at LLA Building, Mount Road, Madras on 22-11-90, *Rilisar Bull* 7(1-4) Jan-Dec 1991:6-7.

Reports about the condolence meeting at the sudden and sad demise of Prof P Gangadhar Rao on 29 Oct. 1990. On this sad occasion Dr P N Mohanrajan, Dr K S Raghavan, Sh C Deenadayalu, spoke among others.

020.92 I Iyyanki Venkata Ramanayya

Adisheshuvu, Hari 239

Teachings of Iyyanki, *Her Lib Sc* 30(1-2) Jan-Apr 1991 : 25-27.

Describes the work and experience of IVR in promoting national service, participation in freedom movement, stressing the use of nature cure, use of books and libraries, and public libraries activities.

Kaula, P N 240

Iyyanki Venkata Ramanayya : Achievements and assessment, *Her Lib Sc* 30(1-2) Jan-Apr 1991 : 35-40.

Reproduces encomia by such personalities as V V Giri, K L Rao, S R Ranganathan, Indira Gandhi, Khandubhai Desai, P N Kaula, Devandra Rao, S R Bhatia. Refers to awards, felicitation address conferred on IVR.

Moorthy, J Satyanarayana 241

Iyyanki Venkata Ramanayya : The good samaritan, *Her Lib Sci* 30(1-2) Jan-Apr 1991 : 13-15.

Makes an assessment of work and contribution of IVR sacrificing his role in freedom movement, social and educational constructive activities, and library movement. Describes him as a good samaritan and considers him among the immortals of the country.

Narasimha Rao, G V S L 242

Architect of the public library movement in India, *Her Lib Sci* 30(1-2) Jan-Apr 1991 : 15-17.

Refers to IVR as 'Karamyogi'. Describes his varied activities specifying his pioneering work for the promotion of public library activities, naturopathy and swadeshi movement. Mentions the honours and awards conferred on him and also the institution of Iyyanki Gold Medal at Andhra University.

Ramalingareddy, C 243

Veteran of public library movement, *Her Lib Sci* 30(1-2) Jan-Apr 1991: 17-18.

Discusses briefly the activities of IVR in the promotion of library movement and its assessment.

Ramanayya, Iyyanki Venkata 244

Iyyanki on himself : Early training career and profession, *Her Lib Sci* 30(1-2) Jan-Apr 1991 : 28-31.

Gives an account of early life of Iyyanki as recorded by himself. States the impact of his grand mother on his life and of environment of his career and activities. Discusses his role for the promotion of library movement as a professional should do and accomplish.

Rao, Kodati Narayana 245

The blessed soul, *Her Lib Sci* (1-2) Jan-Apr 1991 : 27-28.

Refers to the glorious life of Iyyanki and his work in public social service and public library movement which has brought him recognition, honours and awards.

Sarada, K 246

Homage to Iyyanki Venkata Ramanayya, *Her Lib Sci* 30 (1-2) Jan-Apr 1991 : 8-12.

Describes Iyyanki's early life, public library movement, publications of journals, propagation of libraries as potent agency of education, establishment of library associations, organising conferences, and library field activities. Mentions honours and awards conferred on Iyyanki in recognition of his pioneering work.

Sarma, J Madhava Rama 247

At the threshold of light, *Her Lib Sci* 30(1-2) Jan-Apr 1991 : 18-25.

Mentions services of Iyyanki in the field of libraries, specially setting up of library associations, holding of All-India public library conference, organising library pilgrimages and publicity programmes. Describes the movement for national liberation and spread of knowledge, naturopathy, editing of journals, etc. States his life, messages and achievements.

020.92 K Kaula, P N

Chaudhary, Poonam 248

Felicitation and honours conferred and works on Prof Kaula, *DLIS,* 601-602.

Mentions felicitations and honours conferred by various societies, associations, organisations in India and abroad. Also includes works on Prof Kaula.

Curras, Emilia 249

Impact on international documentation : Contribution of Professor Kaula, *DLIS*, 310-321.

Covers some aspects of international documentation and the impact of P N Kaula by his works, views, meetings, and personality. Expresses admiration of P N Kaula for his oratory and depth of knowledge on the subject.

Esperanza, M Sister 250

Going up the ladder : A chronology of events in Kaula's life, *DLIS*, 607-620.

Lists chronology of events from March 13, 1924, Kaula's birth in Srinagar (Kashmir) to 1990.

Esperanza, M Sister 251

An institution by himself, *DLIS,* 553-569.

Makes an institute study of Kaula's work as UNESCO Expert, as Journalist, as learner and as leader of the profession. Gives a personal glimpse of Kaula as a man with tremendous courage, fortitude and ever willing to help others.

Gupta, S R 252

Untold episodes of a dedicated life (3), *Her Lib Sci* 30 (1-2) Jan-Apr 1991 : 58-65.

Mentions earlier two episodes published in *Her Lib Sci*, 13, 1974. Describes 9 episodes from Kaula's life relating to his dashing and risky adventures of early younger days from going to Madras for LIS course to Pilani, Delhi, Aligarh Muslim University, and his association with Ranganathan.

Gupta, S R and **Verma, S S** 253

The sui generis educator, *DLIS*, 475-491.

Describes the genius of Prof P N Kaula as exhibited in his activities of teacher-educator and his contributions to his discipline of LIS. Portraits Kaula as an educator and assesses his work covering the span of 34 years.

Gurtu, Arvind 254

Views and expressions, *DLIS,* 515-522.

Evaluates work of Kaula narrating some of the episodes from his life. Highlights his views on the slow development of libraries.

Khurshid, Anis 255

Multifaceted internationalist : Salutations to Prof P N Kaula,. *DLIS*, 501-503.

Gives briefly the admirable record and influence of the work of P N Kaula who is referred to as a multifaceted internationalist. Pays tributes from Pakistan.

Konnur, M B 256

Friend, philosopher and guide of librarians, *DLIS,* 547-551.

Projects the profoundity of P N Kaula's knowledge and willingness to help researchers.

Kumar, P S G and **Gupta, S R** 257

Works of Professor Kaula, *DLIS,* 583-597.

Lists all the works of Prof P N Kaula. Part A consists of books and monographs written/compiled/edited. Part B includes periodicals edited by him. Part C includes schedules of depth classification. In Part D are given library development plans; while Part E includes draft library Bills. Part F contains Memos submitted; while Part G includes journals in which his writings are published. Further parts include information about lectures delivered, conferences attended, Awards instituted.

Lazar, Peter 258

International librarianship and Kaula, *DLIS*, 303-317.

Discusses international librarianship and the impact of the work of P N Kaula. Brings out the difference between librarianship and information science and projects the view of Kaula on the subject. Also presents the dichotomy created in the field.

Nayeem, M A 259

The ideal librarian and inspiring teacher, *DLIS*, 493-500.

Describes the missionary devotion of P N Kaula which makes an ideal librarian and an inspiring teacher of LIS. Speaks about the awards won, recognitions gained and other activities on other related fields.

Rudich, Salomon M Dorf 260

Prof Kaula's achievements and impact on Cuba, *DLIS,* 331-338.

Describes the development of library and information services in

Cuba and the work of P N Kaula as Unesco Expert. Gives an impact of his activities, his personality, learning, etc.

Satija, M P and **Sukhdev Singh** 261

An essay on Professor Kaula's contributions to library journalism, *DLIS*, 461-473.

Presents an account of the editing work of journals by Kaula starting with Abgila. Evaluates the work of journalism specifying the features and standards set out by him.

Shores, Louis 262

World librarianship for century twenty-one : An essay dedicated to the Editor P N Kaula, *Her Lib Sci* 29(1-2) Jan-Apr 1990 : 63-64.

Refers to the imagination of Don Quixote and quest for life through landing on moon. Discusses Western interest in Physics and work at Duke University. Describes the earthly potential of libraries and predicts an exciting thrust into the unknown. This essay was written on June 13, 1976 for Kaula Festschrift.

Shukla, B B 263

Work and impact of Prof Prithvi Nath Kaula : A study, *DLIS*, 535-545.

Provides information about Kaula's birth and early career. Describes several aspects of his work and their impact on national and international librarianship.

Subba Rao, C V 264

Roses and thorns : A view of Kaula's life, *DLIS*, 505-513.

Presents a critical appreciation of Kaula projecting him as a faithful disciple of S R Ranganathan, and admiring his courage, fortitude, competence, standards and an ideal of his own.

Thakur, U M 265

Prof P N Kaula and Bihar, *DLIS*, 455-460.

Describes the work of P N Kaula in the promotion of library legislation and library education in Bihar. Also refers to the Address of Tributes presented by 22 organisations at Patna.

Venkatappaiah, V 266

Introduction, *DLIS,* 27-37.

Provides introduction about Prof P N Kaula, his struggles and hard work and service, record of contribution, as a man of endearing qualities.

020.92 M McColvin, L R

Arora, R L and **Puri, K Inder** 267

Contribution of McColvin in the field of library science (1896-1976), *Int Lib Move* 12 (3) Sept 1990 : 113-117.

Deals with the early life of L R McColvin born on 30 Nov 1896. Discusses him as a man, his career and position, his personality, as an administrator, as a writer, as an editor, Describes him as a pioneer of the Library Association, and the honours he got.

020.92 R Ramakrishnan Nair, M N

Prof M N Ramakrishnan Nayar : A short biography, *PLSI*, xi-xii. 268

Provides a brief biographical account of Prof M N Ramakrishnan who has recently retired as Head, Dept of Library and Information Science, University of Kerala, Trivandrum.

020.92 RA Ranganathan, S R

Girja Kumar 269

Relevance of Ranganathan, *CLIS Observer* 8(3-4) July-Dec 1991 : 43-48.

Examines critically the relevance of Ranganathan's contributions. Delineates their strength and limitations in the context of recent development in the field of LIS. States that his basic contribution need to be reassessed to make them relevant to present day needs.

Konnur, M B 270

Dr Ranganathan and American librarianship, *DLIS*, 297-301.

Narrates the impact of the works of Dr S R Ranganathan on American librarianship. Refers to the tributes paid to the work of Ranganathan as 'World Librarian'.

Ranganathan International Centenary Volume Committee 271

Invitation for contributions, *Her Lib Sci* 30 (3-4) July-Oct 1991 : 239-240.

Reports an invitation to the professionals for contribution to be included in the Centenary Volume entitled 'International and Comparative Librarianship and Information Systems' to cover all aspects of LIS of which Ranganathan was the fountainhead during his life time.

Ranganathan, S R 272

A librarian looks back : Autobiography of Dr S R Ranganathan, appended with an evaluation of his life and work, by P N Kaula, New Delhi: ABC Publishing House, 1990.

Recollects what the great library scientist Ranganathan has to say about himself, about his 'person' how he led his life, was he really great, and many more questions are answered. It is mostly reproduction of his essays in *Her Lib Sci*, 1962-72. Includes addition by P N Kaula.

Satija, M P 273

Ranganathan : Development of his writing career, *Lib Her* 29 (1-2) Apr-Sept 1990 : 63-71.

Describes contribution of Ranganathan. Considers his *Five Laws* as a fountainhead of his work. Regards Colon Classification as a second great breakthrough after Dewey. Points out that he recovered universal attention in his life time, his work won him wide acclaim. Concludes that he was having futuristic approach.

020.92 S Saxena, T P

Professor T P Saxena, *ULI*, 1-4. 274

Provides a biographical account of Prof T P Saxena who was born in Feb 1916 in Jhansi district of U P, got education at Lucknow and Imperial Library, Calcutta, served at Lucknow University Library, Allahabad University Library, and at Aligarh Muslim University as head of the Dept, and came to PAU, Ludhiana in 1965 where he retired in 1978. Gives account of his significant publications and other contributions.

020.92 SH Sharma, J S

Sharma, Jagdish S 275

My life and work, New Delhi : Ess Ess Publications, 1990. 88 p.

Prepared as a supplement to an earlier publication *Library movement in India and abroad.* This autobiography of the famous librarian, library educator is divided into eight chapters describing his migration to USA and visits to other Scandinavian countries.

020.9 LIS – History
History of Library and Information Science

020.947 LIS – Soviet Russia

Kushnarenko, Natalya N 276

Soviet local studies librarianship : The present-day situation and tendencies of its future development, *Jl Lib and Inf Sci* 14(2) Dec 1989: 128-135.

Discusses importance of local studies activities in libraries. Explains their practical implementation in USSR. Suggests the Type of professional education needed for such activities. Mentions need for cooperation.

020.954 LIS – India

Davis, Donald G (Jr) 277

The status of library history in India : A report of an informal survey and a selective bibliographic essay, *Jl Lib and Inf Sci* 14(2) Dec 1989: 98-114.

Discusses present status of library history in India. Surveys present activities. Reviews systematically English language literature on the subject. Describes findings based on literature survey, interviews with several leaders in profession. Compares with similar efforts in other countries. Brings out gap areas.

Khan, H A 278

Library profession in India : A look back, *PL*, 1-8.

Provides an overview of library profession in India through 20th century giving library development, library education, library literature, library associations, library profession, and government attitude. Deals with development of public libraries, school libraries, children libraries, college and university libraries, research and scientific libraries, national libraries. Discusses the future of library profession in India.

020.954162 LIS – Assam

Buragohain, Alka and **Lahkar, Narendra** 279

Prof Kaula and Assam library movement, *DLIS*, 447-454.

Mentions the work of Prof Kaula in the development of public and academic libraries in Assam during his various visits.

020.95483 LIS – Kerala

Raman Nair, R 280

The emergence of organised library movement in Kerala, *Int Lib Move* 13(4) Dec 1991 : 209-216.

Describes attempts made to organise library movement in Kerala. Explains efforts of Kerala Granthalaya Sanghom, Kerala Granthasala Sanghom, Dewan Sri C P Ramaswamy Aiyer, etc.

020.95484 LIS – Andhra Pradesh

Raju, A A N 281

Library movement in Telangana during 1901-1948, *ILA Bull* 27(3) Oct-Dec 1991: 107-110.

Traces the historical development of library movement in Telangana since 1901, and various conferences organised to give a fillip to it. Concludes that this library movement helped the genesis of literary and linguistic movements and political awakening in the Telangana region of Andhra Pradesh.

020.962 LIS – Egypt

020.962(1) Alexandrian Library

Aman, Mohammed M 282

Alexandrian Library rises again, *Her Lib Sci* 29 (1-2) Jan-Apr 1990 : 3-11.

Relates the past history of the great Alexandrian Library set up in

332 B C. Describes type of literature in its holdings in ancient past Narrates its destruction. Evaluates the project for the establishment of new Alexandrian Library with the support from UNESCO and UNDP. Discusses international significance of the project, subject orientation of the collection, organisation and structure envisaged. Gives also cost estimates of the project.

020.973 LIS – USA

Sharma, Ravindra N 283

Information science and its development in the United States, *ISL*, 23-32.

Traces the development of information science in the USA since the establishment of the American Documentation Institute. Discusses role of LIS schools to adopt information science in their curricula. Describes impact of information science on libraries. Gives the present status and future in view of the development of CD-ROM technology.

020.99611 LIS – Fiji

Ali, F A 284

Library service of Fiji, *Jl Lib and Inf Sci* 15(1) June 1990 : 87-94.

Highlights the main features of library services in Fiji with emphasis on public library services and school library services.

021.2 Library and Society

Library and Community

Nedosa, P S 285

Impediments to democratic process in Africa : The other downplayed variable, *Int Lib Move* 12(4) Dec 1990 : 201-212.

Discusses the concept of democracy. Points that the role of information as it exists in different forms of print and non-print forms including gathering, organisation, storage, retrieval and dissemination by librarians in supporting and stabilising democratic rule in Africa. Also emphasizes role of library and information scientists.

021.24 Libraries and Educational Role

Kaula, P N 286

Observations on education and libraries : Press conference addressed by Prof Kaula at Visakhapatnam, *Her Lib Sci* 30(3-4) July-Oct 1991 : 241-242.

Reports addressing the Press conference on 30 Nov 1991, on policy of the Govt on education and libraries. Reproduces the report published in the *Indian Express* of 1 Dec 1990.

021.24(1) Libraries and Adult Education

Agada, John 287

Towards people-oriented development in the Third World : A case for relevant library services, *Int Lib Move* 12(3) Sept 1990 : 125-136.

Attempts to re-examine the concepts of individual and national development and the human factor collateral. Points out that libraries have failed to touch the lives of 90 per cent of people. Challenges the tradition of illiteracy problem syndrome and seeks new dimensions of relevance.

Mohanrajan, P A 288

Fusion of National Literacy Mission and Raja Rammohun Roy Library Foundation programme : Need for an integrated approach, *Granthana* 1(1) Jan 1990 : 25-39.

Mentions the role of revolutions, industrial revolutions and need of library for it. Describes adult education programme in India. Identifies barriers to adult education programmes. Discusses NLM launched in 1988, its key issues, voluntary agencies, Jana Shiksan Nilayams. Brings out role of libraries in national system of education. Discusses role of RRRLF in the development of public libraries.

Sahoo, K C 289

Role of library in mass education, *Ind Jl Inf Lib & Society* 3(3-4) Sept-Dec 1990 : 291-298.

Defines the terms 'library' and 'education'. Discusses how the public library plays the role of an informal educational institution with special reference to adult illiterates. Explains how the different groups of society are benefitted through extension services.

021.24(1) Libraries and New Education Policy

Sangam, S L 290

The New Education Policy and library services, *Ind Jl Inf Lib & Society* 3(1-2) Mar-June 1990 : 107-115.

Mentions about the different education commissions. Describes the role of libraries in the educational process. Points out various difficulties of academic libraries and remedial measures for the same. Pleads for National Policy on L&I Services. Makes out a case for recognition of the significance of role of libraries in NEP.

021.642 Union Catalogues

Hariharan, A, Keshava Rao, B R and **Somaiah, M S** 291

Design and development of a database on micro-CDS/ISIS-union catalogue of S & T conference proceedings, *Ann Lib Sci and Doc* 38 (2) June 1991 : 53-68.

States that a union catalogue for conference proceedings is not available. Describes the project taken up by INSDOC Regional Centre, Bangalore for covering S&T libraries in Bangalore. Describes their experiences of developing the database on Micro-CDS/ISIS and publishing the first volume of the union catalogue using DTP.

Khurshid, Anis 292

Union catalogue for Arab countries : Problems and prospects, *DLIS,* 409-428.

Provides picture of library infrastructure in the Arab countries. Gives need of resource sharing, meaning, uses, mechanics of union catalogue and its role in resource sharing. Discusses the problems and prospects of union catalogue work for 21 countries in the Arab region.

Malhan, I V and **Satija, M P** 293

Union catalogues of scientific serials in India with special reference to NUCSSI (1988), *Jl Lib and Inf Sci* 14(2) Dec 1989 : 136-141.

Explains usefulness of a union catalogue. Discusses efforts of the ILA and INSDOC towards compilation of union catalogue. Gives in detail the scope, arrangement, etc of NUCSSI.

021.65 Library Networks, Consortia, etc

Kaul, H K 294

Library networks in UK and Spain : The projections for India, *Her Lib Sci* 29(3-4) July-Oct 1990 : 179-192.

Discusses progress of library automation in European countries. Describes in detail the networks in UK and bibliographic networks in Spain. Describes other cooperative projects. Provides broad projections.

Kaul, H K 295

The library networks in UK and Spain : The projections for India, *CALNE*, 224-239.

Explains the networking in Europe particularly the UK and Spain, where some library automation projects exist. Outlines the broad projections of these networks studies by the author by his personal visits.

Katyal, Prem Lata, Gambhir, Sudha and **Rao, Nag Jyotsna** 296

National information system and network in India, *NIPP*, 294-300.

Defines the concept of information system. Highlights the activities of some of the national information systems, i.e., NICNET, INDONET, CALIBNET, DELNET, SIRNET, INFLIBNET. Mentions bibliographic applications in general data networks.

Parida, Baman 297

Networking of libraries and information centres in India, *NIPP*, 113-121.

Gives a brief account of the various networks that are being developed in India using computer mediated communication facilities and of some Asian regional networks of interest to India such as APINMAP, ASTINET, EASYNET, etc.

Raina, Roshan and **Mishra, Rajesh K** 298

Networking the library systems of the national level management schools in India, *IM*, 70.

Discusses the feasibility of establishing a network among the library systems of management schools of India in a three-phase programme. Discusses mechanism of its operation and telecommunication considerations. Highlights telecommunication issues involved in such a network to make it cost effective.

Rajeswari, D 299

Computer and library networking, *CALNE,* 214-219.

States that in view of the rising costs of library materials sharing of resources in becoming more important. Defines network. Gives aims and objectives of library network. Discusses library automation and network in India and abroad. Mentions INFLIBNET as a cooperative network.

Satija, M P 300

Government data network in India, *Rilisar Bull* 7(1-4) Jan-Dec 1991 : 38-40.

Discusses NICNET as a network of Government of India initiated in 1977. Gives its various phases of development.

Sehgal, R L 301

Pica information network : A case study, *NIPP*, 350-354.

Describes Pica. Discusses Pica network and its participation in other projects. Explains its open library network, its features such as resource sharing for the participating institutions, ILL, On line retrieval system, etc. Discusses local library systems. Describes the user support in Pica.

Sharma, R N 302

Workshop on business and information networks, *Her Lib Sci* 29(1-2) Jan-Apr 1990 : 99-100.

Gives the discussion, Keynote address and futures plans on the occasion of the Workshop on Business and Information Networks organised by the Federation of Indian Chambers of Commerce and Industry on 16 Nov 1989.

United States Information Service 303

Computer networking : USIS experience, *INICAE* 9(1) Mar 1991 : 54-66.

Explains networking and the quality of electronic transmission, media used telephone network, data transmission, microwave transmission, satellite transmission. Describes commercial networks, library networks and through illustrations structure of networking. Suggests data networks and their operation in India.

Viswanathan, T, Mittal, Rekha and **Lakshmi, V V** 304

Library networks in India, *Ann Lib Sci and Doc* 38(2) June 1991 : 39-52.

Mentions importance of information and information network. Explains INFLIBNET, CALIBNET, DELNET, SIRNET established in India. Gives importance and need of inter networking. Proposes a SAARC Information Network (SARINET).

021.65(1) CALIBNET

Majumdar, S and **Taneja, Ram D** 305

Calcutta Library Network (CALIBNET) software : New Delhi exposition a curtain raiser, *NISSAT Newsletter* 10(3) July-Sept 1991 : 10-14.

Reports about the demonstration of CALIBNET software organised by NISSAT and DELNET on July 18-19, 1991 in New Delhi.

Roy, Satyabrata, Sen, Jayashree and **Chatterjee, Ashis** 306

Calcutta calls to close the information gap, *CALNE,* 324-330.

Deals with the CALIBNET plan being developed with the help of NISSAT. Gives its overview, possibilities and requirements, critical issues. Concludes that CALIBNET is striving to adapt to the needs of information age.

021.65 (1) CANARANET

Mohandas, M K and **Shet, K C** 307

CANARANET : A proposal for data network for Dakshina Kannada district, *ILA Bull* 27(3) Oct-Dec 1991 : 126-129.

Proposes a data network for Dakshina Kannada district which is fast developing, and is expected to meet its information dissemination, assimilation requirements, particularly to meet the needs of the academic institutions in the matter of library resource sharing, and also to help the Government of India NICNET, etc.

021.65 (1) Ch I N

International Chemical Information Network (Ch I N), *NISSAT Newsletter* 9(4) Oct-Dec 1990 : 13-14. 308

Describes the objectives of Ch I N, the Ch I N programme, activities, pilot projects, and membership of Ch I N.

021.65(1) DELNET

Guha, B 309

Synopsis of the report as feasibility study on automation and networking of Delhi libraries (DELNET) prepared by CMC Ltd, New Delhi : NISSAT/DSR, 1991. 51 p.

Describes in gist the feasibility of automation and networking of a number of libraries in Delhi. Gives figures representing the network configurations to be followed in Phase I and Phase II. Includes other important data regarding the collection, manpower, user services, funds, etc of the libraries.

Kaul, H K 310

DELNET : A brief introduction, *NIPP*, 328-335.

Mentions origin of DELNET. Gives pre-requisites for participation. Discusses actions initiated in this regard. Explains the achievements of DELNET during the last three years with the creation of bibliographic database.

Kaul, H K and **Taneja, Ram D** 311

Computerised network of Delhi libraries : DELNET E-mail launched, *NISSAT Newsletter* 10(2) Apr-June 1991 : 3-5.

Reports about the launching of DELNET E-mail on 19 March 1991 with the support of NISSAT. Mentions about the project and libraries already started activities on computerised catalogues in the zero phase.

021.65(1) ERNET

Project Ernet, *NISSAT Newsletter* 9(4) Oct-Dec 1990 : 6-10. 312

Explains the implementation of Project ERNET initiated during the Seventh Five Year Plan (1985-90) aimed at setting up a computer network for academic and research community. Outlines methodology, objectives, infrastructure, standards and protocols, strategy, participating agencies, etc.

021.65(1) I-NET

I-NET: Packet switched service for reliable data communication, *NISSAT Newsletter* 10(4) Oct-Dec 1991 : 5-7. 313

Explains I-NET being introduced by the Dept of Telecommunication as a bearer network for fast, reliable, flexible and cost-effective transport of information. Gives the concept, terminal equipment, benefits, typical applications and facilities.

021.65(1) INDONET

Basu, R N 314

National information networks: INDONET, *NIPP*, 371-379.

Gives evolution and need of networking in India. Discusses objectives of INDONET. Describes its development in Phase I with higher speed data transmission in Phase II, access to public databases, advanced scientific software packages, etc.

021.65(1) INFLIBNET

Arora, O P 315

Information and Library Network (INFLIBNET), *NIPP*, 313-321.

States that INFLIBNET is a nationwide computer communication network linking libraries. Describes that in view of the limited resources available during Eighth Plan the number of nodes have been reduced to 60-80 which will be expanded to cover all the 400 nodes in the Ninth Plan. Mentions that all the participating nodes will have requisite computer and communication hardware/ software and trained staff.

Baba, Abdul Majid 316

Information and Library Network (INFLIBNET), *CALNE,* 296-302.

Gives concept of INFLIBNET. Discusses its objectives linking libraries and information centres in universities, institutions of national importance, R & D centres, colleges, etc. Describes its functioning, network services at different levels, management mechanism, communication system, personnel needs, implementation, and cost implication.

Banerjee, Bimal Kumar 317

Library network and resource sharing in the context of INFLIBNET and CALIBNET, *CALNE*, 303-315.

States that sharing of resources is the major objectives of INFLIBNET. Discusses need of resource sharing in accessibility of information. Describes shared acquisition, shared cataloguing, NUCSSI and its machine-readable database, saving in duplication, need of networking. Gives Indian scenario of scientific information system such as CALIBNET, INFLIBNET. Also gives document delivery scene in India.

Borkar, V M 318

Academic library system and development of INFLIBNET, *NIPP*, 249-252.

Explains that an academic library system with some modification can make a success of INFLIBNET because UGC is the vital force behind. Explains the process of information communication with a network structure where academic library system is depicted as the centre. Describes INFLIBNET and its salient features.

Dwivedi, P N 319

The problems of standardisation in operations systems and services in the field of INFLIBNET *Ind Jl Inf Lib & Society* 4(2) June 1991 : 104-111.

Explains aims of INFLIBNET. Lays emphasis on inter connecting university and academic libraries. Outlines some problems of standardisation in operations systems and services.

Kamaiah, P 320

INFLIBNET, *NIPP,* 322-327.

Points out need for information policy. Brings out need for national information system to achieve optimum results in the use of information. Describes the genesis and growth of INFLIBNET. Deals with the follow up action by the UGC. Discusses the problems faced by it. Offers suggestions for effective implementation of the objectives of INFLIBNET.

Kumarappa, G and **Balakumari, N** 321

Indian languages in INFLIBNET : Role of National Library, *CALNE*, 316-323.

Deals with the need of using Roman alphabet for bibliographic contorl in Indian languages. Gives the state-of-the-art of transliteration of Indian languages mentioning problems relating to Indic names, corporate bodies, place names, subject headings, etc. Mentions efforts of switching from one language to another through computers. Explains role of National Library in this context.

Pawar, S S, Thakar, G S and **Sharma, Neelam** 322

Establishment of information and library network : A critical appraisal, *NIPP,* 301-307.

Gives overview of libraries and information centres in India. Examine the scope and objective of INFLIBNET and the problems to be faced in the implementation of the programme.

Sharma, S K and **Vinod Kumar** 323

National information networks : National information systems, *NIPP*, 290-293.

States that INFLIBNET is a cooperative network and will contribute to pooling, sharing and optimization of resources facilities and services of libraries and information centres in university system. Describes that it is a major programme for modernisation of libraries and information centres in the country with application of modern technologies of information dissemination.

University Grants Commission (India), Inter Agency Working Group 324

Information and Library Network (INFLIBNET) : A summary of the report of the Inter-Agency Working Group, *INICAE* 9(1) Mar 1990 : 68-90.

Gives the background and constituting the 'Working Group' on INFLIBNET. Describes objectives and its focus. Discusses services of INFLIBNET as multiple function/service network. Describes organisation of information management in INFLIBNET and location of different centres. Explains areas of standardization in information handling, software requirement, computer hardware in various libraries, sectoral information centre.

Zaidi, S Mustafa 325

Information and Library Network (INFLIBNET) : The proposal and some possible constraints, *OSUL*, 197-210.

Gives the genesis of INFLIBNET and its needs. Mentions how it will function. Describes recommendations in each areas, the progress made, prospects and constraints. Gives some critical comments. Gives terms of reference for the Working Group and recommendation in the two Annextures.

021.65(1) INWDS

Inamdar, N B 326

Planning and Training Workshop for Information Network for Women and Development Studies : A report, *Her Lib Sci* 30(1-2) Jan-Apr 1991 : 85-88.

Reports about this three day Workshop held at Osmania University, August 10-12, 1990. Discusses about inauguration session, Session 1, Discussion Sessions, Valedictory function, vote of thanks, etc.

021.65(1) ISDN Network

Asia Pacific Telecommunity, Pattaya, Thailand 327

Integrated Services Digital Network (ISDN), *INICAE* 9(1) Mar 1990 : 107.

Explains the ISDN networks. Reports about the regional seminar organised by the Asia Pacific Telecommunity in Pattaya, Thailand, from 24 to 27 May 1988.

021.65(1) NELIBNET

Lahiri, Ramansu and **Subramaniam, Krishnan** 328

NELIBNET, a promise of prospect for North-East India : An outline, *NIPP*, 336-343.

States that online network system in the North-eastern region is a necessity. Proposes to have an online network system called NELIBNET connecting all the documentation centres, university libraries, college, and special libraries. Mentions that linkage between NELIBNET and INFLIBNET would be set up. Points out that the proposal has been taken up by the Manipur University.

Lahiri, Ramansu and **Subramaniam, Krishnan** 329

NELIBNET – a promise of prospect for North East India : An outline, *Univ News* 29(34) 26 Aug 1991 : 9-13.

Makes a case for NELIBNET to be set up for Northeastern states, and thereby connect all the libraries, documentation and information centres for the purposes of resource sharing.

021.65(1) NICNET

District Informations System of the National Informatics Centre, *HLAICI*, v 7, 26-33. 330

Describes the District Information System of the NIC under the Govt of India plan extending NICNET to cover the entire country. Explains the plan to create district databases, monitoring databases, administrative database, socio-economic database, DISNIC infrastructure, training etc.

Panigrahi, Jyotirmaya 331

NICNET (National Information Center Network), *NIPP*, 308-312.

Provides the scope and objectives of NICNET. Gives the network description, the facilities and services available through it, such as bibliographic applications, MEDLARS operations in India, etc. Gives also the future plans.

Seshagiri, N et al 332

NICNET ; a hierarchical distributed computer communication network for decision support in the Indian government, *HLAICI*, v 7, 47-58.

Describes in detail the origin and development of NIC from 1973 and setting up of NICNET in 1977. Gives hierarchy of government informatics from national to grass-root level. Explains NICNET architecture-computer, communication, master and micro earth station, network features, terrestrial communication and network.

021.65(1) PAISNET

Ragavan, M C, Suresh Kumar and **Gulati, Sunita** 333

National Public Administration Information Services Network (PAISNET): A Proposal, *CALNE*, 266-286.

Outlines need of national information systems in public administration. Lists objectives of PAISNET. Describes organizational structure and model for various institutions. Discusses role of IIPA as the national coordinating centre. Deals with the structure and model including characteristics, working together, etc. Discusses network activities involved.

021.65(1) RINSCA Network

Akopov, A 334

Regional Informatics Network for South and Central Asia (RINSCA), *NISSAT Newsletter* 9(4) Oct-Dec 1990 : 3-5.

Discusses the new project proposal on RINSCA for evolving Regional Informatics Network for Asia and Pacific in cooperation with NIC of India in accordance with the recommendations of the previous meeting of the National Coordinators held in Kathmandu, Nepal in Oct 1989.

021.65(1) SIRNET

Sirnet Electronic mail system, *NISSAT Newsletter* 10(1) Jan-Mar 1991 : 3-6. 335

Explains the setting up of SIRNET as a computer communication network for the CSIR labs. Gives equipments required, mail node set up, etc. Mentions how INSDOC helps in developing expertise in establishing E-mail facilities. Describes what is E-mail. Lists institutions on E-mail network.

021.65(1) SSIRNET

Rab, S Fazle 336

Managing information : Need for the planning of Social Science Research Institute's Network (SSIRNET), *CALNE*, 253-265.

Traces growth of social science research organisation in India, regional centres of ICDDR. Discusses use of social science knowledge to academicians and society. Explains concept of information network. Describes growth of networking in India and barriers to networkings. Stresses need for establishing SSIRNET with computers.

021.65 (1) TECHNET

Joshi, Jayshree 337

Technical Education Libraries Network (TECHNET) – Gujarat : A proposed plan, *CALNE*, 240-249.

Explains the concepts of network and information network. Makes a proposal for a network plan for libraries under the Dept of

Technical Education in Gujarat. Outlines its goals and objectives, services and other inputs.

021.65(1) LAN

Ahuja, J P S 338

Building a micro-computer based local area network for libraries : From concept to precept, *Lib Sci slant Doc and Inf Std* 29(2) June 1991 : 58-64.

Describes need for networking a library with various constituent units of its parent organisation. Puts forth a case for building a micro computer based LAN. Compares characteristics of a mini computer based system with those of microcomputer based system. Defines the concept of network, networking, etc.

Desikan, R S and **Muthuswamy, R** 339

Configuring a Local Area Network system for a technical information centre : A case study, *AGLIS Jl* 8 (1-4) Jan- Dec 1990 : 41-49.

Emphasises the need for planning while buying computer hardware for information retrieval and library automation. Discusses plus points of LAN and draws comparison with a distributive system. Analyses system, component, peripherals and justifies selection of the right one for the LAN configuration in terms of technical and financial considerations.

Natarajan, M 340

Local Area Network: Requisites for structure and applications. *NISSAT Newsletter* 9(2) Apr-June 1990 : 3-7.

Defines LAN. Gives its need. Explains design concept of LAN and technology required. Discusses applications of LAN, its advantages and disadvantages.

Selvi, M G 341

Current technology in the library-Local Area Networks (LANs), *Ann Lib Sci and Doc* 38(3) Sept 1991 : 108-118.

States that LANs have been developing rapidly. Defines LAN, states characteristics, position and classification. Deals with four main technological aspects essential for LANs. Describes importance of application of LANs in libraries.

021.65(1) Resource Sharing

Chopra, H R 342

Resource sharing in university libraries in India, *OSUL*, 146-152.

Defines resource sharing. Explains need of resource sharing in university libraries. Identifies areas of resource sharing. Describes various levels of resource sharing and how it can be done. Also mentions INFLIBNET.

Dubey, Yogendra P 343

The economics of information transfer using Resource Sharing Simulation System (RSSS) : A decision support system, *Lib Sci slant Doc and Inf Std* 28(2) June 1991 : 82-86.

Discusses features of INFLIBNET. Identifies the economics component of the network. Points out the problems of the governance of the system and suggests a computer based decision support system for the network.

Joshi, S C 344

Resource sharing, *Ind Jl Inf Lib & Society* 3(3-4) Sept-Dec 1990 : 153-160.

Gives importance of resource sharing. Defines ways and means of resource sharing. Mentions resource sharing trends in India.

Pusty, Jatindra Nath 345

Sharing the resources of text-book library in a scientific and technological library system, *College Libn* 69(1-4) 1990 : 8-12.

Explains reasons of sharing textbook in this era of technological development. Discusses sharing at undergraduate level. Mentions the participants and gives procedure of getting books issued. Discusses merits and limitations. Mentions areas of success.

Ramaiah, L S 346

Resource sharing among the Indian university libraries: The need for a network, *CPT*, 294-300.

Provides an overview of higher education in India. Makes a case for networks of university libraries. Discusses pre-requisites for resource sharing. States that university libraries should be provided with microfilming facilities, xeroxing, micro-processors, etc. Describes the tools and the operations needed for an effective network.

Raman Nair, R 347

Resource sharing networks for higher education at state level, *CALNE,* 331-345.

Defines Resource Sharing Networks (RSNW). Outlines its need and objectives. Gives its implications. Discusses range and requirements. Describes RSNW in India in higher education including efforts of UGC. Discusses RSNW for higher education including INFLIBNET. Describes higher education situation in Kerala and need for RSNW for Kerala.

Soma Raju, P 348

Resource sharing among university libraries, *ULI*, 115-122.

Discusses functions and problems of a university library. Brings out importance of resource sharing among university libraries and how they should go about. Says that resource sharing at state/regional level is feasible. Gives a proposal for resource sharing for Andhra Pradesh universities through the A P University Library Network.

021.7 Public Relations (PR)

Karisiddappa, C R, Sangam, S L and **Konnur, P V** 349

Professional excellence through library public relation with special reference to Karnataka library system, *ILA Bull* 27(3) Oct-Dec 1991 : 97-101.

States that image of the public library in most cases is not good. Mentions that the negligence of public relations concept and programmes by professional librarians is one reason. Highlights the role of PR in public libraries in the achievement of professional excellence in Karnataka. Suggests improvement of PR to rebuild its finer image.

Prafulla Chandra, T V 350

Application of public relations research techniques for improving the professional image of library/information personnel, *SALP,* 68-70.

Discusses the role of PR to change the attitude of indifferent politicians, non-assertive public towards the library and information professionals. Describes the strategy to effectively utilise the various media in order to enhance the image.

021.7(1) Foreign Cultural Centres Libraries

Amudhavalli, A 351

Library services of foreign cultural centres at Madras, *CPT,* 104-113.

Attempts to provide a descriptive account of the American Centre Library and the British Council Library at Madras regarding their genesis, book resources, staff resources, users and services. Also gives a comparative view.

021.8 Exchange of Librarians

Konnur, M B 352

Transnational library relations : The Indo-American experience, *Lib Her* 27 (3-4) Oct 1988 – Jan 1989 : 128-134.

Provides summary of the Ph D thesis submitted by the author in 1986 to the University of Poona under the supervision of Prof M R Riswadkar.

Konnur, M B 353

Transnational library relations : The Indo-American experience, New Delhi : Concept Publishing Company, 1990. xiv, 191 p.

Includes 8 chapters based on a Ph D work of the author. Studies library relations which emerged and were strengthened between India and the USA during more than the past 75 years.

021.82 Commissions and Libraries

Education Commission (India) (Kothari Commission) (1964) 354

Recommendations, *OSUL,* 256-259.

Gives recommendations of the Kothari Commission (1964-66) on development of libraries, finance and expenditure, collection development plan of a university library in Appendix III.

Kalia, D R 355

A Library Commission of Inquiry and technical audit of academic libraries, *CLIS Observer* 8(1-2) Jan-June 1991 : 1-2.

In this Editorial, the Editor makes a case for appointing a 'Library Commission of Inquiry' to report on university and college libraries and provide guidelines for promoting library-based education.

022.3 Library Buildings – Planning and Design

Deshmukh, P P 356

The planning of a library building, *ULI*, 214-222.

Gives guidelines for planning a library building. Pleads for a collaboration of librarian and architect. Gives norms for site selection keeping into view growth factor. Provides guidelines for planning exterior and interior. Discusses location of various sections and work areas.

022.3172 University Library Buildings

Rajwant Singh 357

Planning the university library building in India, *OSUL*, 187-196.

Gives importance of library building. Explains need of planning the library building. Lists principles of planning and views of authorities. Describes lighting and airconditioning, equipment and furniture selection.

Rajwant Singh 358

Who's who in planning university library building, *ULI*, 223-230.

States that planning of a university library is a team-work. Suggests the composition of planning team. Discusses in detail the role and responsibility of university librarian, architect and the consultant. Deals with various aspects of cooperation between university librarian and architect. Discusses librarian's brief for the architect.

Tejomurty, A and **Shukla, K H** 359

University library buildings in Gujarat, *ILA Bull* 26(2) July-Sept 1990:80-94.

Discusses importance of university library buildings. Explains concepts of principles of planning and library building committee. Explains location of university library buildings in Gujarat. Discusses floor areas with space dimensions, stack area, general reading area, etc. Indicates future considerations.

022.9 Library Equipments, Furniture, etc

Grover, D R and **Gupta, Urmil** 360

Library furniture, *ULI*, 231-240.

Brings out importance of a well-designed university library building and qualities of furniture. Discusses various items of furniture and their specialisations. Deals in detail with bookracks, catalogue cabinets, display racks, storage racks, reading tables, chairs, trolleys, charging trays, atlas stands, etc.

Mahajan, S G 361

Establishing a microfilming unit in the Poona University Library, *CPT*, 147-154.

Describes the preparation of the proposal, terms and conditions of donation. Lists problems faced while setting up the Microfilming Unit. Mentions selection of the equipment, items of equipment to be purchased. Mentions the problems that lie ahead.

023 LIBRARY PERSONNEL MANPOWER DEVELOPMENT STAFFING

Aguolu, C C 362

Staffing in Nigerian university libraries, *Her Lib Sci* 29(1-2) Jan-Apr 1990: 24-37.

Makes a study based on a sample of six oldest Nigerian university libraries. Evaluates librarian's perceptions of their responsibilities, their academic and professional background, work environment, job satisfaction, and opportunities for continuing education and professional development. Reveals that effective library service has been hindered by the inability of library administrators to conceptualise proper role of librarian, rigid bureaucratization of libraries, etc.

Anand, C M and **Sen, B K** 363

Manpower development for computer applications to library and information activities – role of INSDOC, *IASLIC Bull* 36(4) Dec 1991 : 157-169.

Describes that INSDOC has been offering a two year training course in information science since 1964. Retraces the development of the course content in respect of computer applications in LIS activities. Reviews also INSDOC's programmes of short-term courses on computer application between 1987-92.

Bhargava, G D 364

Library personnel in university libraries, *OSUL*, 12-27.

Gives objectives of university libraries. Discusses about library standards. Analyses existing norms of library staff in university libraries in India. Describes basic and optimum norms of library personnel. Describes types and levels of manpower required. Deals with status and qualifications.

Chatterjee, Ashish and **Roy, Satyabrata** 365

Human relations : A problem in college libraries in India, *Luck Libn* 22(1-2) Mar-June 1990 : 13-16.

Deals with the relationship of the librarian with the management, students, teachers, colleagues, and others and the problems encountered by him in the course of his work.

Dasgupta, A K 366

National Technical Manpower Information System : A structure description, *HLAICI,* v 8, 1-10.

Describes the need for technical manpower. Raises some fundamental questions and issues and objectives of NTMIS. Discusses the structure of determinants of the information system, information flow system, organisation of input structure, output structure.

Devarajan, G 367

Professional manpower resources and prospective requirements in special libraries in Kerala, *PL*, 65-74.

States that professional power resources in libraries constitutes important component. Discusses relevance of manpower planning. Gives a brief account of special libraries and LIS education in India with a scene from Kerala also. Analyses data on special libraries in Kerala collected through questionnaire. Discusses qualifications of staff, their present position, positions frozen, library services, etc. Discusses prospective needs and problems.

Dosa, Marta 368

International cooperation in human resource development, *DLIS*, 81-91.

Emphasises role of human resources. Gives professional practice, education and research. Discusses some issues in human resources development. Describes problems solving in interdisciplinary areas. Makes proposals of international collaboration.

Gopalakrishnan Nair, P 369

Librarianship and professional development : An evaluation, *PL,* 34-43.

States that librarianship is at cross-roads and to survive personnel have to improve their skills through professional development. Explains factors necessitating professional development. Describes methods of professional development and role of library schools and library associations. Makes some suggestions.

Ijari, S R and **Kannappanavar, B U** 370

Development of professional manpower in public library system of Karnataka state, *PL,* 59-64.

Gives need of manpower in libraries. Discusses public library situation in Karnataka since 1965. Identifies present professional staff structure; assesses quality of service. Finds out reasons for inadequacies. Suggests a re-structure of staff to provide effective and efficient library services.

Isaac, D 371

Staff morale in libraries, *Luck Libn* 23(1) Jan-Mar 1991:31-35.

Discusses role of staff morale in libraries. Points out that organizational culture and emotional adjustment are important for raising the morale of staff. Suggests measures like counselling, workers participation in management and motivation as corrective measures to raise the morale of staff.

Isaac, K A 372

Professional development of librarian, *PL,* 9-13.

Emphasises on the need of professional development without which it will be rendered obsolete and redundant. Describes methods such as LIS education, continuing education programmes, acquaintance with current literature, publications, conferences, seminars, workshops, etc, work environments, duty v/s right, for development of library personnel.

Kapoor, S K 373

Role of IASLIC in manpower development, *IASLIC Bull* 36(4) Dec 1991 : 175-176.

Outlines briefly the role of IASLIC as a professional body in enhancing the competence of professionals in the new emerging areas of professions practice, particularly in IT. Outlines IASLIC's approach to manpower development in future.

Kemparaju, TD 374

Manpower development in library and information science – present and future need in the context of emerging technologies, *Ann Lib Sci & Doc* 37(2) June 1990 : 63-66.

Identifies role and impact of IT on LIS activities. Depicts changing scenario in the profession due to emerging IT. Identifies knowledge and skills requirements in LIS personnel to interact with changing environs. Suggests measures for its development and future challenges.

Lahiri, Ramansu 375

Manpower syndrome of university libraries: A case for serial unit, *Her Lib Sci* 30 (3-4) July-Oct 1991 : 195-204.

Studies the backdrop of dissatisfaction over serials service, the manpower syndrome of the serial unit of university libraries of North East region of India. Observes that all the units have become inefficient partly due to the absence of a proper supervisory position and required manpower. Makes an analysis and suggests some measures for overcoming the problem.

LIS Manpower needs in India : An assessment, *NISSAT News-letter* 10(30 July-Sept 1991 : 16-17. 376

Reports about the major findings of a survey of LIS manpower needs in India conducted jointly by Burdwan University and IASLIC, and sponsored by NISSAT.

Maheswarappa, B S and **Salmani, G K** 377

The demand for library and information workers in India : Analysis of advertised vacancies during 1988, *ILA Bull* 27(1) Apr-June 1991 : 8-21.

Studies the demand for library and information science workers in different types of libraries including education institutions in India based on the vacancies advertised in ll newspapers including the Hindu, the Statesman, Indian Express, The Times of India, Employment News, University News, etc.

Manorama Srinath and **Nithyanadam, K** 378

NISSAT manpower development programmes : Awareness among librarians, *NIPP*, 413-418.

Highlights role of information in the present information age and complicated needs of present society. Describes objectives of NISSAT. Discusses programmes on manpower development and IT. Conducts a survey of library professionals in Pondicherry and Madras city to determine the awareness of manpower development programmes and to assess how many were benefited.

Misra, Jogesh 379

The contribution of manpower planning to national development : The developing library workforce in South-East Asia, *CPT*, 42-52.

Advocates that the design, development, operations and management of a service to meet the needs of informations seekers and users, requires expertise of various kinds to create the document database, to ensure that users get the required information, to design and effectively manage the systems. Presents an integrated view of manpower development in LIS. Gives features of national policy for manpower development in LIS. Gives certain recommendations.

Mohandas, M K and **Shet, K C** 380

Evolution of library and information science professionals in Karnataka, *NIPP*, 408-412.

Gives data regarding manpower development in Karnataka for the last five years. Projects manpower needs for the beginning of the 21st century. Proposes a three-tier structure for imparting computer education for library professionals.

Pulla Reddy, V 381

Professional developmental activities of librarians working in university and special libraries in Andhra Pradesh, *Lib Her* 30(2-4) July 1991-Jan 1992 : 162-180.

Analyses data collected through a questionnaire from a random sample of 195 librarians working in university and special libraries of A P. Reveals an active involvement of senior librarians in different activities of professional development. Concludes that there are no significant differences between professional librarians working in university and special libraries and men and women librarians in the level of involvement.

Raina, Roshan 382

Fulbright experience in the US (July 26, 1990 – Jan 31, 1991): A report, *Luck Libn* 23(1) Jan-Mar 1991 : 36-46.

Reports about the visit to US under the Fulbright Internship Programme and gives account of the activities undertaken at the Syracuse University Library System while in the USA.

Ramaiah, L S 383

Motivation and training for the staff in university libraries in India, *Univ News* 28(30) July 23, 1990 : 8-10.

Deals with the issue of motivating the library personnel in universities in India for further training as part of continuing education programmes so that they could update themselves and provide better information services.

Reddy, J Yadgiri 384

Manpower planning for university libraries : An analysis, *Ind Jl Inf Lib & Society* 4(2) June 1991 : 112-121.

Emphasises importance of human resource and its planning in all kinds of institutions. Explains factors to be considered for effective and efficient manpower planning. Enumerates steps involved in planning process. Provides a method of job analysis, description and evaluation. Offers certain suggestions.

Rewadikar, Shalini 385

L&IS manpower development : Some social, psychological and organisational considerations and constraints, *CALNE*, 201-207.

Deals with the computer infrastructure, importance of information and manpower development. Describes decision groups which influence manpower development in L&IS profession. Discusses some social and psychological aspects of change. States need for proper perspective of computer.

Rewadikar, Shalini 386

National information policy for manpower development : A conceptual framework, *NIPP*, 393-402.

Explains the aims of national information policy and importance of manpower. Brings out interdependence of manpower development on organisational environs. Stresses need for preparing professionals for dynamic role with latest IT. Indicates the changing roles of the professionals in the information infrastructure of India.

Saini, M L 387

Turning library staff to efficiency, *ULI*, 195-202.

States that quality education is dependent on efficient libraries which in turn depends on its staff. Identifies facets that contribute to low efficiency. Describes positive factors that could ensure efficiency in libraries. States that proper guidance is also desirable.

Seetharama, S 388

Staffing of libraries and information centres, *CPT*, 138-146.

Explains that the quality of personnel governs the efficiency and effectiveness of library and information centres. Suggests some documents as basis for estimation of manpower. Gives the staff formula for professionals. Discusses centres and universities offering courses for professional personnel development. Mentions motivation.

Sewa Singh and **Jasmer Singh** 389

College library personnel in Punjab : A survey, *Jl Lib and Inf Sci* 14(2) Dec 1989 : 145-156.

Reveals the results of a survey relating to the existing strength of different categories of library personnel in college libraries of Punjab and Chandigarh. Discusses the implications of the Cadre Review Committee of the Punjab Govt. Mentions recommendations of UGC Committee on university and college libraries and the UGC Workshop held at Khandala. Suggests the adoption of the recommendations of the UGC Standing Committee on university and college libraries.

Surinder Kumar, Ray, Dibakar and **Chinnappa, S L** 390

Manpower development activities at National Informatics Centre, *IASLIC Bull* 36(4) Dec 1991 : 171-174.

Gives a brief account of training programmes, workshops, seminars in modern methods of IT aimed at beginners as well as qualified professionals conducted by NIC under its manpower development programme.

Thaty, R K and **Choudhury, B K** 391

Motivating library personnels of the university libraries of Orissa: A study, *Ind Jl Lib Inf & Society* 3(3-4) Sept-Dec 1990 : 171-184.

Explores the factors motivating the library professionals working in the university libraries of Orissa. Mentions that salary and status are found to be the two most important motivators. Stresses the professional competencies motivation to increase the productivity of the individual.

Viswa Mohan, V and **Raju A A N** 392

Management of information resources of human resources in India: A proposal, *IM*, 37-38.

Brings out the existing channels of human resource information in India such as employment exchange, directories, other agencies having their own limitations. Points out need for developing a system/centre for power control, organisation, and dissemination of human resource information in India.

023(1) Staff Formula

Srimurugan, A , Kumaravel, J P S and **Shunmuganathan, S C** 393

Staff formula for the automation and technical services section of the university library, *CALNE,* 174-178.

States that all university libraries are at infant stage in the use of computers in library services. Suggests to set up a computer division in a university library and Automation and Technical Services Section. Proposes the staff structure in this Section.

023 (1) Academic Status . Professional Status

Banerjee, Bimal Kumar 394

Library professional status – a critical appraisal, *SALP*, 85.

Examines professional status of librarians on the basis of various definitions and attributes propounded by eminent personalities. States that the principal criteria in enhancing professional status and social recognition is commitment to serve the needs of users.

Basak, Nanda Dulal and **Das, Binod Behari** 395

New communication techniques and status of LIS profession, *SALP*, 84.

Argues that the status of librarians could be increased by utilising various communication channels and providing different services as ILL, reference service, CAS, SDI, etc, and adopt new IT to the benefit and satisfaction of users.

Bavakutty, M 396

Academic status for university library staff, *ULI*, 162-172.

Gives recommendations of various commissions on the importance of libraries and librarians. Explains the concept of academic status for librarians. Proves that librarians also teach like teachers. Informs about the status of librarians in UK, USSR, and USA. Discusses the status of university library staff in India. Suggests that librarians too should get it.

Beghum, Khaiser Jahan 397

Present status of librarians in a few specialised institutions in South India, *SALP*, 90.

Examines, on the basis of a survey of 33 library staff from 15 special libraries, the present status of librarians and associated job factors that influence the work attitude of individual workers occupying different positions in different special libraries.

Bhattacharyya, Amarendra Nath 398

Academic librarians in search of an identity : A study on the status and authority of college library professionals in West Bengal *vis-a-vis* the emerging needs of higher education, *SALP*, 48-53.

Defines status in society and profession, scaler status and functional status. Gives status-needs and self-realisation. Describes the status of college librarians in West Bengal. Discusses authority and responsibility of college librarians. Explains newer role of college librarians and need for status.

Bose, Sree Kanta and **De, Biswajit** 399

Status and powers of non-government college librarians of West Bengal, *SALP*, 84.

States that non-government college librarians of West Bengal have not gained status and authority to manage their libraries.

Pleads to librarians to rise up to the required standard to attain proper status and power.

Chatterjee, Amitabha

400

Status and authority of public library personnel as envisaged in State Library Acts and rule in India, *SALP*, 64-67.

Refers to status and that of public library personnel. Mentions factors for authority. Studies status and authority of different categories of public library personnel in six states, viz, Tamil Nadu, Andhra Pradesh, Karnataka, Maharashtra, West Bengal and Manipur under their library acts. Gives suggestions for incorporation in the existing laws.

Dutta, Arati

401

Image of responsibility and status of library professionals in the age of automation in library service : A look at the National Library, *SALP*, 83.

States that the library and information services environs are changing and national libraries will be challenged to perform their traditional roles in different manners. Lists some suggestions which may help increases effectiveness of library professionals.

Gautam, Anil Kumar

402

Academic status for university library staff, *OSUL*, 28-45.

Defines status. Explains need of academic status. Gives logical analysis of the problem. Describes academic status vs faculty status giving advantages of the latter. Mentions librarian as teacher. Discusses Ranganathan's contribution in this regard. Gives efforts of government. Describes also international scene.

Govi, Pushpaveni

403

New demands on professionals in library management for increasing authority and status, *SALP*, 86.

States that to enhance status and authority concerted efforts to promote information are to be made. Mentions that they should give advice, user education, user survey to assess the impact of services, etc.

IASLIC, Calcutta 404

Status and authority of library profession in library management; *Papers* presented at the 14th National Seminar, Mysore, 14-17 Nov 1990; edited by Amitabha Chatterjee, Subir Sen, S K Kapoor and M N Nagaraj, Calcutta : IASLIC, 1990. 97 p.

Includes 45 papers, extended abstracts and abstracts of papers presented at the 14th National Seminar of IASLIC, held at Mysore during November 14-17, 1990. Deals with the status and authority of library profession in the country.

Jana, P 405

Some factors determining the status and authority of library and information professionals, *SALP*, 95-96.

Discusses status and authority as two correlated terms. Mentions aim of librarianship and limitations regarding the status and authority. Discusses ambiguities in qualifications, declining services, hence profession should be evaluated covering all aspects. States that associations should work to achieve the status.

Kannappanavar, B U 406

Status and pay scales of the college librarians in Karnataka, *SALP*, 82-83.

States that though recommended by the UGC college librarians in Karnataka have not been included in the modified UGC scheme. Observes that professional associations have not been able to be effective except the College Librarians' Association.

Manorama Srinath and **Stephen, S Lawyed** 407

Faculty perception about the professional image and status of university library staff, *SALP*, 25-26.

Makes a survey of image and status of Anna University and Madras University Library staff among the faculty on the basis of 14 questions. Reveals that the librarians are proceeding towards their goal of attaining faculty status. Suggests that they should adopt new technological innovations before they are taken over by computer specialists.

Pownikar, Shriniwas Sharadrao 408

Status of academic librarians in India : Some observations, *SALP*, 45-46.

Discusses role of academic librarian in the educational process.

Describes status of librarian *vis-a-vis* faculty. Discusses difference between academic and faculty status. Explains status of librarians and reasons for low status. Lists steps for improving status.

Prins, Hans 409

Status, image and reputation of librarianship : Results of an empirical study, *Jl Lib and Inf Sci* 16(1) June 1991: 11-24.

Observes that the status, image and reputation of librarianship is considered low. Examines the reasons given by an empirical study conducted by RTMLA. Follows survey research method, and analysis is done using statistical techniques including rank method.

Rajan Pillai, C V 410

Status of library and information professionals : Its meaning, implications and suggestions for improvement, *SALP*, 13-16.

Discusses the question of the professional status of librarianship by giving essential elements of a profession which it qualifies. Outlines factors involved in establishing the status. Points out that status for library and information professionals has several implications. Offers suggestions for improvement.

Saha, Ramakrishna and **Paul, Anil Chandra** 411

Status, pay and authority of West Bengal librarians, *SALP*, 71-75.

Attempts to illustrate the activities of the organizations of librarians and their achievements and sought to find out ways and means for reaching their goals. Gives library movement in post-independence period as a background. Discusses the role of Bengal Library Association in college and university library sector, school library sector, and strategies adopted and to be adopted.

Samantaray, Moortimatee and **Rath, Pravarkar** 412

Status of librarians in government libraries of Orissa : A case study, *SALP*, 94.

Gives an idea of the status and salary of the public librarians in Orissa. Finds arbitrary designation and haphazard pay scales. Suggests some measures for the professional development and improvement of status of librarians.

Satish, N G and **Takalkal, Anil** 413

Occupational status of librarianship – an empirical note, *SALP*, 17-20.

Takes up the question of status of library professionals. Conducts a survey to rate 15 professions on the basis of a questionnaire given to 80 individuals from different walks of life, and response was 82.5%. Reveals that librarians occupy as low as 9th and documentation 15th rank.

Selvi, M G 414

Status and authority of library profession in library management, *SALP*, 93-94.

Describes librarian as a teacher because he assists library users in locating information and has therefore to develop an efficient communication skills. Discusses role and status of women in librarianship.

Sen, Bharati 415

Status of college librarians based on some colleges under Bombay University within thc limits of Bombay City, *Lib Sci slant Doc and Inf Std* 28 (1) Mar 1991 : 5-17.

Identifies factors that determine the status of librarianship. Reveals from a sample survey of 37 college libraries under Bombay University that the librarianship is yet to gain its true status. Indicates that the librarian does not feel the necessity in developing himself intellectually, his role as administrator is not strong, and is not assertive of his expert authority. Suggests that they need to think to enhance their status and prestige.

Shukla, R K and **Sethi, Rashmi** 416

LIS professionals in special libraries : Strategies to secure status, *SALP*, 91-92.

Discusses that professional bodies should prepare minimum standards for different types of libraries with regard to staff, services, finance, etc. Pleads for continuing education by associations in view of professional obsolescence. States that quality education be given in LIS schools. Suggests various strategies with use of IT.

Subba Rao, C V 417

Conflict in authority : A furniture case study, *SALP*, 87.

Makes a case for financial and administrative powers with the librarian on the basis of practical examples where certain non-standard furniture articles were thrust upon the librarian which speaks of conflict of authority.

Vaishnav, A A 418

Status and authority of academic librarians in Marathawada, *SALP*, 83-84.

Reports, on the basis of a survey, areas of responsibility, measure amount of authority, areas of accountability and status of college/university librarians working in Marathawada region. Finds that amount of authority is very less than the responsibility. However, they are given status.

Vishwa Mohan, V 419

Strategies for securing due status and authority for library and information professionals, *SALP*, 61-63.

Defines status and authority which are generally denied to library and information professionals in India. Enumerates strategies at the level of individual library, through professional associations, to gain due status and authority.

Yoganandarao, Chillarigi 420

Library and information services in engineering design organisation : Status and authority for professional management, *SALP*, 86.

Stresses need for reducing time-lag between acquisition and supply of information to the engineering professionals. Explains new role of the librarian to be played to acquire status, authority and power towards better management of library and information services. Suggests the role of professional organisations.

023.2 Professional Positions

Devraj Singh 421

Career of librarians in India, Pakistan and USA : A review of literature, *Lib Her* 29 (3-4) Oct 1990 – Jan 1991 : 183-198.

Provides an extensive survey of past literature on the topic of study. Reveals that no comprehensive study has been reported in developing countries. Includes all related aspects. Reviews major aspects such as socio-economic background, educational background, choice of librarianship as a career, job mobility, etc.

Devraj Singh 422

Factors related to career advancement of special library professionals in Delhi, *Lib Her* 27(3-4) Oct 1988 – Jan 1989 : 95-104.

Identifies various factors that lead to advancement in professional career. Examines significance of relationship between some professional and personal characteristics and advancement.

Misra, Budhendu Bijoy 423

Responsibility of library professionals in the emerging IR scenario, *SALP*, 85.

Discusses how the responsibility of information personnel has increased in view of the increasing service demands by users for which they have to analyse, evaluate and synthesise the data for easy access.

Roy, Satyabrata and **Chatterjee, Ashis** 424

Changing role of academic librarians in India, *Her Lib Sci* 29 (1-2) Jan-Apr 1990 : 42-45.

Discusses present situation of academic librarians in India and that of the users in the changing role of academic libraries. Identifies related problems. Suggests solution for the fulfilment of new type of library and information services. Concludes that new breed of librarians will be required possessing both scientific knowledge and training in the application of appropriate information handling techniques.

Sarkar, Pradip Kumar and **Saha, Amit** 425

Position of subordinate professional staff: Some studies, *SPAL*, 87.

Focusses on the important role *vis-a-vis* the position of the subordinate professional staff on the basis of observation in different libraries in Calcutta. Contends that with the new modes of library services involving modern tools and techniques, subordinate professionals should enjoy reasonable amount of authority and status.

Subba Rao, C V and **Prabha Krishnan** 426

Chattopadhyaya Review Committee on Government of India libraries : A critique, *Her Lib Sci* 30(1-2) Jan-Apr 1991 : 50-58.

Examines the categorisation of staff announced by Chattopadhyaya Review Committee which lead to anamoly. Specifies points allotted in the categorisation formula. Points out that unmentioned work in the library like weeding, staff administration, research papers and surveys etc have to be woven into categorisation formula. Suggests the withdrawal of this defective formula.

Subba Rao, C V, Khatri, Nirmal and **Prabha Krishnan** 427

Categorisation formula of "Review Committee Recommendations" : An experimental reconstruction, *ILA Bull* 27(2) July-Sept 1991 : 76-90.

Examines critically the staff categorisations formula as given in the *Review Committee Report* of the fourth Pay Commission. Lists anamolies and suggests remedies. Gives a new staff categorisation formula based on their own experience and with proper explanations.

023.3 Semi-Professionals

Bilesanmi, S A 428

Using of part-time professionals and para professional librarians in public and college libraries in Nigeria : Ogun state as a case study, *Int Lib Move* 12(2) June 1990 : 64-68.

Makes a case for the use of part-time professionals and para professionals in public and college libraries on Ogun state in Nigeria. Examines their advantages and disadvantages in terms of management, wages and fringe benefits.

023.9 Job Performance

Basak, Nanda Dulal and **Das, Binod Bihari** 429

Performance appraisal system in a government-financed library of a higher learning institute, *AGLIS Jl* 7(4) Dec 1989 : 38-42.

Brings out library's objectives and its staff. Discusses need for personnel management, assessment of potentials, training needs, performance conduct, etc. through appraisal system, self-evaluation report, supervisor's report. Provides also sample data regarding format.

Gopinath, M A 430

Performance appraisal of the library professionals: A normative approach, *Lib Sci slant Doc and Info Std* 27(3) Sept 1990 : 183.

Discusses the facets of performance, performance diagnosis, and performance appraisal. Identifies performance criteria in different professional activities such as collection development, technical processing, circulation of documents, maintenance and preservation of services, and information services. Delineates norms for performance appraisal on the basis of the five laws of library science.

Rajyalakshmi, D 431

Administrator's role in quality performance in academic libraries, *ILA Bull* 24(4) Jan-Mar 1989 : 221-226.

Examines the desired attributes of administrators in academic libraries. Emphasises upon their role in improving quality performance. Discusses variables/factors such as education background, management style, collection size, job satisfaction, etc.

023.9(1) Job Satisfaction

Navalani, K 432

Job characteristics of library and information work as satisfiers and dissatisfiers a survey, *Ann Lib Sci and Doc* 37(3) Sept 1990 : 85-95.

Analyses data gathered on level of satisfaction with job characteristics of library and information work through a questionnaire from professionals and semi-professionals working in university libraries in India. Reveals that majority of the respondents are satisfied with most of the attributes of their work.

Navalani, K 433

Manpower in university libraries in India : A study into the level of its satisfaction with its status, *CLIS Observer* 7(1-2) Jan-June 1990 : 20-24.

Studies into the level of satisfaction of library personnel working in university libraries in India through statistical methods and questionnaire. Finds out that a majority of them seem to be satisfied with their status. Mentions that men have a higher rating of satisfaction than women.

Navalani, K 434

Promotion : The least satisfying aspect of library profession, *CPT*, 126-137.

Defines promotion. Studies the job satisfaction on the basis of a nation wide survey of job satisfaction of professionals and semi-professionals working in university libraries in India with opportunities, criteria and practices of promotion. Presents data in tables.

Prasad, H N and **Singh, S N** 435

A study into the effect of job anxiety on job satisfaction of professional library staff : A case study, *ILA Bull* 25(4) Jan-Mar 1990 : 199-213.

Studies the relationship between job satisfaction and job involvement. Measures job satisfaction and job anxiety with the help of two separate scales on the sample of 50 drawn on the basis of stratified sampling technique from the Central Library, BHU.

Pulla Reddy, V 436

Job satisfaction of librarians working in university and college libraries of Delhi : A study, *Lib Her* 29(1-2) Apr-Sept 1990 : 34-43.

Analyses data gathered through questionnaire, on random sampling, of librarians working in university and college libraries of Delhi to reach at findings on correlates of job satisfaction and similarities and differences among various subgroups of librarians. Throws light on incentives for job satisfaction.

023.9(1) Library Ethics
Professional Ethics

Mehboob, S and **Abdul Majeed, K C** 437

Ethics of librarianship-a general view, *PL*, 105-109.

Deals with ethics of librarianship owing obligations to library users, books, the library profession, library staff, to librarian himself.

023.9(1) Qualifications

Subbaiah, R 438

Academic and professional qualifications of staff in university libraries *ULI*, 173-181 .

Depicts changing scenario of libraries in view of proliferation of literature, modern IT, etc. Mentions qualifications of academic librarian and role of UGC. Discusses qualification in relation to the job requirements. Opines that qualification of academic librarian should be based on their job requirements only. Concludes that more stress be given on professional qualifications.

023.9(1) Salary Scales

New Pay scales for library staff under purview of the Government of India, *CLIS Observer* 7(3-4) July-Dec 1990 : 119-127. 439

Gives the new pay scales for library staff as revised by the Government of India based on the report of the Review Committee.

Revised Pay structure for library staff announced, *NISSAT Newsletter* 9(3) July-Sept 1990 : 3-10. 440

Reproduces the office Memorandum issued by the Ministry of Finance, Govt of India, regarding the Govt decision on the recommendations made by a Review Committee set up by the Dept of Culture in Sept 1987.

Steering Committee, Central Government Library Staff, New Delhi 441

Joint Memorandum on Review Committee on library staff, *Her Lib Sci* 30(1-2) Jan-Apr 1991 : 70-79.

In view of the Review Committee report describes Joint Memo to the 4th Pay Commission. Discusses comments on recommendations, suggested pay scales and promotion scheme anamolies of Office Memo, categorisation of libraries, qualifications, charter of demand. Also gives extract from the Pay Commission Report.

025 Documentation. Information

Aguolu, C C 442

The concept of bibliographic access to scientific information and knowledge in developing countries, *Int Lib Move* 12 (1) Mar 1990 : 19-30.

Defines information. Explains knowledge. Discusses implications of growth of knowledge on the researchers, scientists, etc. Gives elements of bibliographical services concerned with written and un-written records. Lays emphasis on bibliographic control. Mentions importance of secondary and tertiary services.

Arunan, M C and **Mendes, Jennle** 443

Wanted new information order, *Univ News* 29(37) 16 Sept 1991 : 1-2.

Explains the need for new information environment in the changing situations in libraries and information centres as a result of the applications of the IT, etc. Lays emphasis on the needs of a new breed of information specialists.

Butola, B S 444

Social origin and function of information, *SSI*, 365-367.

Gives importance of information. Discusses the structure and origin of information. Describes information and its social functions as hegemonic function and counter hegemonic function.

Curras, Emilia 445

Information and a cosmovision of ecology, *INICAE*, 9(2) Sept 1990 : 163-171.

States the panorama of possible paths for human activity and happiness. Describes ecological systems and phenomena of universe as known to us through human intelligence and information. Discusses evolutionary process of life through increasing use of knowledge and 'cosmovision' of ecology. Examines role of information in social transformation and in diffusion of science and culture.

Gopinath, M A 446

Information economics as an area of specialization, *Lib Sci slant Doc and Inf Std* 28(2) June 1991 : 64-67.

Defines information economics as a field of interdisciplinary interaction between Information Science and Economics Information Science in a helpful area of theoretical and practical implications of library and information specialists. Identifies some area of interactions seen through published literature in different fields.

Joshi, S C 447

Role of information in the 21st century, *Ind Jl Inf Lib & Society* 3(1-2) Mar-June 1990 : 29-

Deals with the information explosion and importance of information. Defines information. Gives its characteristics. Treats information as an indispensable resource. Discusses current trends in production of information sources. Describes the impact of technology in terms of computer, micrographics, telecommunication, AV media. Discusses emergence of IT and micrographics. Describes the current scene of paperless society.

Kaushik, Purnima 448

Documentation services in India, *ISL*, 228-253.

Focusses on the role and contribution of national organisations of India such as INSDOC, DESIDOC, NASSDOC, etc in promoting and furthering the documentation and information activities in the country.

Keenan, Stella 449

Research reviews in information and documentation, *INICAE* 9(2) Sept 1990: 211-218.

States that the FID has started a new series of research reviews-Research Reviews in Information and Documentation. Describes ISORID established in 1971 as an international information system to serve the field of documentation. Mentions reference tools for identification of research. Describes the *Current research in LIS* of the LA (UK). Gives reasons for changing the FID publications. Discusses research and IT conference held in July 1989 at Cranfield. Gives current research topics and future development.

Kejariwal, O P 450

Information back-up for historical studies : The need and the availability, *SSI*, 368-376.

States that history relies on information back-up. Mentions various information centres for history. Observes that historical scholarship in India is not upto the mark. Discusses imbalance between availability and needs of scholars. Tells about the privileged American scholar. Discusses problems in information gathering. Describes service attitude in libraries. Offers various suggestions.

Mishra, Manoj K and **Mishra, Sanjaya** 451

Conflict : Its management in information organization, *Lib Her* 30(2-4) July 1991-Jan 1992 : 257-263.

Defines and explains conflict as difference of opinion in interpersonal and group communication. Describes different types of conflicts, their causes, identification and resolution techniques necessary for conflict management in information organization.

Neelakantan, K and **Srimurugan, A** 452

Information: Becoming informed, *Univ News* 28(45) Nov 5, 1990 : 8-9.

Defines information and human quest for information. Discusses uses in the information system approach. Describes how to become will informed from various library sources.

Ray, Dipak Kumar and **Chaudhuri, Aruna** 453

Information and its application by applied technology, *Ind Jl Inf Lib & Society* 3 (1-2) Mar-June 1990 : 76-86.

Defines documentation and gives its scope. Discusses relation between documentation work and documentation service; documentation work and systematic bibliography. Describes importance of information. Discusses types of information to make it information system.

Sharma, R N and **Taneja, Ram D** 454

Technical communication : Fourth training course, Jodhpur, *NISSAT Newsletter* 9(3) July-Sept 1990 : 14-16.

Reports about the Fourth Training Course on Technical Communication, organised by SIS and NISSAT at Central Arid Zone Research Institute, Jodhpur during 28-31 Aug 1990.

Swaroop Rani, B S 455

Information environment: From storehouse to databanks, *SALP*, 89.

Identifies new roles of librarians, which have changed over the years, as that of information resources managers, marketing manager, information integrator, system designer, etc. Stresses that these be made public to attain professional status.

025(1) Information Explosion

Kaula, P N 456

Information revolution and its impact on libraries, *Ind Jl Inf Lib & Society* 4 (3-4) Sept-Dec 1991 : 167-186.

Refers to the dynamics of change resulting in change in working of libraries. Discusses information revolution and its impact on libraries. Analyses advent of documentation and information and communication technology. Discusses computer networking and library networking programmes. Presents a paradoxical situation of new and old versions of librarianship. Describes manpower planning, changes needed for training and education of LIS personnel.

Lahiri, A 457

Facing the deluge-I, *NISSAT Newsletter* 10(3) July-Sept 1991:1.

Discusses the use of a combination of conventional and hi-tech methodologies to aid the process of hinting for information in this age of deluge.

Lahiri, A 458

Facing the deluge – II, *NISSAT Newsletter* 10(4) Oct-Dec 1991 : 1.

States that apart from further development of information on hardware and software, we need to go back to basic science and more importantly to psychology and explore solutions to problems.

Lazar, Peter 459

The "information revolution" and the library and information profession in developing countries, *ISL*, 1-22.

Aims at providing some realistic views on information revolution, its impact on society and future of library and information services. Takes a cautious view between underrating and overrating the future role of information and the library and information infrastructure. Discusses main trends of development of library and information ser-vices in India.

025 (1) Information Society

Bhattacharyya, G 460

Information society and the place of conventional techniques for information work an service, *Lib Sci Slant Docu and Inf Std* 26(2) June 1989: 108-113.

Considers the place of conventional professional software technologies, such as classification, cataloguing, and indexing along with their associated tools in the context of emerging information society.

Girja Kumar 461

Towards an information society in India, *IM*, 1-8.

Delivered as the presidential address at the XVIII IASLIC Conference held at Kurukshetra during Dec 26-29, 1991. Discusses the changing situation from knowledge to information where society is progressing towards information society in which system design, socio-technology design, information management are important. Describes that information has to be cost-effective for which MIS and DIS has to play important role. Points out that role of librarian as manager shall get transformed.

Mudhol, Mahesh V 462

2001, paperless society, *Indian Exp* Apr 1990 (Hyderabad Edition).

Discusses the changing scene of the information world as a result of the advent of the new technologies in the 21st century.

Srivastava, A P 463

Biotech and information society in India? *ILA Bull* 26(4) Jan-Mar 1991 : 165-178.

Examines the present day life in India in the context of scientific and technological development, rational thinking, value system, etc. Attempts to gauge the future of 'Bio-tech' and 'Information Society' in this context in India. Points out that in the absence of constant review of social and metaphysical thought quality of Indian life remains the same.

025(1) Documentation and Information Centres/Systems

Mangla, P B 464

Information system and services in India: Trends and prospects, *Jl Lib and Inf Sci* 14(2) Dec 1989 : 84-97.

Highlights developments in the field of library, documentation and information services in India after independence. Emphasises need for information systems and services. Discusses objectives and functions of NISSAT, INSDOC, DESIDOC and proposed NISS and INFLIBNET. Mentions emergence of certain non-bibliographic information systems such as NICNET, INDONET. Mentions some problems.

Ramaiah, L S and **Prafulla Chandra, T V** 465

A review of information systems and centres in India, *Her Lib Sci* 30(3-4) July-Oct 1991 : 234-237.

Points out the genesis and development of library literature in India. Mentions that two series in LIS – CICIL and HLAICI – are doing a good job. Reviews the Volume 7 of HLAICI on the activities, programmes, services of various information centres and networks in science and technology; while Volume 8 covers the social sciences. Mentions the utility of these volumes.

Seetharama, S 466

Guidelines for planning of libraries and information centres, Calcutta : IASLIC, 1990. xix, 257 p.

Divided into 10 chapters from A to J includes details on planning process, total system view, information sources development, library and information services/products planning, manpower planning, furniture/equipment planning, space planning, financial planning, IT and system planning. In chapter K gives bibliographical reference and appendices in chapter L.

Subramaniam, J B 467

Information systems, services and networks for development, *CPT*, 316-339.

Mentions importance and problems of information, and UNISIST-II. Presents outlines of some of the more important national and international organisations, information system, services, and networks, such as ASTINFO, UNIDO, INIS, FAO ILO, WIPO, EURONET, ESA, APINESS, etc. Concludes that with the changing scenario though India has NISSAT, yet much remains to be done in resource sharing.

025 (1) DESIDOC

DESIDOC, Delhi 468

A brief note on the computerization activities of DESIDOC, *DRTC 1989,* P 1-5.

Mentions in brief the computerization activities of DESIDOC, Delhi. Packages used are user-friendly and written in COBOL.

DESIDOC – an overview, *DESIDOC Bull* 10(1) Jan 1990 : 3-5. 469

Traces genesis of DESIDOC. Describes its activities and services such as collection of information, processing of information. Discusses dissemination of information through online searching, sharing the resources, computerisation of information services. Mentions its translation services, supporting services and other activities.

DESIDOC, Delhi 470

Information processing and dissemination activities, *DESIDOC Bull* 10(3) May 1990 : 11-14.

Describes the computerization of information at DESIDOC, the Defence Science Library Management System (DELMS) as a comprehensive package which allows the user to create and manage structured databases and to perform all library management functions. Mentions also online searching of information.

DESIDOC, Delhi 471

Publications – a means of communication science, *DESIDOC Bull* 10(2) Mar 1990 : 3-5.

Highlights the role of the various DESIDOC publications in communicating science, dissemination of information on current developments in defence science and technology.

Murthy, S S and **Rangra, V K** 472

Defence Scientific Information and Documentation Centre; organization and functions, *HLAICI,* v 7, 89-102.

Mentions role of R & D in defence and DRDO. Gives formation and functions of DRDO. Explains organization of DESIDOC including library, information processing and dissemination, translation, publications, training, union catalogue project, etc. Gives information about seminars/conferences, membership, new building, etc.

025 (1) DRTC

Bhattacharyya, G 473

Documentation Research and Training Centre, *HLAICI,* v 8, 222-229.

Outlines the origin and development of DRTC, Lists its objectives and programmes. Describes activities in order to achieve these objectives. Discusses its research programme, advisory service programme, extension programme, publication programme, training programme, continuing education programme. Gives a list of its Annual Seminars and Refresher Seminars.

025 (1) IDSA

Subba Rao, C V and **Chopra, Uma** 474

Institute of Defence Studies and Analysis : Documentation activities, *HLAICI,* v 8, 118-123.

Gives importance of documentation activity in defence. Explains the library and documentation activities of Institute for Defence Studies and Analysis, clipping, collection, indexes, reference tools prepared, microfilming, etc.

025 (1) INIS

Ebinuma, Yukio 475

Special aspects on INIS operations in Japan, *DLIS*, 223-230.

Mentions purpose of INIS and part the Japan Atomic Energy Research Institute is playing. Describes internal committees for INIS operations, reference tools for input processing for coverage base and selection of Japanese literature. Discusses use of INIS data by JAERI.

Gupta, Sangeeta 476

International Nuclear Information System (INIS), *Int Lib Move* 13(1) Mar 1991 : 44-49.

Deals with INIS – a computerized bibliographic database organised for retrieval of information on atomic energy. Gives objectives of INIS. Mentions its organization. Describes various characteristics of INIS.

025 (1) INSDOC

Chadha, O N and **Gupta, B M** 477

Indian National Scientific Documentation Centre, *HLAICI*, v 7, 59-88.

Gives history, organisation and management. Tabulates various information services of INSDOC. Describes information dissemination (through *ISA*, etc.), information retrieval, information access tools as union catalogues, directories, etc. Explains information resource management. Discusses various manpower development programmes. Mentions about regional centres, national centre on Bibliometrics, international and national collaboration, participation in SAARC. Gives appendices.

Shukla, B B 478

Role and activities of the Indian National Scientific Documentation Centre (INSDOC), *Ind Jl Inf Lib & Society* 3(1-2) Mar-June 1990 : 139-148.

Gives an account of the establishment of INSDOC. Elaborates various activities of INSDOC that include document procurement service, information service, etc. Gives an account of publication, various projects, regional centres, etc.

025 (1) INSIS

Commission on European Communities, Brussels 479

INSIS – Integrated Information Services, *INICAE* 9(1) Mar 1990: 67-68.

Describes INSIS as an attempt to improve communication between the CEC nations. Discusses priorities for INSIS, and its three pilot projects.

025 (1) NASSDOC

Agrawal, S P and **Manohar Lal** 480

Documentation activities and services in social sciences : Role of NASSDOC and ICSSR Regional Centres, *HLAICI*, v 8, 78-108.

Describes in brief ICSSR. Describes in detail the genesis of NASSDOC, its objectives, organization, programmes and activities, collection, ILRC, documentation programmes, regional centres programmes, continuing education programmes, document delivery, consultancy, membership, future programmes, etc.

Vajahat, Abida, Tejpal, Rama and **Gambhir, Sudha** 481

Present status of social science information infrastructure in India with particular reference to NASSDOC, *NIPP*, 265-274.

Discusses importance of social sciences, role of ICSSR-NASSDOC in the development of dissemination of information in the field of social sciences. Explains the present and future programmes and role of NASSDOC in developing National Information System in Social Sciences. Gives future plans also.

025 (1) NBSS

Patil, Y M 482

Documentation centre of NBBS and LUP, (ICAR), *HLAICI*, v 7, 261-265.

Discusses the establishment of the National Bureau of Soil Survey and Land Use Planning (NBSS and LUP) under IARI in 1956. Gives its objectives. Describes Documentation centre, its objectives, services, etc.

025 (1) NDCMC

Verma, P K 483

National Documentation Centre on Mass Communication, *HLAICI*, v 8, 38-42.

Traces the development of National Documentation Mass Communication. Gives its objectives, activities, CAS, bibliographical services, reference and information services, clipping service, media memory, etc.

025 (1) NICILL

Murthy, Sulochana S 484

National Information Centre for Indian Languages and Linguistics (NICILL): A proposal, *CPT*, 301-315.

Deals with the development of library and documentations services at the Central Institute of Indian Languages. Emphasises need for setting up a NICILL at the Institute. Attempts to give a draft model for the proposed plan describing objectives, structure, functions, and various documentation services in detail, including preparation of computerised database.

025 (1) NICSAI

Pathan, N S 485

A need for National Information Centre for Sugar and Allied Industries, *NIPP,* 181-187.

Examines the need for an information centre for sugar industry. Presents in brief the idea of setting up a NICSAI (National Information Centre for Sugar and Allied Industries) and explains its utility to the industry. Appeals to the Government for supporting the creation of such a Centre.

025 (1) NIHFW

Meshram, Siddarth G, Hans Raj and **Gowtham, M S** 486

National Documentation Centre for Health, Population and Family Welfare, *HLAICI*, v 8, 210-221.

States the importance of population and health information. Describes the various activities of NIHFW. Discusses the setting up of the National Documentation Centre and its objectives and merger of the NIFW Library and NIHAE Library in the Centre. Describes the organisational structure through Library unit, Documentation unit, Reprographic unit, Computer unit. Also mentions its training programmes, network development, participation in regional and international programmes, publications, etc.

025 (1) NIRD

Inamdar, N B and **Satish, N G** 487

National Institute of Rural Development: Centre on rural documentation, *HLAICI*, v 8, 192-198.

Describes the renaming of the library and documentation section of this Institute as Centre on Documentation in 1983 which functions under NIRD. Describes the library activities of the Centre, documentation services as CORD Index, CORD Abstracts, bibliographies, national register of research consultancy services, reprographic and SDI services. Appends a list of bibliographies compiled by CORD after 1977 and NIRD publications.

025 (1) NISHI

Kanakachary, M 488

National Information System for the Humanities in India, *NIPP*, 282-289.

Defines humanities and gives its scope and value in the present information age. Describes growth of humanities literature in India. Emphasizes the need of a National Information System for the Humanities in India (NISHI). Gives a design for a model and lists out the important activities of the proposed system.

025 (1) NISSAT

Accessing S & T information : NISSAT emerges as key component, *NISSAT Newsletter* 9(2) Apr-June 1990: 11-15. 489

Explains the role of NISSAT in promoting and supporting easy and quick access to information through organized information centres integrated into a network.

Lahiri, A 490

NISSATCARD – a passer-partout for library users, *NISSAT Newsletter* 9(4) Oct-Dec 1990 : 1.

Describes the idea of a scheme of providing NISSATCARD against a deposit to users by NISSAT for enabling them to use libraries of other institutions.

National Information System for Science and Technology, *HLAICI*, v 7, 34-42. 491

Describes various sectoral centres under NISSAT. Mentions two new centres: NCB and NICORD. Gives information analysis and data centres under NISSAT, NUCSSI, online and SDI service, library networking, computer based bibliographic information, manpower, development studies, directories, etc. Also gives international activities.

NISSATCARD: A feasible study: Progress report, *NISSAT Newsletter* 10(4) Oct-Dec 1991 : 3-4. 492

Reports about the progress made on the concept of NISSATCARD in view of feasibility study about identification of users, cost-pricing model, etc.

025 (1) PAIC

Suresh Kumar 493

Public administration information system, *NIPP*, 275-281.

Defines public administration. Explains the objectives, functions, manpower development, services and financial outlay for setting up a National Information Center in public administration.

025 (1) SENDOC

Gupta, B M 494

Small Enterprise National Documentation Centre, *HLAICI*, v 8, 109-117.

Describes the establishment of SENDOC, its aims and objectives, activities, library, central information file, information services, computerisation, seminars and workshops, training programmes, and special projects.

025.02 Technical Processes

Gopinath, M A 495

Technical processing in libraries : Limitations and prospects, *AGLIS Jl* 7(4) Dec 1989 : 7-8.

States that classification and cataloguing are two techniques and tools of libraries. Describes organisation of collection, variety and specificity. Discusses functional aspects of technical processing. Outlines problems in flow of documents. Offers solutions for some of these problems.

025.0285 Computerization of Library Operations
Library Automation
Library Computerization

Alabi, G A 496

Computer applications in libraries in Africa – now, in the year 2000 or when?, *CPT*, 212-220.

Underlines role of computer in library operations. Describes the current trends in computer applications in Africa. Gives computer scenario in Nigeria. Discusses constraints in the use of new technology in Africa. Stresses the need computer literacy in Africa, and need for automation of library and information systems.

Balbir Singh 497

Computer and its application in library work, *Int Lib Move* 13(3) Sept 1991 : 168; 13(4) Dec 1991 : 169-174.

Continued in next issue pp 169-174.

Explains the computer application in acquisition, periodicals, circulation, and technical section of libraries.

Chakraborty, Arun Kumar 498

Managerial approach to computerisation of library and information work and services, *CALNE*, 31-44.

Mentions importance of computers, functions offered, and limitations. Describes a mechanized system with typical library computer applications, management of such a system. Describes change related factors. Concludes that computerization will help in greater speed and ease of access.

Chandran, Ranjita 499

Development of directory of agents using dBase III Plus, *DRTC 1989*, Q 1-15.

Highlights methodology for developing a computer readable directory of agents on a PC using dBASE III Plus. Discusses various menus used for creation of files, updating of files, conducting interactive searches and generating printed output in a specified format.

Choudhuri, Abhijit 500

Selection of library and information software: A checklist, *DRTC 1989*, X 1-17.

States that selecting right kind of model of computerised system, and setting it up properly are creative intellectual tasks. Discusses problems of selecting suitable software package for library and information systems. Provides a checklist for choosing and evaluating software packages.

DESIDOC, Delhi 501

SANJAY: Augmented CDS/ISIS package for library automation, *NISSAT Newsletter* 10(3) July-Sept 1991 : 3-6.

Explains a library automation package based on CDS/ISIS version 2.3, named SANJAY developed by DESIDOC. Describes the development of software package and special features. Discusses the automation of Technology Bhavan Library. Mentions system implementation.

DRTC, Bangalore 502

Annual seminar, 23, 1989 : Computer softwares for information work and services, edited by I K Ravichandra Rao, Bangalore : DRTC, 1989. various pagings.

Includes 26 articles by various experts on different aspects of computer software and their applications in library and information work.

Dwivedi, P N 503

Role of the micro-computer services and information systems, *Ind Jl Inf Lib & Society* 3(1-2) Mar-June 1990: 87-96.

Gives importance of information and information system. Examines the current hardware, software for microcomputer system relevant to computerisation of libraries in India. Concludes that librarians should learn about this new high technology tool.

Ehikhamenor, Fabian A 504

Rationalising the development of scientific and technical informa tion systems in Nigeria, *Ann Lib Sci and Doc* 38 (4) Dec 1991 : 148-152.

Discusses the concepts of organisational structures and their coordinating functions in the application of library automation and STI systems in Nigeria. Shows that there is some awareness of the need of such systems.

Goel, D R and **Beryah, Parvinder** 505

Development of computer based library management system software, *Media and Tech for Human Resource Development* 2 (1) Oct 1989 : 35-44.

Introduces library and its rich collection. Gives library management system of Devi Ahilya Vishwavidyalaya, Indore. States that it is not functioning very systematically, efficiently and effectively. Discusses the development of a Computer Based Library Management System Software and finds out the usability of this System.

Harinarayana, N S 506

Concept of library automation, *CPT,* 174-184; Also in *Her Lib Sci* 30(3-4) July-Oct 1991 : 174-184.

Describes libraries as important component of modern society and undergoing transition. Mentions need for automation. Points out that 'library automation' has no universally accepted definition. Gives scope of library automation. Describes three stages in automation: Planning, designing, operational which include feasibility, logical and physical design, and implementation and evaluation of the project.

Harvey, John F 507

A computer software glossary for libraries, *ISL*, 264-281.

Gives the glossary of terms popular in the computer software field. Divides them under general definitions, programming, programs. Also gives sources of software information.

Kamath, V A 508

Computer application in library and information services: A brief survey of the world and Indian scenario, *CPT*, 199-211.

Gives importance of information and information handling with computer. Narrates briefly in a chronological order the most significant landmarks in the evolution of the computer starting with Abacus comes to modern day 5th generation computers. Discusses computer applications to library and information work in western countries. Makes a survey of computer scenario in India with their applications to libraries and information centres.

Kanakachary, M, Reddy, J Yadgiri and **Rao, S Sudarshan** 509

Approach to library automation : Some basic issues, *CALNE*, 72-77.

Describes the objectives of library automation. Mentions advantages of library automations and its features. Discusses the planning process for the success of automation in any kind of library. Concludes that planning of library automation should be according to the needs.

Kashyap, M M 510

Design and development of computerized information system for the Ratan Tata Library, University of Delhi with the aid of

CDS/ISIS software, *Lib Her* 28 (3-4) Oct 1989-Jan 1990 : 92-117.

Discusses the four phases consisting of planning and analysis, data design, creation of databases and maintenance on functional phase. Provides general observations based on author's experience, indicating pitfalls to be avoided in the process. Gives suggestions regarding security control to ensure that data is properly safeguarded.

Katna, A K 511

CLMS Computerised college library management system : An experience, *ILA Bull* 25(4) Jan-Mar 1990 : 214-219.

Attempts to discuss the various problems, their solutions and few suggestions for the success of computerization of catalogue with CDS/ISIS. Describes the first phase of this activity briefly under CLMS.

Khurshid, Zahiruddin 512

Library automation – a new dimension in Arabian Gulf librarianship, *DLIS*, 141-152.

Mentions manpower situation in Gulf region, application of modern technologies. Discusses Kuwait scenario since 1975 with regard to bibliographical services, circulation, STAIRS, etc. Gives Saudi Arabia scenario regarding library automation, and also in other countries.

Krishan Kumar and **Shailendra Kumar** 513

An overview of computer activities in library and information science in India in the year 1988, *Lib Her* 28(3-4) Oct 1989-Jan 1990 : 118-123.

Describes importance of computer application in the present day context. Provides chronology of activities. Gives an overview of the activities. Concludes that special libraries and information centers are more active and networking of libraries and information centres/documentation centres is likely to gain added importance in near future.

Kumar, P S G 514

Computers and university libraries in India, *OSUL*, 176-186.

Deals with the early period of computers and university libraries giving reasons for non-popularity of computers in academic libraries. Describes the Indian scene of computers in university libraries. Discusses issues as employment, cost, viability, authority, etc. Gives an action plan. Describes the selection of hardware and software. States that computers are taking us towards a network.

Library Automation: The real crunch, *NISSAT Newsletter* 9(2) Apr-June 1990 :1. 515

Discusses need of library automation, packages developed in dBase, COBOL, etc. States that in view of the CDS/ISIS of UNESCO on the one hand and local library management packages libraries have to move carefully.

Mohandas, M K and **Shet, K C** 516

Development of database file in KREC Library, *DRTC 1989*, C 1-9.

Proposes for automation for K R E C Library with dBase III plus package. Describes two files of cataloguing operators. Proposes creation of more files for library automation. Recommends the purchase of PC/AT to meet the demands of users.

Murthy, S G K, Prasanna Kumari, K N and **Garudadwajan, B** 517

Integrated library automation – experience of NAL using PCs, *Lib Sci slant Doc and Info Std* 26(3) Sept 1989 : 196-216.

Presents library automation system dBase 3 in ICA/NAL including Library Documentation Acquisition System. From the system we can generate various service by-products. Discusses the salient features of the system.

Murthy, S S and **Rangra, V K** 518

Use of personal computers in library and information systems, *DLIS*, 189-198.

Mentions library in a desk concept and rise of PC. Gives characteristics of PC, constituent of PC system. Mentions criteria in the choice of PC industry in India, and application of PC in library and information system. Explains use of PC in DESIDOC.

Narinder Kumar and **Sharma, Ajay Kumar** 519

Nucleus for LAN : For a university library, *CALNE,* 85-96.

Defines LAN. Gives its essential part. Discusses its need as a nucleus of total information network of international level. Gives the overall analysis of institutional activities departmentwise. Describes selection of micro computers for LAN. Outlines advantages of new technology. Makes a case study of Kurukshetra University.

Patil, Y M 520

Computer applications for library and information work at the Documentation Centre of NBSS & LUP (ICAR), *CALNE*, 14-30.

Lists activities of NBSS & LUP. Gives information services of the Institute. Enumerates reasons for introducing computerised information services. Describes Micro CAIRS Software and its use at NBSS. Discusses its various applications. Also mentions projected plans.

Patkar, Vivek N 521

A generic design science approach to library computerisation, *Jl Lib and Inf Sci* 15(2) Dec 1990 : 129-138.

States that introduction of computer in a library generally raises users' and staff's expectations. Points out that the success of library computerisation depends on appropriate selection of hardware and software. Proposes a generic design science approach combining subjective judgement with analytical tools.

Patkar, Vivek N and **Iyer, P V** 522

Determining priorities for computerisation in libraries, *Ann Lib Sci and Doc* 37(3) Sept 1990 : 110-116.

Provides importance of computer technology in libraries. Gives the Bombay University Library scenario. Discusses the problems while undertaking computerisation by large libraries concerning deciding the sequence of activities to be computerised so as to satisfy the expectations of various groups. Applies Interpretive Structural Models Method.

Paul Pandian, M 523

Use of dBase IV and dBase/SQL for information processing and retrieval in libraries, *Lib Sci slant Doc and Info Std* 28(1) Mar 1991: 31-35.

Discusses the features of dBase/SQL. Identifies the factors that help information retrieval. Provides format for entry details for bibliographic database. Illustrates search query formats using dBase/SQL.

Rajasekharan, K 524

Computerisation of library and information activities in Kerala University : A proposal, *Int Lib Move* 13(2) June 1991 : 89-97.

Recognises importance of information in agriculture. Explains the needs for computerisation. Discusses advantages of library computerisation. Describes pre-requisites for computerisation. Gives planning of various processes. Describes functional activities that can be computerised such as acquisition, cataloguing, circulation and serial control.

Rajinder 525

The library in the information explosion : Computer effectively relevant to the challenge, *Int Lib Move* 13(4) Dec 1991: 204-208.

Mentions importance of information and growth of literature has put difficulties in acquisition, storage, retrieval and dissemination. States that use of computer has overcome these obstacles. Emphasises need for computer based information to have greater efficiency, new services, etc.

Ramachandran, V 526

Barcode applications in libraries, *Rilisar Bull* 7(1-4) Jan-Dec 1991 : 27-37.

Traces origin of barcode technology, and its use in libraries. Defines barcodes and gives its use with computers. Explains basic requirements for barcode application. Describes their use in circulation system. Discusses difficulties in the manual system. Explains computer based circulation system and merits of barcodes.

Ramaiah, L S and **Reddy, J Yadgiri** 527

Computerisation of record and archival collections: Need for the holistic view of information, *CALNE,* 117-123.

Discusses need of information and nature of information. Defines records and archives. Gives classification of archives. Mentions finding aids and search strategy. Describes the need for the modernisation of records and archives. Gives the global trends for modernisation.

Rama Reddy, E 528

Automation in libraries : Job design, staffing and training requirements, *Ind Jl Inf Lib & Society* 3(3-4) Sept- Dec 1990 : 227-234.

Describes briefly the job design evaluation of positions needed, integrating the change with automation, staffing the activities, performance standards, education and training of manpower while introducing automation in the libraries.

Rama Reddy, E 529

Planning automated library services, *Univ News* 29(51) 23 Dec 1991: 10-14.

Describes in detail the introduction of automation and its proper planning for computerising the library services so that the users needs could be satisfied more efficiently.

Rao, Kalyani and **Vyasmoorthy, P** 530

Word processing and its applications to the library, *CPT*, 221-230.

Defines word processing. Gives types of work processing. Mentions common features of word processing. Lists special features of WP packages. Describes advantages and limitations of using WP. discusses library applications of WP.

Ravichandra Rao, I K 531

Functions of automated systems, *DRTC 1989*, Al-22.

Discusses need for computerization of library activities,, procedures for automation of library functions, and functions of automated systems are discussed.

Suryanarayana, G 532

Computer maintained library system, *DRTC 1989*, Jl-7.

Describes computer maintained library system which is user friendly and tailored to suit a person without having a knowledge of dBase. Discusses various modules of the system.

Systems Data Controls Pvt Ltd, Bombay 533

Library manager, *DRTC 1989*, Tl-3.

Discusses a package based relational data model for library applications. It is well tested package, it states.

Tagore, P et al 534

MAITRAYEE : Library computerisation and networking software, *NISSAT Newsletter* 10(3) July-Sept 1991 : 7-9, 15.

Describes MAITRAYEE, the software package, an attempt to library computerisation and networking. Gives the philosophy behind it, the DBMS backbone, network backbone. Explains application software in various housekeeping operations. Gives future enhancements.

Tiwana, Paul 535

Computerizing a small library, *Her Lib Sci* 30(3-4) July-Oct 1991: 229-232.

Mentions the application of microcomputers in library work. Gives a brief account of Nova Scotia Teachers College Library and the decision to automate it unit by unit. Describes process of automation by having Bib-Base Modules, Bib-Base Acq, Bib-Base MARC, Bib-Base Public. States the use of technology in circulation work, etc.

Vaithilingam, N , **Ranganathan, T** and **Jacob, P J** 536

dBase software for library automation, *DRTC 1989*, Bl-26.

Explains the need for computerisation of library activities. Chooses dBase III Plus as software. Explains databases employed and software environment developed at HAL Engine Technical Library, Bangalore. Explains thc activities covered such as Members profile, Books cataloguing, Circulation control, etc.

Vij, Rajeev and **Mehta, S N** 537

Computerphobia : Are library professionals really aware of health hazards caused by computers?, *CALNE*, 179-191.

Gives classification of computer based library functions. Examines the known evidence of a variety of medical complaints such as eye strain, headache, bodyache, etc from VDU on the basis of a survey of library professionals through questionnaire. Concludes that VDU causes health hazards. Offers suggestions to minimise this sickness.

Wilsys – Software for library computerization, *INICAE* 9(1) Mar 1990 : 100-103. 538

Explains two major components of WILISYS : WILIMAX and WILITRAX. Discusses the WILIMAX package and its functions such as acquisition, circulation, maintenance, search and query and periodicals. States that WILITRAX package is meant for storing and retrieving abstracts information. Gives also its activities.

025.0285 (1) Gatekeeper Technology

Kaula, P N 539

Trends in informations handling system: Gatekeeper technology, *INICAE* 10(2) Sept 1991 : 185-197.

Based on the address delivered at the International Forum on Information System held at Kanagawa University, Hiratsuka (Japan) on 25 Oct 1990. Discusses information handling activities, IRS, IT, communication software, gateway systems and services, electronic information sources, and role of technological gatekeeper. Refers to the second computer age and research on thinking computers, AI, etc. Mentions major R & D programme of the 5th Generation computers.

025.04 Automated Information Storage and Retrieval Systems

Bakshi, Urvi 540

Consumer Information Resource Centre : Present activities and future plans, *HLAICI*, 124-129.

Describes the activities of Consumer Education Research Centre since its inception. Discusses activities of CERC's consumer library particularly its use of CDS/ISIS for computerised management of information storage and retrieval. CERC is functioning as Consumer Information Resource Centre.

Balakrishana, M R 541

Magnetic and optical storage of information, *NISSAT Newsletter* 10(1) Jan-Mar 1991 : 7-9.

Dwells on some fundamental aspects of optical recording, production of CD-ROM and the equipment required to 'read' it. Gives advantages of optical storage media over magnetic media. Refers to the physical layouting of data on the discs, logical file, and directory structures, etc.

Chandrasekhar, M S and **Jain, Sandeep** 542

WILISYS : WIPRO Integrated Library Information System, *DRTC*, 1989, HI-19.

Discusses various functions of a library and need for making use of computers in day to day operations. Describes WIPRO Integrated Library Information System (WILISYS) Software for library computerization.

Dubey, Yogendra P 543

International information systems and services and their relevance to India. *SSI*, 279-289.

Defines an information system, information service, online information system, database, information network. Discusses types of databases available. Describes characteristics of databases. Explains relevance of international information systems and its complex nature.

Grover, Vinod Kumar 544

Computer based information system for India, *NIPP*, 130.

Mentions need for developing a computerbased information system at national level. Gives constraints for such a system in India, but it is becoming viable. Gives some suggestions. (Abstract only).

Pitroda, Sam 545

Keynote address, *DESIDOC Bull* 9(1-2) Jan & Mar 1989 : 10-11, 13.

Excerpts from the Keynote Address delivered at the International Conference on Bibliographic Databases and Networking, etc. in which he talked about the role of information technology in social transformation.

Rajkumar, P V and **Gopalakrishnan, S** 546

User approach in designing of information retrieval systems, *CALNE*, 53-58.

Discusses information generation, information requirement aspects keeping in view user groups and their needs. Describes qualities of information and causes of IRS failure. States that user acceptance is important component in a system. Describes that user consultation is a vital element in library computerisation hence user approach and his needs should not be neglected.

Rao, R Sangeeta 547

Urban and Regional Information System, *HLAICI*, v 8, 11-15.

States the need for urban and regional information with the adoption of planned development. Promotes establishment of Urban and

Regional Information System (URIS) in Town and Country Planning organisation. Lists conceptual, technical and administrative problems relating to URIS.

Tell, Bjorn 548

Establishment of automated information system, *INICAE* 9(1) Mar 1990 : 25-34.

Refers to the automated information system and computerised search as a masking off technique. Discusses information retrieval in batch processing through conventional and non-conventional indexing techniques. States the evolution of document retrieval technique, online processing through such networks like MEDLINE, SDC, ORBIT, NASA, RECON, DIALOG, etc. Points out that information, knowledge and related technologies are resources. Examines ES in information system. States the characteristics of the system.

Unified Medical Language System, *INICAE* 10(2) Sept 1991 : 220-223. 549

Describes UMLS as an intelligent automated system. Discusses its components and use of UMLS knowledge source. Describes it as a semantic network and arrangements for distribution of its components. Gives its application procedures.

Vijaylakshmi, B 550

Computer based library system, *DLIS*, 161-169.

Defines computer based library systems, their advantages and disadvantages. Describes housekeeping activities like acquisition, circulation, cataloguing, and serial control where computers are used including formating and generation of indices.

025.04 Databases. Bibliographic Databases

ACCIS, Geneva 551

ACCIS Working Group on Database Access, *INICAE* 10(1) Mar 1991 : 95-97.

Reports about the proceedings of the meeting held in December 1989 at the ILO in Geneva.

ACCIS, Geneva 552

United Nations system databases on CD-ROM, *INICAE* 10(2) Sept 1991 : 226-234.

Describes 16 databases known to ACCIS within the UN system which are either operational or planned and which are or will be available on CD-ROM to external users. States that all these are also available on COM; diskette; magnetic tape; online; and print.

Cuadra, Carlos A 553

Growth of online databases, *INICAE* 9(2) Sept 1990 : 225-226.

Reports increase in online and portable databases at the current growth rate. Describes range of databases in every kind of subject matter with 4465 databases by January 1990. Describes common type online databases. Mentions their other features also.

Deshmukh, Subhash, Bhattacharya, Jaydeb and **Srinivasan, T R** 554

Comparative study of bibliographic database with Mini-Micro CDS/ISIS Version 1.0 and Version 2.3, *Lib Her* 28(1-2) Apr-Sept 1989: 1-9.

Provides an analytical view of advantages of Mini-Micro Version 2.3 over Mini-Micro Version 1.0 in real working environs.

Deshmukh, Subhash, Hiremath, J P and **Srinivasan, T R** 555

Development of user friendly bibliographical database using Micro-CDS/ISIS Version 2.3 at National Council for Cement and Building Materials, *Ann Lib Sci and Doc* 36(4) Dec 1989 : 111-124.

Presents overview of the efforts made in developing bibliographic database on cement and building materials industry using Micro-CDS/ISIS. Emphasises on the design of additional help menus for each command to make the system more user friendly.

Gambhir, Sudha, Kapoor, Sarita, Mam Chand and **Rao, N Nagjyotsna** 556

Bibliographic databases and networks : The Indian scenario, *CALNE*, 287-295.

Describes various bibliographic networks and databases developed in India. Classifies them in three categories: (1) general data/information network services, (2) bibliographic applications in general data networks, (3) specialized information network. Also mentions India's participation in international database development activities.

Hadagali, Prakash B 557

CD-ROM databases : Information storage and retrieval, *Luck Libn* 22 (1-2) Mar-June 1990 : 1-5.

States that CD-ROM is a new technology for information storage and retrieval. Mentions its advantages and disadvantages. Gives librarians attitude towards CD-ROM. States that it is gradually being adopted by Indian libraries. Mentions its benefits and hurdles. Concludes that professional training is a must for its proper use.

Hukam Singh, Neogi, R N and **Chadha, O N** 558

Towards creation of a national database on science and technology, *Ann Lib Sci and Doc* 37(1) Mar 1990 : 20-27.

Describes computerization of *Indian Science Abstracts* which will reduce the time and help bring out the final output on target. Contemplates to create a readable, searchable, national database on CDS/ISIS, Version 2.3 of Indian scientific and technical literature.

Jagga Rao, N V, Kankachary, M and **Chandra, T V P** 559

Management of manual database, *IM*, 55-56.

Describes various aspects of the databank designed and developed in the field of linguistics and literature which is being maintained manually at the CIEFL Library. Discusses database design and development and database working.

Jaipal, Kumar S and **Dewan, B N** 560

Development of database and query language at National Data Centre, Pune, *HLAICI*, v 7, 244-248.

Deals with the database created at India Meteorological Department of storing more than 25 types of data from a large number of data recording stations.

Kasiviswanadham, S 561

Role of commercial database in information retrieval systems – a case study with CAN/SDI package, *DLIS,* 231-242.

Discusses commercial databases for information retrieval services. Emphasizes on the need for creation of databases at institution level giving the example of Environmental Information System Centre, Madras which creates awareness and provides information retrieval services.

Mukhopadhyay, A 562

Experimental design of a bibliographic database with variable structure fieldlength for dBase 3+ applications, *IASLIC Bull* 36(2) June 1991 : 69-76.

States that library use of general purpose software has concentrated on routine applications. Describes that relational databases like dBase have potential to solve problems of variable length of field, variable record structure and repeatable fields. Discusses a pilot project designed to address these issues. Demonstrates that dBase can provide workable solutions.

Murthy, S S 563

International Conference on Bibliographic Databases and Networks, *INICAE* 9 (1) Mar 1990 : 104-106.

Reports about this international conference held in New Delhi during February 22-25, 1989. Describes the topics, discusses about databases, networks, etc in various technical sessions of the Conference. Also gives Panel discussion.

Network Advisory Committee, Washington 564

Non-bibliographic databases in a network environment, *INICAE* 10(1) Mar 1991 : 97-100.

Explains about the focus of the NAC on non-bibliographic databases. Gives users perspectives, sharing and use of non-bibliographic data, network for 21st century, etc.

Rajashekar, T B 565

Database service for S & T researches : Options and strategies, *NIPP,* 35-50.

Gives importance of electronic databases. Mentions their categories. Gives flow of information from print to database production and use. Gives a list of important S & T bibliographic databases. Gives an action plan to reduce gap in information accessibility of scientists in India and western countries.

Rajashekar, T B 566

GENBIBCON : A generalised software procedure for adapting heterogeneous bibliographic databases, *DRTC 1989*, Rl-20.

Describes the features of GENBIBCON which includes both a methodology and a set a software procedure for converting heterogeneous bibliographic formats into a target format which can then be imported into a local database.

Sapra, R L and **Pitroda, R S** 567

Database management plant germplasm system, *HLAICI*, v 7, 201-210.

Describes database information system as a tool with genetic resource manager. Deals with genetic resource activities, plant exploration, evaluation and characterisation, germplasm introduction and exchange, germplasm conservation, utilization, etc. Gives the need for genetic resource management and germplasm database.

Sathyanarayana, N V 568

Database industry for India : An agenda for action, *NIPP*, 71-91.

Focusses on the need for developing a strong base for information industry in India to promote and accelerate the growth of database industry. Presents a global view of information industry market. Reviews emerging Indian scenario for industry. Discusses infrastructural needs for promoting database industry. Discusses to set a performance goal for Indian database industry and defines broad strategies for success.

Soni, Rajendra, Jaffery, Farhat N and **Viswanathan, P N** 569

Creation of a computerized databank on chemical safety at Industrial Toxicology Research Centre, *Ann Lib Sci and Doc* 37(2) June 1990: 74-82.

Explains the details of a computerized databank created by ITRC, Lucknow for identifying chemical risks in occupational and community environs, to develop capabilities for avoiding of chemical accidents, and to formulate regulatory guidelines.

Srinivasan, S and **Gupta, R C** 570

Designing and updating of databases of building experts, *IM*, 71-72.

Deals with the designing and updating the list of CBRI experts on committees etc with BIS which is difficult to handle manually. Describes use of computer program using dBase III plus in handling the updating problem.

Sukhdev Singh 571

Anatomy of local databases at IGNOU Library and Documentation Division,*CALNE*, 97-116.

Mentions setting up of IGNOU, its Library and its activities. Describes the use of CDS/ISIS for creating three databases. Discusses the use of CLB Database, its FDT, Worksheet, FST. Also describes Database RSB and Database JAE and other associated details.

UNESCO 572

UNESCO databases, *NISSAT Newsletter* 9(3) July-Sept 1990 : 20-21.

Explains that UNESCO produces three types of databases : bibliographic, referral, and numerical in the fields of education, science, culture, social and human sciences, communication and information. Describes in detail these three types of databases with the listing.

025.04 (1) Software Packages

Ravichandra Rao, I K 573

Computer softwares for information work and services, Bangalore : DRTC, 1989.

Includes 26 articles written by library and information professionals in the country in this DRTC Annual Seminar number 23 for the year 1989.

Vyasmoorthy, P and **Gunjal, S R** 574

Software packages in India for library and information work, *DRTC 1989*, El-10.

Includes information on indegenously produced software packages. Gives details of hardware needed, library functions for which the package offers solutions.

025.04 (1) CDS/ISIS

DESIDOC, Delhi 575

Use of CDS/ISIS, *INICAE* 9(1) Mar 1990 : 91-96.

Reports about the first meeting of CDS/ISIS User's Group sponsored by NISSAT organised at DESIDOC, Delhi. Describes the discussions held in various sessions on papers presented : Two in Session 1; three in Session 2; one paper and demonstration in Session 3; two papers in Session 4; two in Session 5; and two in Session 6.

Devadason, F J 576

Setting up a bibliographic database using Micro CDS/ISIS software, *MLC,* 1-15, 189-193, 157-166.

Involves the identification of relevant data elements, defining them, describing their content and form of representation, searchable data elements, etc. Presents these factors as a case study using CDS/ISIS Microversion. Presents bibliographic database design for CDS/ISIS that takes care of books, articles, reports, conference proceedings, theses, patents, etc.

Makhija, Hem Lata and **Datta, Subrata** 577

Salient features of CDS/ISIS and dBase III plus package in designing and creating a bibliographic database, *IASLIC Bull* 36(2) June 1991 : 61-68.

Describes a database conceived to provide an online facility to identify and locate a document. Database consists of reports, survey reports, draft and final report of various projects undertaken by CMDA. Two packages in CDS/ISIS and dBase III plus were developed to find out actual difficulties and advantages of the two. Compares them in relation to database structure, method of interaction, data feeding, indexing, sorting and retrieval.

Muddumoolya, S and **Koganurmath, M M** 578

Technical institute libraries information management : File management in micro CDS/ISIS Version 2.3, *IM,* 70.

Explains the mechanics involved at different stages in initiating information management of technical institute libraries. Describes various steps involved in file management with CDS/ISIS software.

Prasad, A R D 579

Database management systems, *DLIS*, 263-271.

Provides origins of database and its advantages. Describes the CDS/ISIS package and its functional capabilities and levels of interaction. Compares it with commercial databases. Discusses the applications of CDS/ISIS in libraries.

Use of PCs and **CDS/ISIS** in library and information environment – INFOTEK Workshop, *NISSAT Newsletter* 10(4) Oct-Dec 1991: 8. 580

Reports about the Workshop on 'Use of Personal Computers and CDS/ISIS in Library and Information Environment' organised by Institute of Information Technology during 7-12 Oct 1991 at the NIPM, Madras.

025.04 (1) CD-ROM Technology

Kanwar, Vinod 581

Acquiring CD-ROM technology for libraries, *IM,* 51-54.

Brings out importance of CD-ROM technology. Discusses equipments needed. Discusses its advantages and limitations. Describes selection of CD-ROM for libraries. Mentions its cost on market potential. Explains future of CD-ROM products and technology.

Kanwar, Vinod 582

Acquiring CD-ROM technology for libraries, *NIPP*, 454-460.

Defines CD-ROM. Mentions equipment needed for it. Discusses advantages and limitations of CD-ROM technology as applicable to libraries. States that selection of CD-ROM products to be acquired is made in view of user needs, cost of the product and funds available. Mention future prospects.

Kanwar, Vinod 583

CD-ROM technology : Its merits and demerits, *CALNE*, 160-166.

Defines database and CD-ROM. Discusses developments of CD-ROM databases, CEC Projects, DEC databases, silver platter, UMI databases. Describes selection of CD-ROM products keeping in view datafiles, search software, hardware, cost and terms of purchase. Enumerates applications of CD-ROM. Describes CD-ROM as a medium giving advantages and disadvantages.

Kottai, A 584

CD-ROM technology for library and information retrieval applications, *NIPP,* 445-453.

Discusses CD-ROM technology for library and information retrieval applications, CD-ROM based systems configuration, online vs CD-ROM, advantages, disadvantages, and applications in library operations. Also mentions future trends.

Narendra Kumar and **Sen, B K** 585

SCI CD-ROM in the service of scientific community, *ILA Bull* 27(2) July-Sept 1991 : 54-57.

States that while online access to databases was a boon, its prohibitive cost of searching did not allow many scientists to reap its benefits. Describes that CD-ROM technology has given new dimensions to information storage and retrieval. Mention that many databases are now available in compact disk editions.

Natarajan, M 586

Information management on CD-ROM network and its implications, *IM,*66.

Deals with CD-ROM as an optional storage. Mentions accessibility of CD-ROM through network with advantages. Suggests that once this network is installed, there will be variety of valuable information resources that are available over it.

Panda, Krishna C 587

CD-ROM in LIS : Superb or sombre, *IM*, 64-65.

Describes the uses of CD-ROM as a convenient and attractive storage and retrieval tool for distribution and accessing bibliographic databases. Provides insight into various issues such as technology, production devise, its basic components, costs merits, and pitfalls of CD-ROM.

Rama Reddy, E and **Nagaraja Rao, K** 588

CD-ROM technology : A library perspective, *Univ News* 28(25) June 18, 1990 : 8-10.

Traces history and computers. Discusses CD-ROM Technology, its sources, CD-ROM Disk drives, software, prices. Describes database searching with CD-ROM. Mentions its advantages for libraries.

Satish, N 589

CD-ROM technology : A viable alternative to online database search, *CALNE*, 167-173.

Deals with the hypothesis that if external databases are converted onto CD-ROMs and are made available to library/information centres, the users information needs can be effectively satisfied. Discusses CD-ROM technology and online database search with their strength and limitations. Also discusses effectiveness of CD-ROM technology in INFLIBNET.

Siddiqui, Moid A 590

Can CD-ROM replace online? *INICAE*, 10(1) Mar 1991 : 40-48.

Mentions CD-ROM being used commercially since 1985 is not just a simple replacement for online services. States that it being a new medium be unified with online to make multimedia information service that offers the best of both.

Taneja, S K 591

CD-ROM in S & T libraries with special reference to India, *ILA Bull* 27(3-4) Oct-Dec 1991 : 115-125.

Discusses CD-ROM, its applications, recording and reading mechanism, IR methods and designing of retrieval software and system components. Mentions problems of standardisation and interchangeability. Examines role of CD-ROM in libraries and networking. Gives its pros and cons. Suggests improvements needed to increase its utility. Gives selection methods and impact of CD-ROM on libraries in India. Mentions some of the CD-ROM products available in the market.

Vengan, R 592

Information management with CD-ROM technology, *NIPP*, 426-444.

Lists various storage media. Describes what is CD-ROM. Gives its geneology, storage capacity, publishing system. Illustrates merits and demerits of CD-ROM. Outlines CD-ROM vs online and CD-ROM networking technology. Makes suggestions for CD-ROM publications in India.

025.04 (1) Expert Systems (ES)

Ajith Kumar, G 593

Development of Expert Systems for information retrieval : An introduction, *AGLIS Jl* 8 (1-4) Jan- Dec 1990 : 17-22.

Discusses computerised information retrieval. Describes database and knowledge-base and ES. Provides conceptual design of ES and knowledge-based system. Gives production aspects of knowledge-based systems, and its applications.

Manorama Srinath 594

Expert System for information management, *ILA Bull* 27(2) July-Sept 1991 : 63-67.

Explains the basic concepts which lead to the evolution of Expert Systems and provides a description of the significance and role of ES in decision-making process. Indicates various types of ES which can be designed for certain purposes.

Subramanian, K R, et al 595

An Expert System to aid classification and referencing work in libraries, *Lib.Sci slant Doc and Inf Std* 26(2) June 1989 : 97-107.

Explains how an ES has been designed and implemented on a PC/XT to aid classification and referencing work in libraries so that any classification scheme can be adopted to help librarians in depth classification of books. The system is fully driven.

025.04 (1) Online Searching

Ajith Kumar, G 596

Infrastructure for online access, *AGLIS Jl* 8(1-4) Jan- Dec 1990: 38-40.

Describes in detail the infrastructure required to access such online databases as DIALOG. Also provides the various costs involved in setting up such a facility.

Harish Chandra 597

On-line data base technology : A trend setter for a library system, *DLIS*, 153-160.

Gives objectives and advantages of data base technology, and online database. Mentions components of online database, its types, characteristics. Discusses functions of DBMS. Explains applications of online database technology, and network model.

Kasi Rao, V, Ramesh Babu, B and **Kaliyan, S** 598

Online information system for industrial growth : Need for a policy, *NIPP,* 134-135.

Mentions technologies contributing to the development and use of online database services. Defines a database; gives its types and subdivisions. Defines 'online'. Describes steps involved in online search and applications of online systems. (Abstract only).

Neelameghan, A , Sarvamangala, G and **Lalitha, M R** 599

Training in the use of online services, *DRTC 1989*, Y1-25.

Discussed role of online information retrieval services in the present day context and future needs. Emphasises advantages of simulation packages – the computer aided teaching-learning aid for online information retrieval. Presents an overview of some such package available at DRTC.

Panda, Krushna C 600

Online database : Some basic issues, *NIPP*, 57-70.

Provides an insight into how online databases bring numerous advantages. Highlights some of the basic issues such as growth and development, conceptual framework, classification, searching device, supporting technologies, merits and pitfalls from users' point of view. Shows that inherent limitations of conventional IR system can be minimised.

Ramnath, Radhika 601

TIFACLINE – an online networked technology information system, *NISSAT Newsletter* 10 (2) Apr-June 1991 : 6-8.

Describes the efforts of the Technological Information Forecasting and Assessment Council (TIFAC) under the DST in developing TIFACLINE. Explains the concept, information content, pilot project, and implementation including hardware, software, etc.

Seetharaman, M N 602

An introduction to online networks and services and a case study of an experimental project in NAL, Bangalore, *CPT,* 279-293.

Divided into two parts, discusses the dynamics of information.

Outlines impact of technology in information handling. Mentions importance of machine readable databases, online systems and services, online networks. Points out users of online searching. Mentions future developments. In Part II describes the online networks of the European Space Agency, access to it from India, online demonstration in Bangalore and New Delhi and implementing the project with service.

Summit Roger K 603

Online information : A ten-year perspective and look, *ISL*, 33-42.

Discusses the primary technological developments which have been combined for selection and transfer of knowledge. Describes the current trends in the areas of PC, CD-ROM, telecommunication, software and application, databases markets and users, etc which may be utilised in information services product development.

Vijaylakshmi, B 604

Online information networks, *DLIS,* 243-255.

Discusses computer based networks goals and types of networks. Describes their relevance for online information retrieval systems. Gives also a brief account of internal online services. Mentions use of DIALOG and Information Retrieval Service of European Space Agency (ESA/IRS).

Yamamoto, Takeo, et al 605

Tool IR : An online information service, *INICAE* 10(1) Mar 1991 : 29-40.

Describes TOOL-IR (University of Tokyo On Line Information Retrieval) as the first online bibliographic information service of practical scale in Japan. Gives its genesis. Discusses briefly the service and the software. Analyses users reaction to the system.

025.04 (1) Information Technology (IT)

Achyutha Rao, H R and **Ramasesh, C P** 606

Implications of information technology on librarians, *SALP*, 81-82.

Describes various implications of IT on librarians and they will be information specialists, library as paperless institution, etc. Speculates whether in the new society of future librarian will be an endangered species.

Agrawal, I K 607

Proposed infrastructure and facilities for the development of information industry in India, *NIPP*, 419.

Explains that we are on the treshold of revolutionary changes effected by IT having impact on our economic and social life. States that online information services are growing fast but in India it is facing problems. Proposes infrastructure and services to meet information needs of various groups. Also proposes strategies needed make the venture viable.

Harinarayana, N S 608

Impact of technology on the changing role of librarians, *SALP*, 33-37.

Studies the impact of new technologies on libraries such as powerful and portable computers, user interface software, storage media, communication technology, and AI. Discusses libraries in relation to technology to increase their image; but the image of librarian has not increased. Describes impact of technology on librarians' status; other riles to be considered to improve the status.

Khattar, Nandini 609

Newer roles and responsibility of library/information professionals in the emerging information scenario, *SALP*, 76-77.

Discusses the role of library manager in the changing information scenario. Gives role of management for changes in information environs. Describes the knowledge, skills and attitude required of the information professional in the new environs of IT.

Kuldip Chand 610

S & T information scene in India, *SISCOM* 11 (4-5) Apr-May 1991:1-2.

Describes about the activities of NISSAT and its Sectoral information centres, NICNET, INDONET, SIRNET and other networks which are indicative of the importance given to meet the need of S & T sector.

Kumar, R P 611

Emerging technologies and the state of health science libraries in India, *CPT*, 261-269.

Mentions value of information and modern technology. Discusses use of computer microcomputer, WP, online bibliographic databases in processing information. Describes role of teletext and videotext, fibreoptics, EM, facsimile transmission, etc. Gives state of health science libraries in India and the introduction of modern technology, and role of libraries in changing situation. Gives few suggestions for promoting IT in these libraries.

Kumar, R P 612

Frontiers in modern technologies and public libraries in India, *Int Lib Move* 12(1) Mar 1990 : 40-47.

Mentions importance of information. States that modern technologies have brought out sophisticated innovations such as computer satellites and techniques. Explains computer technology, Expert Systems, teletext and videotext, fibre optics electronic mail, CD ROM, etc. Discusses impact of modern technology on public libraries in India. Gives few suggestions in this regard.

Lahiri, A 613

Let technology and work environment go hand-in-hand, *NISSAT Newsletter* 10(2) Apr-June 1991 : 1.

Points out that development of IT have nearly reached a saturation level. States that in developing countries problems are compounded by the absence of work culture and environment. Mentions that information users' wants are less known.

Lahiri, A 614

Retrospect and prospect, *NISSAT Newsletter* 10(1) Jan-Mar 1991 : 1.

Takes stock of the trend of IT in the last two decades which includes computers, photocopying technology, micrographics technology, telecommunication technology, further revolutionary development in IT as CD-ROM, online, etc.

Mangla, P B 615

Second Pacific Conference on New Information Technology for Library and Information Professionals held at Glass Hotel, Singapore, May 29-31, 1989 : A report, *Jl Lib & Inf Sci* 15 (1) June 1990 : 95-97.

Gives a report of this Second Conference organised by Dr Ching-chih Chen of Simmons College, Boston in which 238 persons from 17 countries participated. In all 64 papers were presented at the three day Conference.

Moorthy, A Lakshmana and **Rajendran, V** 616

Information technologies for libraries and information centres, *AGLIS Jl* 8 (1-4) Jan-Dec 1990 : 6-16.

Defines IT. Makes an attempt to overview the impact of the IT on libraries and information services. Presents a brief discussion of electronic message and document delivery systems, and electronic mail.

Navlani, K 617

National seminar on information technology and libraries : Report, *Her Lib Sci* 30 (3-4) July-Oct 1991 : 251-253.

Reports about the UGC National Seminar held at the Punjabi University, Patiala, during 2-3 Feb 1990 which was inaugurated by the Vice-Chancellor, Mr S C Biswas, then President of ILA, gave the Keynote Address and Prof P B Mangla delivered Presidential remarks. About 25 select teachers spoke on four Sessions : IT and university libraries; IT and LIS education; IT : Problems and prospects; and Information centres and tools.

Nweke, Ken M C 618

Patterns of availability of information technology in Nigerian special libraries: A study of present status, *IASLIC Bull* 35(1) Mar 1990 : 25-34.

Reports the results of a survey to types and quantity of available IT in Nigerian special libraries. Discusses patterns of availability, groups of special library sizes, groups of degrees of use of IT in special library services.

Paramesvar, K R and **Harchandran Singh** 619

Standardization in information technology (International and national scene), *HLAICI*, v 7, 273-285.

Provides the world scene of IT, the international standard bodies. Gives the national scene and Bureau of Indian Standards and other national organizations. Discusses future strategies.

Parida, Baman 620

Strategic use of information and information technology, *IM,* 43-45.

States that telecommunication and computers constitute major part of IT. Describes computer network, databases and India's participation in these data-bases. Discusses general and specialised networks in India such as NICNET, INDONET, BTISNET, etc. Concludes that India has not yet grown to the desirable extent, efforts of NISSAT notwithstanding.

Prabhakar, S S 621

The role of modern technology in the changing world of information, *Ind Jl Inf Lib & Society* 4(2) June 1991 : 147-152.

Brings out importance of information and IT. Discusses impact of IT in the information field. Describes computer scene in the world and its impact on the libraries and information world.

Prem Singh 622

Managing technological change in libraries, *Lib Sci slant Doc & Info Std* 28(4) Dec 1991 : 137-149: Also in *Administrator* 36(1) Jan-Mar 1991 : 67-84.

Discusses the various faces of information technology that are emerging. Identifies their impact on library and its services. Discusses the strategies that are to be followed for adopting IT in a phased manner.

Rajashekhran, K 623

The impact of information technologies in increasing information access in developing countries, *NIPP*, 420-425.

Stresses need to use IT. Provides a bird's eyeview of the emerging technologies for increasing access to information in library and information centres of the developing world in order to have broad guidelines for library and information policy in India. Points out need for integrating planning of library and information activities. Suggests that libraries in India should concentrate on rapidly developing technologies for better information access.

SAARC Workshop on technology information and its linkages, *NISSAT Newsletter* 10(4) Oct-Dec 1991 : 10-11. 624

Reports about the two-day SAARC Workshop on 'Technology

Information and its Linkages' held in New Delhi on Sept 24-25, 1991 attended by delegates from Bangladesh, India, Nepal, Pakistan, Bhutan, and Maldives.

Satyanarayana V V V and **Savale, V T** 625

Influence of information technology on IRM in R & D environment, *IM*, 39-42.

States that information is as important as people, machine, capital. Aims at industrial research and development environment, information resources and their acquisition. Describes impact of IT on information resource management regarding acquisition and storage of information resources and retrieval of information from information resources.

Saxena, S C and **Mehta, S N** 626

Impact of new developments in information technologies on library/information professionals in the library/information centre management, *SALP*, 39-42.

Identifies modern information technologies as a tool which will change the roles and responsibilities. Discusses new roles of system analyst, system designer, information manager, database manager, information analyst, network manager, and intermediary to give effective management of library/information services.

SEMATECH 627

Developing advanced technology in SEMATECH, *INICAE* 10 (2) Sept 1991 : 213-216.

Discusses the development of advanced technology by a unique consortium of 14 semi-conductor manufacturers and the US government known as SEMTECH. Also supports research centres in universities.

Shukla, B B 628

Information technology transfer : A study of theories in abstracting and their application, *Ind Jl Lib Inf & Society* 4(3-4) Sept- Dec 1991 : 290-292.

Delineates the importance of correct abstracting for research work. States that abstract should be the substitute of original. Formulates a set of suitable theories in abstracting. Gives methods of abstracting. Stresses significance of study in existing information.

Shunmuganathan, S C and **Kumaravel, J P S** 629

Changing role of librarians in the electronic age, *SALP*, 80.

States that in the changing environs librarians have to play the role of traditional librarian and as a modern information scientist for which he has to equip himself with modern IT and have thorough knowledge of computer and its applications.

Sinha, Arun K 630

Trends in information technology, *DLIS*, 199-221.

Defines IT. Gives historical background. Mentions components of IT such as computers, telecommunication, databases, information systems, microforms, E S, videotext, etc. and their applications.

Sivaprasad, Y V 631

Library and information technology, *IM*, 75.

States that with the advent of computers, compact discs, online facilities, and other tools of IT, the term 'library' becomes obsolete and it should be replaced by 'Information centres'.

Tejomurty, A and **Bose, Kaushik** 632

ISDN : Evolution of a new information technology, *Her Lib Sci*, 30 (3-4) July – Oct 1991 : 184-189.

Discusses the chief characteristics of ISDN. Describes factors responsible to the evolution of ISDN. Mentions stages for its implementation. Discusses technical details of ISDN regarding system architecture, interface, etc. Outlines ISDN services some of which are already available in USA, Japan and Europe.

Varghese, M and **Ambili, K S** 633

Library/Information scientist in the emerging information scenario: Newer roles and responsibilities, *SALP*, 79.

Highlights the advantages of IT, information explosion, emergence and growth of bibliographic tools, automation of library operations which have changed the nature of library profession and the role of librarian who has to play dynamic role.

Viswanathan, T 634

Application of information technology in libraries, *Ann Lib Sci & Doc* 38(1) Mar 1991 : 1-7.

States that for automating the housekeeping operations, IT offers two approaches. Discusses integrated systems approach and distributed systems approach. Lists the variety of computer systems and ITs available. Discusses in detail the configuration for libraries of different sizes. Explains interlibrary network. Concludes that as the time passes resource to automation and employment of IT is inevitable.

Wisenberger, I K 635

Technology transfer as a field of study, *INICAE* 9(1) Mar 1990 : 17-24.

Stresses the need for information studies, and utilization of modern technology and relevant services for users through technology transfer. States three types of knowledge and transfer of professional knowledge between individuals and groups, between organizations and between various regions of a country. Discusses international transfer of knowledge through database from international organisations. Emphasises modernisation of technology of international transfer of knowledge.

Wormell, Irene 636

Gatekeeper as relayer of information : Implication for training and education of information professionals, *INICAE* 10(2) Sept 1991 : 145-152.

States the role of 'gatekeeper' in handling information products and dealing with communication issues in S & T. Discusses characteristics of role of gatekeeper. Mentions development of gatekeeping role and growing needs of gatekeepers. States their qualifications, communication skills, analytical skills, scholarship, technical competence and multidisciplinary insight.

025.04 (1) Information Systems

Chakraborty, Arun Kumar 637

Role of library and information managers in emerging information scenario, *SALP*, 94.

Describes significant technological advances. Points out how information system has moved out of book room to be nerve centre of organisation. Opines that status and authority of library managers should be commensurate with the new role he has to play.

Chandran, D and **Navaneethan, R** 638

Changing role of information systems and status of information professionals, *SALP*, 43-44.

Gives importance of information as a resource. Mentions parameters of information system and major environmental changes which affect the operation of information system. Suggests to adapt such changes for effective management.

Dixit, R P 639

Information systems – MEDLARS, AGRIS and UNISIST, *ISL*, 133-186.

Describes in detail the growth and development of information systems in the area of MEDLARS in order to achieve health for all; AGRIS to secure food for all; and UNISIST to make available the benefits of modern S & T to all.

Dubey, Yogendra P 640

Rapid changes in information environment : Implications for information systems design, *SALP*, 97.

Gives importance of IT and the resultant information age and information society. Discusses that text base information systems fall short of what they could and should be. Mentions importance of AI in changing information environs, and calls for new philosophy and sense of mission that must guide in the provision of information to the users.

Kuldip Chand 641

Environmental Information system (ENVIS), *SISCOM* 11 (6-7) June-July 1991: 1-2.

Describes about the ENVIS as a decentralised system using the distributed network of databases to ensure integration of national efforts in environmental information.

025.04 (1) Information Transfer

Panda, Krushna Chandra and **Padhi, P** 642

Information transfer through digital computer : Some parameters, *CPT*, 232-238.

Provides importance of computer. Gives its types. Explains parts of a digital computer. Compares digital and analog computer.

Describes how information can be transferred through a digital computer in libraries.

Rajyalakshmi, D 643

Free information transfer in national information policy, *NIPP*, 28-34.

Discusses the need for free access to information transfer, need for international and intra-national information transfer, transborder data flow and their impact on national policy making broad considerations of areas to be covered in national policy and implications in implementations of a national policy.

025.06 Information Storage and Retrieval (ISRS)

Kesarwani, S K and **Bhat, S G** 644

Information support for R & D in environmental engineering and science in India, *ALIS*, v 2, 165-183.

Emphasizes the interconnected and independent nature of air, water, land, flora and fauna and interdisciplinary nature of environmental engineering and science. Analyses approaches of variety of persons, involved in R & D activities in this field and their information needs. Justifies role of NEERI as information support system. Discusses its future plans.

Menon, N C 645

INSAT -ID Delta, *INICAE* 10(2) Sept 1991 : 216-210.

States that INSAT-ID was launched on the night of 11 June 1991 from Cape Canaveral. Mentions it as a joint venture launched from USA. Describes it as a period of revolution. States that it was 9th satellite from the foreign soil.

Rab, S Fazle 646

International information systems and their relevance to India : Some observations, *SSI*, 390-402.

Describes information which leads to transform the industrial society to an information society. Mentions role of information in our society. Describes new international information order of UNESCO which led to a number of information activities at international level with information programmes, international information systems, information systems in social sciences. Explains barriers to international information system. Gives their relevance to India.

Sapupria, J S and **Kuntee, P D** 647

Integrated inventory information system, *HLAICI*, v 7, 214-218.

Deals with the collection of oceanography data with the standard form for the Report of Observations and Sample Collection during Oceanographic Programme (ROSCOP). Discusses organization of data in three information systems. Mentions retrieval system through Integrated Inventory Information System, its advantages and the future.

Sengupta, I N 648

Ferocity of AIDS : The deadly disease : Extension lecture, *Ind Jl Inf Lib & Society* 4 (3-4) Sept-Dec 1991 : 285-290.

Reports about the Extension lecture delivered at the Aligarh Muslim University on 8th Feb 1991. Presents AIDS as the deadly disease spread through various media, hence requires education of people.

Shaibu, Samaila 649

A conceptual framework for a Nation Information System (NATIS) during hard times in Nigeria, *Int Lib Move* 12(2) June 1990 : 75-89.

Describes the concept of NATIS and role of UNESCO. Discusses the planning of NATIS infrastructure in Nigeria. Gives trends in LIS in Nigeria, and framework of NATIS in Nigeria. Highlights crucial steps to be taken at national level.

025.0602 ISRS -LIS

Kumar, P S G 650

Management information system for librarians, *CALNE*, 66-71.

Describes computerised information systems and systems for library and information work. Discusses management information systems (MIS) such as Personnel Information System, Workgroup Information System. Describes organisational information systems to bring integration of the activities of various departments.

025.06020218 ISRS – Standards

Bahl, A K and **Bhatia, Anita** 651

National information system: Standards, *NIPP*, 197-208.

Describes need for setting up of the Bureau of Indian Standards. Discusses its main functions. Explains the need for standards for information systems. Gives scope of the sectional committees. Reviews the achievements in standardisation of L & I work. Presents the international scene in this connection. Discusses further developments.

025.063 ISRS – Social Sciences

Binwal, J C, Chandel, A S and **Saraf, Veena,** *Eds.* 652

Social science information : Problems and prospects, New Delhi : Har-Anand Publications, in association with Vikas Publishing House, 1990. xvi, 494 p.

Includes 42 papers presented at a Seminar organised at NEHU, Shillong during May 19-21, 1988 on the area of (1) Structure and development of social sciences, (2) social science research in India, (3) characteristics/types and use of social science literature, (4) information needs and behaviour, and (5) information systems and services. Reviews existing situation and outlines futuristic design.

Binwal, J C, Chandel, A S and Saraf, Veena 653

Social science research and information in North-East India : Problems and prospects, *SSI*, 107-122.

Discusses the development of social science in pre-independence and post-independence period in the area of North-East India. Also provides the current scenario of research and the consequent problems of information access.

Borah, M N 654

Social science information needs of extension education scientists and students of agricultural university, *SSI*, 333-335.

Gives a brief introduction of Assam Agriculture University. Describes extension education and social science in the context of agriculture and allied sciences. Describes the need of social science information for extension education scientists and students on the basis of a survey of their citations in dissertations, published articles and interviews.

Buragohain, Alka 655

A plan for North-Eastern Regional Social Science Documentation and Information System coordinating the national social science information system, *SSI*, 476-482.

Gives introduction of the North-Eastern region. Discusses sources of information in social science studies in this region. Enumerates various research organisations and initiatives of the NE council in the improvement of information and library services.

Foskett, D J 656

Structure and development of social sciences, *SSI,* 3-15.

Defines information, data, and knowledge. Discusses general systems theory and structure of social sciences. Describes relationships in social sciences and documentary classification schemes like DC, LC, BC2.

Giridhari Singh, N 657.

Social science information for health care service, *SSI*, 467-471.

Deals with thc hcalth care information needed for primary health care service, information for curatibe service, and information for specialised treatment. Makes a mention of the Programme of the WHO to attain health for all by 2000.

Kaula, P N 658

Information activities in social sciences in India : Genesis, development and trend, *SSI*, 403-416.

Mentions identification of social sciences as a discipline. Discusses emergence of documentation and its spread to social science subjects. Describes various seminars on social science documentation held since 1959. Mentions activities of NASSDOC.

Kundu, A K and **Sinha, R R** 659

Flow of social science information and their dissemination technology, *SSI*, 450-457.

Explains social science literature and social science disciplines. Discusses literature growth and the agencies responsible for it. Outlines information sources and services. Describes activities of ICSSR through NASSDOC. Mentions factors affecting IT transfer.

Mukhopadhyay, A 660

Social science information system and information technology : Problems and possibilities, *SSI*, 427-442.

Mentions importance of information in changing society where an information policy is required as a result of information explosion. Gives definition and scope of social sciences. Laments on document non-availability. Discusses impact of new technology on resource sharing and networking. States that it can lead across the international gateway for resource utilisation.

Murthy, T A V and **Nagaraj Rao, K** 661

Social science information dissemination : A case study, *SSI*, 464-466.

Discusses the social sciences as being established at University of Hyderabad. Describes the resource building, special collection, documentation activities, networking, computerization activities.

Rab, S Fazle 662

A N S Institute of Social Studies : Library information and publication activities, *HLAICI*, 261-272.

Traces the origin and development of the A N S Institute of Social Studies, Patna. Gives its objectives such as research and training activities, publications. Describes activities of library and documentation centre. Appends a list of ANSISS publications.

Rab, S Fazle 663

Access to information : The growth and development of information systems in social sciences and the pioneering work of Kaula, *DLIS*, 279-296.

Describes the role of information in Information Society. Discusses New International Economic Order v/s New International Information Order. Narrates the UNESCO activities in the growth and development of other international agencies and their programmes. Mentions social science information system in India.

Sharma, Narendra Nath 664

North eastern region and social science information : A brief analysis, *SSI*, 472-475.

Discusses some characteristics of North Eastern region of India and initiation of social science in this area. Points out agencies for storage of social science literature of this region. Makes a case for a Regional Documentation and Information Centre empowered to provide various services.

Srivastava, A P 665

Some characteristics of social science literature, *SSI,* 184-193.

Explains social science literature. Discusses characteristics of social science literature and criterial for evaluation. Gives some estimates of volume of production and scattering of social science literature. Outlines characteristics of storage and retrieval of such literature.

Vyas, S D 666

Need for a national information system for social sciences, *NIPP*, 258-264.

Discusses a proposal for National Information System for Social Sciences. Explains objectives, functions and need of National Social Science Library, sectoral centres, regional centres. Suggests cooperation with INFLIBNET and other information systems at regional and international level.

025.063022 ISRS – Communication

IPDC 667

International Programme for the Development of Communication (IPDC), *INICAE* 10(2) Sept 1991 : 224-225.

States that about 100 nationals have benefitted from IPDC fellowships in 1989. Discusses some pipeline projects such as library projects, national and regional information networks, national archives, etc.

025.063046 ISRS – Population

Pathak, Lalit P 668

Population studies : Development, structure and information system, *SSI*, 95-103.

Traces the development of population studies. States that population studies are of inter-disciplinary nature and are measurable to some extent. Discusses the development pattern of population studies after the Second World War.

025.063054 ISRS – Women Development

Vyas, Anju 669

Centre for Women's Development Studies (library, information & networking activities), *HLAICI*,v 8, 60-74.

Traces genesis of the Centre. Gives its objectives. Describes activities of the Centre. Discusses library and information services of the Centre. Proposes a national information network for women and development studies as no databases or comprehensive bibliographies are available.

025.06333 ISRS – Natural Resources

Raghavendra, S R 670

National Natural Resources Management System, *HLAICI*, v 7, 43-46.

Traces the concept of remote sensing, and its present developments with ISRO. Discusses NNMRS to have effective utilization of earth resources data for maximum national benefit. Gives its components, application projects, manpower development, etc.

Subhan Khan 671

Natural Resources Data Management System (NRDMS) *HLAICI*, v 7, 1-13.

Gives origin of NRDMS under DST, Govt of India. Describes file structure, grid reference system, remote sensing application, database updation and applications in NRDMS. Explains NRDMS software, plan for district database, usefulness, status of NRDMS – district database, Gurgaon.

Water and Power Information System, *HLAICI*, v 7, 211-213. 672

Relates the establishment of WAPIS based on cooperative efforts of Central Water and Power Research Station, Pune, CBIP & CWC, New Delhi. Describes its integrated information system based on computer.

025.063337 ISRS – Environment

John, B 673

INFOTERRA : International Referral System for Sources of Environmental Information, *DLIS*, 257-261.

Discusses role of information in modern society specially in environmentally sound development. Describes the role of INFOTERRA as a referral system in organising environmental information.

025.06334 ISRS – Cooperatives

Kulkarni, M M 674

Vaikunth Mehta National Institute of Cooperative Management : Library, information and publication activities, *HLAICI*, v 8, 256-260.

Traces history of the Institute. States the objectives of the Institute. Describes its activities such as training programme, research activities, publications, management consultancy, international collaboration. Discusses the role and activities of its Library in systematic handling, management and monitoring of information.

025.06338 ISRS – Industry

Chetty, P Rajarathnam and **Reddy, B Pratapa** 675

Need for national information programme for small scale industries in India, *NIPP*, 154-158.

Describes need for information and information policies. Gives organizational structure of small scale industries in India. Lists information problems in small scale industries. Describes in detail about the National Information System for Small Industries (NISSSI). Gives also its functions.

Khan, P K 676

Information for small industry development : Need and sources with special reference to NE Region of India, *SSI*, 483-488.

Points out need of industrial information for small industry. Describes various sources of information for industry. Discusses infrastructure of the National Institute of Small Industry Extension Training (NISIET), NER Centre for collection, storing and disseminating information.

Mahmood Ali, M, Reddy, P J and **Hussain, Asghar** 677

Information storage and retrieval system for thermophysical properties, *HLAICI*, v 7, 233-239.

Describes the computerised DBANK (Data Bank) developed as a

growing large storage, computing and retrieval system for the physical and thermodynamic properties of industrially important substance.

Pandurangan, S 678

National information system for small scale industries, *NIPP*, 136-142.

Gives overview of small scale industries and industrial policy in India. Mentions importance of information for industry as it is basic need for its development and modernisation. Gives types of information needed. Describes that for collecting and organising industrial information various government institutions such as SENDOC are busy. States that a computerised network for free flow of industrial information should be established.

Peter, K M and **Peter, Susy** 679

Information needs of small scale industries : A study based on industries at Bangalore, *NIPP*, 143-153.

Describes that small scale industries provide employment to many and play an important role in nation's socio-economic development. States that technical information is a vital ingredient for small industries to lean upon for solving many of its problems. States that unlike the heavy industries, the information infrastructure of the small scale industries are rather very poor.

025.0633574 ISRS – Corporate Sector

The Corporate Studies Group, India Institute of Public Administration, New Delhi 680

Corporate Information System, *HLAICI*, v 8, 16-23.

Explains the difficulties in collecting data on corporate sector. Mentions the need of Corporate Information System (CIS) to compile information on various aspects of Indian corporate sector. Provides a brief outline of the basic features, scope, and coverage of the CIS to its prospective users.

025.0634 ISRS – Law

Rao, Dittakavi Nagasankara 681

Special features of Westlaw, *INICAE* 9(2) Sept 1990 : 171-174.

Introduces Westlaw – a computer assisted legal research service.

Describes its special features. Also provides the examples to explain the stated special features.

025.0637 ISRS – Education

Central Institute of Educational Technology (NCERT), New Delhi 682

Information, Documentation & CLF Division : Activities and expectations, *HLAICI*, v 8, 241-243.

Describes the activities and expectation of the Central Institute of Education Technology (CIET) set up in 1984. Gives the resource base of media collection. Discusses the functions and activities of Information, Documentation and Central Film Library. Lists facilities, services, and future programme of IDCFL.

025.06381 ISRS – Trade

Gupta, B M 683

Trade Information System in India (with special reference to TDA), *HLAICI,* v 8, 24-32.

States the need for an appropriate and efficient trade information system. Gives organisation of Trade Information System in India of the TDA. Identifies sources of information, technical processing, information dissemination, promotional activities and upgradation of TCS to the National Centre for Trade Information.

Kumar, P 684

Management of trade information in STC, *HALICI,* v 8, 33-37.

States the need of an efficient and reliable trade information system. Describes STC's information base on commodities, information base for manufactured products. Gives brief account of STC's Library/Information Centre.

025.653 (1) ISRS – INSPEC

Galliste, Adrian R 685

Digital signal processing, *INICAE* 9(2) Sept 1990 : 222-224.

Describes signal processing and digital signal processing. Deals with INSPEC database for coverage of developments in this fast developing area in respect of optical information, acoustic signal processing, signal processing and dection, optical information processing, pattern recognition, information theory communication etc.

Riar, Harbinder Singh 686

Optical computing, *INICAE* 10(2) Sept 1991 : 210-212.

States the implications of modern era of optical computing and advantages of digital image processing. Analyses INSPEC Database covering the whole spectrum of optical processing and describes the main classification codes for optical computing, pointing out the principle terms in controlled indexing.

Ware, C 687

Intersteller moleculer, *INICAE* 10(1) Mar 1991 : 75-76.

Refers to different molecules and molecular ions identified in intersteller space. Makes a study of intersteller molecules and related topics found in *Physics Abstracts* (Section A of the INSPEC Database).

025.0653 ISRS – NPL

Tiwari, D K 688

Data activities in radio physics at National Physical Laboratory, New Delhi, *HLAICI*, v 7, 266-269.

Deals with radio science, solar activity predictions, and other activities at NPL, New Delhi. Mention about data exchange facilities.

025.065397 ISRS – Atomic Energy (BARC)

Balakrishana, M R 689

Bhaba Atomic Research Centre (Library and Information services), *HLAICI*, v 7, 194-200.

Deals with BARC, its library and information activities, resource development, information services, publishing and printing, training facilities, etc.

025.0654 ISRS – Chemistry

Singh, R S 690

Chemical reactions information system, *CALNE*, 145-151.

Discusses handling of chemical characteristics for IR. Describes the sectors involved in chemical research activities in India. Describes existing products and services such as CASREACT, ORAC, MACCS, Chembase, Chemtext, etc. Also describes efforts made in India by NISSAT in setting up NICHEM. Gives its functions and advantages.

025.0654 (1) ISRS – NICHEM

National Information Centre on Chemistry and Chemical Technology (NICCHEM), *HLAICI*, v 7, 166-169. 691

Describes the functions of NICCHEM set up under NISSAT in 1986. Explains its activities and services. Discusses the proposed additional services.

025.06548 ISRS – Crystallography

Manorama Srinath and **Ambuja, R** 692

National Information Centre for Crystallography (NICRYS), *NIPP*, 131-133.

Explains briefly the scope and activities of NICRYS for using the Cambridge Structural Data which is accessible through INDONET. Reports the results of a study of the use of the database services by the scientists of the A C College of Technology, Madras.

Srinivasan, R 693

National Information Centre for Crystallography (NICRYS), *HLAICI*, v 7, 170-175.

Explains crystallography as a discipline. Discusses crystallography database and its characteristics. Mentions training programmes, and promotional activities of NICRYS. Gives the future plan of action.

Subramanian, M S 694

Crystallographic information dissemination in India : An investigation, *CLIS Observer* 7 (3-4) July-Dec 1990 : 93-98.

Highlights the concept of crystallography and information needs of scientists. Catalogues the activities of National Information Centre for Crystallography (NICRYS). Gives suggestions on the basis of national workshop reports, for future development.

025.0655146 ISRS – Oceanography

Desai, B N, Kunte, P D and **Bhargava, R M S** 695

National Oceanographic Information System, *NIPP*, 167-176.

States that in view of the importance of information relating to ocean study Indian National Oceanographic Data Centre (INODC) has been set up. Describes objectives, functions, data holding of INODC. Discusses how oceanographic data is organised through database management systems, databanks, etc. Deals with library and documentation system, the local database called 'Oceanline'.

Tapaswi, M P 696

Indian national information programme for marine science, *NIPP*, 209-219.

Gives importance of information relating to marine science. Explains the steps to be taken for a better utilization and management of information resources available in institutions concerned with marine sciences in India. Describes the role and services and facilities of the NIO Library as a case study.

Tapaswi, M P 697

Proceedings of the Offshore Technology Conference – quantitative and qualitative assessment, *Ann Lib Sci & Doc* 38(4) Dec 1991 : 119-126.

Evaluates the proceedings of this Conference. Finds that very few core journals are devoted of offshore technology alone, and these proceedings considered with journals ranks fourth. Suggests that publications in OTC proceedings be considered at par with the journal articles.

025.06574 ISRS – Biology

Ramachandran, S and **Kolaskar, A S** 698

Bioinformation system in India, *HLAICI*, v 7, 14-21

Gives need for developing bioinformation system in India. Discusses the planned bioinformation system, micro level planning, soft information, hard data, culture banks, biopolymer databases, bioprocess, engineering, energetics, management of information system, etc.

025.066 ISRS – Technology and Industry

Rahman Khan, A and **Carroll, Bonnie C** 699

Industrial and technological information; who has it and who needs it? The role of NTIS in acquisition and dissemination, *INICAE* 9(2) Sept 1990 : 139-155.

Stresses the information and communication process as the basis to the effective advancement of science and its application. Describes STI transfer process. Discusses generators, products and services, and users of STI and programmes to facilitate this process. Highlights technical reports as significant information product. Presents some future directions for NIIS to help meet needs of users and acquire information more effectively. Gives benefits and requirements for international cooperation.

025.06608 ISRS – Patents

Mohapatra, B S 700

Patent Information System of India, *HLAICI*, v 7, 225-228.

Describes establishment of the Patent Information System at Nagpur in 1980, its objectives, acquisition of foreign patents documents. Discusses patent information service including SDI, abstracting, copy supply, etc.

Paranjpe, P P 701

Patent Information System : Present status and future plans, *NIPP*, 188-196.

Explains the nature, scope and use of patent specifications as an important source for industrial information, technology transfer, and identification of technology trends. Gives an account of the activities of the Patent Information System in India, its present services, and its plan for modernization through computerization.

Ramachandran, R 702

Patent system in India, Japan, UK and USA : A comparative study, *Luck Libn* 22 (3-4) Sept-Dec 1990 : 58-67.

Traces the origin of patent system. Defines patent and legal provisions of patent protection. Compares some aspects of the existing patent system in India, Japan, UK and USA.

Ramachandran, R 703

Patent Information System in the USSR : A personal experience, *ILA Bull* 26(1) Apr-June 1990 : 14-25.

Describes management of inventive activity in USSR and objectives of patent information. Discusses structure and composition of patent information, patent files, patent abstracts information of NPO 'Poisk' and VINITI. Discusses international cooperation. Mentions training of patent professionals.

Stembridge, Amanda 704

The importance of patents information and the role of Derwent Publications Ltd in processing this information, *CPT*, 36-41.

Gives a brief history of patents. States that 70% of the information contained in patents is not published elsewhere, but they reveal existing technology. Describes the patenting procedure. Explains the role of Derwent Publications, London in meeting the need of patent information.

025.0661 (1) ISRS – MEDLARS

Chinnappa, S L, Pandita, Naina, Paul, Shravani and **Kumar, I** 705

MEDLARS services in India, *NIPP*, 159-165.

Gives the scope of MEDLARS, MEDLINE, online access to MEDLARS Database at NLM and NIC, available CD ROM database procedure for searching the databases training programmes and various catalogues of medical periodicals. Gives statistics for the services rendered by the MEDLARS Service Section at NIC.

Isaac, N P 706

ICMR - NIC Centre for Biomedical Information (MEDLARS operations in India), *HLAICI*, v 7, 186-188.

Explains MEDLARS and its operations in India in the National Library of Medicine. Describes various support services of the Centre, such as union lists, user awareness programmes, software development, etc.

Kottai, A 707

MEDLINE of CD ROM : A comparison of DIALOG on Disc and Silver Platter interface, *IM,* 59. (Abstract only).

Enumerates factors influencing the design of the two CD ROM interfaces. Makes a comparative study of DIALOG On Disc and Silver Platter. Points out, on these bases that DIALOG interface is better than Silver Platter interface.

025.066151 ISRS – Drugs and Pharmacology

Jain, H C and **Taneja, Ram D** 708

Development of pharmaceutical industry – UNIDO meet discusses network for information exchange, *NISSAT Newsletter* 9(2) Apr-June 1990 : 16.

Discusses the topics taken up at the interregional meeting of UNIDO in New Delhi from 19 to 22 March 1990, particularly information on development of potential of pharmaceuticals and herbal medicines.

Naresh Kumar and **Sengupta, K N** 709

Drugs and pharmaceuticals information services in India : The role of NICDAP, *HLAICI*, v 7, 145-157.

Explains the need for specialised information centres. Gives importance of drug industries in India. Gives establishment of NICDAP at CDRI. Discusses library resources development. Mentions objectives of NICDAP, its various activities, computer activities and NICDAP - WHO collaborating Centre on Drug Information.

025.066213 ISRS – Electrical Engineering

Verma, Promod Kumar and **Nagaraja Rao, K** 710

BHEL's libraries/technical information centres network, *HLAICI*, v 7, 181-185.

Deals with BHEL, and its library and information services. Discusses computer application in library and information activity for SDI, CAS, union catalogue, book acquisition, circulation, etc.

025.0662138152 ISRS – Semiconductors

Talwar, V G 711

Mobility of specialists in the field of semiconductor device technology, *INICAE* 10 (2) Sept 1991 : 204-210

Discusses mobility of specialists who have contributed documents in the field of semiconductors device technology based on sectorwise mobility, from industrial sector to research laboratories and universities and from one country to another. Observes that intercountry movement of specialists indicated the transfer of knowledge and do-how. Suggests increased movement of specialists from developed to developing countries and vice versa.

025.06621902 (1) ISRS – NICMAT

Vasudeva Rao, K N 712

National Information Centre for Machine Tools and Production Engineering, *HLAICI*, v 7, 136-144.

Discusses role of Central Machine Tools Industries. Describes establishment of NICMAP, and its objectives. Gives holdings of CMTI Library. Explains information services of NICMAP, the database it has generated, technical enquiry services, bibliography services, supporting services, promotional· activities. Also gives publications, special projects and services.

025.0663 ISRS – Agriculture

Bose, P C 713

Indian Council of Agricultural Research (Agricultural Research Information Centre), *HLAICI*, v 7, 189-193.

Mentions establishment of ICAR in 1929. Gives its main functions and organisational set up. Explains the need for ARIC. Describes establishment of ARIC, its current research information system, products and publications, and collaboration with international organisations.

Bose, P C 714

National Agricultural Research Information System, *NIPP*, 177-180.

Gives the need and scope of the Agricultural Research Information Centre (ARIC) of ICAR and a proposal for setting up a National Agricultural Research Information System for India including a network KRISHINET. Gives its objectives and computerization.

715

Management Information System for agricultūral research – international workshop, *NISSAT Newsletter* 10 (1) Jan-Mar 1991 : 12.

Reports about the objectives and proceedings of the two – week Workshop held on Management of Information System for agricultural research at NAARM, Hyderabad from 17 to 29 Sept, 1990.

Ojha, D C 716

National and international systems for agricultural sciences, *CPT*, 251-260.

Gives need and importance of information systems. Mentions information activities in India. Describes agricultural information systems in India. Gives overview of agricultural research in India. Describes various information centres and their services in India. Also discusses international agricultural information system.

Rajasekharan, K 717

Computer-aided information access in agriculture, *CALNE*, 152-159.

Gives need of information in agriculture. Mentions uses of computer and allied technologies in client-oriented information ser--vices. Gives merits of online access to external databases. Mentions important databases in agriculture. Describes participation of India in AGRIS since 1974, CAB Abstracts online data base. Discusses CD ROM and agriculture data base available on it such as Agricola, AGRIS, CAD Abstracts.

Srivastava, S and **Dey, A** 718

IASRI: Agricultural field experiment information system, *HLAICI*, v 7, 270-272.

Gives functions of the Indian Agricultural Statistics Research Institute. Describes the computer centre and data processing facilities at IASRI. Discusses about the agricultural field experiment information system.

025.06631523 ISRS – Plant Genetics

Siddiqui, A M and **Kar, Debal C** 719

National Bureau of Plant Genetic Resource Library : An overview, *Luck Libn* 23 (1) Jan-Mar 1991 : 25-30.

Gives in brief objectives of NBPGR and its Library. Outline the collection development and services of the NBPGR Library. Examines the existing library and information services such as CAS, SDI, etc. in the field of plant genetic resources.

025.0663932 ISRS – Marine Fisheries

Krishnakartha, K N and **Kanakasabapathi, K** 720

Central Marine Fisheries Research Institute library, information and documentation services, *HLAICI*, v 7, 229-232.

Describes the setting up of library of the CMFRI, the information sources and research divisions. Discusses the activities of the library and documentation division having information network, etc.

025.0666 ISRS – Chemical Engineering

Dadarkar, Pratibha R 721

Information management in Indian chemical industry, *IM*, 15-18.

Points out importance of technology. Mentions growth of chemical industry, importance of chemical information. Enumerates information acquisition problems which can be minimised by proper information management. Discusses its need, techniques and economy factors of information.

Gokhale, Pratibha A 722

Information management for the chemical industry, *IM*, 9-13.

Defines library, special library, information centre and chemical information centre. Gives overview of chemical industry mentioning nature of information and its information needs. Discusses planning of an information centre with emphasis on network for information management cost effective strategies. Outlines advantages of such planning.

Kudchadker, Arvind P 723

The Kanpur Critical Data Centre, *HLAICI*, v 7, 240-243.

Mentions its establishment in 1970 at IIT Kanpur and carried out literature search on some properties of haloalkanes.

025.066606 ISRS – Biotechnology

Biotechnology Information System, *NISSAT Newsletter* 9 (3) July-Sept 1990: 12-14. 724

Describes the structure of BTIS with Biotechnology Information Centre, Distributed Information Centres, User Centres. Explains formation of a computer network BTNET taking advantage of NICNET. Mentions services to be given, training, and international collaboration in Bioinformatics.

National Centre for Biotechnology Information, Bethesada (US) 725

Biotechnology information, *INICAE* 9(2) Sept 1990 : 228-229.

Mentions responsibilities of NCBI. Reports about the lecture series initiated to facilitate use of databases and software. States that NCBI is establishing a technology reports series also.

Ramachandran, S and **Arora, J R** 726

Biotechnology Information System – a national biotechnology information network, *NIPP*, 165.

Deals with the information explosions as a result of developments in biotechnology and researchers need to access information base in biotechnology. Mentions the need for a broad based information support service. Describes objectives of biotechnology scheme, important achievements and futuristic areas of work in the development of techniques and tools for handling biotechnology information.

025.06664 ISRS – Food

Tibbles, Jane 727

The International Food Information Service, *CLIS Observer* 8(1-2) Jan-June 1991 : 23-32.

Traces the origin of IFIS set up in 1968 by four international firms to provide information services in the field of food science and technology. Lists the abstracting services it brings out with online facilities and databases.

025.06664 (1) ISRS – NICFOST

Sangameswaran, S V 728

National Information Centre for Food Science and Technology, *HLAICI*, v 7, 114-126.

Mentions importance of food information and role of CFTRI. Describes NICFOST under NISSAT, the FOSTIS Plan and its implementation. Discusses information resources development, information service development. Mentions collaboration with other agencies. Discusses computerization.

025.06677 (1) ISRS – NICTAS

Shah, P C 729

National Information Centre for Textile and Allied Subjects (NICTAS), *HLAICI*, v 7, 158-165.

Deals with ATIRA, its library and information services, collection, membership, communication with industry. Describes its services. Discusses the establishment of NICTAS at ATIRA, gives objectives of NICTAS. Reports the finding of the survey of information need of user of NICTAS. Gives activities of NICTAS.

Shah, P C 730

A nodal point for textile information - NICTAS, *IASLIC Bull* 35 (1) Mar 1991 : 1-8.

Gives need of textile industry. Discusses ATIRA Library. Describes National Information Centre for Textile and Allied Subjects (NICTAS) giving its concept, genesis, objectives, organisation, support users group interaction, information services offered. Describes its computerisation, its publications and charges for providing information products and services. Mentions marketing of NICTAS information services and products.

025.06685 (1) ISRS – NICLAI

Rau, M V and **Hariharan, Chitra M** 731

National Information Centre for Leather and Allied Industries, *HLAICI,* v 7, 127-135.

Gives importance of leather industry and role of CLRI. Mentions information facilities at CLRI. Gives main objectives of NICLAI, users' needs and library resources. Describes information services and bibliographical services, supporting services. Mentions about Technological Information Bank, Management Information System for R & D Projects and thesaurus of leather science and technical terms.

025.067 ISRS – Arts

Biswas, S C 732

Art and Culture information and preservation; the Indian scenario, *HLAICI*, v 9, Pt 1, 1-8.

Traces history of art and culture in India. Describes the Indian scene in preservation of cultural heritage including printed material, manuscripts, visual arts, etc. Gives the role of Indira Gandhi National Centre for Arts, its library, databank on art and culture.

025.1 LIBRARY ADMINISTRATION
LIBRARY/INFORMATION MANAGEMENT
LIBRARY ORGANIZATION
LIBRARY RESOURCE MANAGEMENT

Alafiatayo, Benjamin O 733

Leadership and decision-making in organisation : A focus on governance in libraries, *Int Lib Move* 12(2) June 1990 : 99-112.

Defines organisation. Discusses leadership and decision-making, allocating resources, library organisation, library management, participatory management, committee system, etc.

Baba, Abdul Majid 734

Information management as a prerequisite for better library and information service, *IM*, 59. (Abstract only).

Defines information and information management. Describes that information needs to be managed effectively, just like other resources like men, material, money, etc to improve decision making, productivity, etc.

Chakraborty, Arun Kumar 735

Strategies of information management, *IM*, 60-62.

States that information management has made tremendous advances in view of importance of information. Traces origin and development of organising intellectual contents of Bliss through Ranganathan. Explains his five laws of library science in modern content of information management.

Chakraborty Ganguly, Krishna 736

Information resource management, *IM*, 64. (Abstract only).

Explains that traditional library tools are to be modified and improved upon to cope with emerging problems of information explosion. Describes factors to be counted in information management.

Chatterjee, Amitabha and **Sen, Subir,** *Eds* 737

Information management in library and information centres in India : Papers, Calcutta : IASLIC, 1991. iv, 75p.

Includes 13 papers with text, and another 13 with extended abstracts and abstracts only. Brought out as Special Publication Number 31, it covers papers presented at the 18th IASLIC Conference, held at Kurukshetra during Dec 26-29, 1991. Sh Girja Kumar delivered the Presidential Address.

Chowdhury, N B 738

Information management for information services, *IM*, 68.

States that information management and IT are interrelated. Describes information and information system. Discusses that through IM greater effectiveness, more work, design, development, etc. are possible. Outlines some problems also.

FID/SIG 739

Training for information resources management, *INICAE* 10 (2) Sept 1991 : 239.

Reports about the first meeting of FID/SIG on Training Information Resources Management held in Washington, D C on 28 November 1990. Discusses mission statement, training opportunities, etc.

Girja Kumar 740

Crisis management of libraries in India, New Delhi : Har-Anand Publishers, 1990. 180 p.

Presents two case studies of Delhi Public Library and BHU Library divided into two parts. Part 1 includes conceptual framework and case studies; Part 2 includes studies in conflicting management. States that these are based on some reports and write ups of the author.

Gopalakrishnan, S and **Annadurai, R** 741

Adequate disclosure – A strategy for information management, *IM*, 47-49.

Brings out need for adequate disclosure. Explains what is adequate disclosure. Mentions characteristics of disclosure of information. Points out facets of adequate disclosure. Gives classification of disclosure. Mentions quality of disclosure.

Gopalakrishnan, S and **Rajkumar, P V** 742

Information management system evaluation factors, *IM*, 57-58 A.

Explains information management system and the factors needed for its evaluation. Gives evaluation models such as Vector model, economic model, user model.

Gopinath, M A 743

Professionalism in library management, *PL*, 14-24.

Defines library as a complex system of humans, documents, finances, capital assets, movable assets. Describes the areas of activity in librarianship that centre round collection development, collection organisation, and users services. Discusses structural changes required in library profession. Gives professional competency analysis on the basis of essentials for various posts, librarian as communicators, silent teachers, etc.

Gupta, R C 744

Management of routine correspondence in library and information activities, *IM*, 69 (Abstract only).

Describes that in library and information centres routine correspondence involves lot of time and manpower in handling. Discusses a case of CBRI where a mailing list database is developed in dBase software and is found useful. Pleads for developing similar programmes for efficient information resource management.

Gupta, S P and **Mehta, S N** 745

Management of scientific and technical libraries, *AGLIS Jl* 7(4) Dec 1989 : 34-37

Gives importance of management as an activity in an organisation, library, etc. Explains need for library management to formulate objectives, management depends much on management skills rather than on technical skills.

Havard-Williams, P 746

Modern management in academic libraries, *DLIS*, 51-57.

States that all libraries are suffering from lack of money. Mentions role of librarian as manager rather than a scholar in such situations. Discusses change in libraries, impact on staff development, management of change, leadership qualities. Gives situation in developing countries. Mentions responsibility of LIS departments in producing future librarians.

Jayaswal, P K 747

Bureaucracy in library organisation : An empirical assessment, *ULI*, 182-194.

Explains the concept of bureaucracy. States its important characteristics. Brings out that women librarians are less involved in decision making; no influence of professional qualifications on bureaucracy; sizable group of librarians in all ranks show low level of specialisation ; higher degree of centralisation in university and public libraries. etc.

Maheswari, M Uma 748

Information resources management, *IM*, 66-67.

Outlines purposes of IM in an organisation. Refers to the information Resource Management to the management of information whereas Information Resources Management to management of information sources of an organisation. Defines IRM. Enumerates ways to have better management of information sources. Development in hardware and software are offering new opportunities.

Management of data COMAD 90, *NISSAT Newsletter*, 10 (1) Jan-Mar 1991 : 10. 749

Reports the discussion held at the International Conference on Management of Data (COMAD 90) during Dec 12-14, 1990 at New Delhi preceded by two-day tutorials.

Manorama Srinath 750

Organisational climate of university libraries in South India, *Jl Lib & Inf Sci* 15(2) Dec 1990 : 170-178.

Defines organisations. Determines the association between variables of climate and other variables. Examines feasibility of study of organisational climate of university libraries. Suggests a theoretical model of organisational climate for university libraries.

Penland, Patrick R and **Mathai, Aleyamma** 751

Managerial communications, *CPT*, 9-21.

Discusses the problem of communication of information from the point of view of the user and also the library manager. States that as far as possible it should be client-oriented facilitation for free flow of information.

Priscilla, N Mary 752

Information management : A look, *IM*, 69. (Abstract only).

Brings out importance of information in modern times. Describes that IM changes the organisation to make possible a new way of including a physical change, or creates a new physical possibility that did not exist before.

Ramesam, V 753

National Management Information System (NMIS) for science and technology sector, *HLAICI*, v 7, 22-25.

Describes the National Management Information System, its objectives, creation of NMIS Database, Information products, distribution of database, etc.

Rangra, V K 754

Library management and organisation : Some theoretical aspects, *AGLIS Jl* 8 (1-4) Jan-Dec 1990 : 1-5.

Discusses various aspects of management, levels and goals of management, planning, steps in planning, points for consideration in library planning, organisation, personnel management, administration, role of library committee, motivation, etc.

Reddy, J Yadgiri and **Satish, N** 755

Information resource management : Some basic issues, *IM*, 63-64.

Explains information and communication media. Discusses

management problems of information resources. Prescribes means to tackle with resource management problems.

Sharma, Pandey S K 756

Report of the rapporteur general of the conference, *AGLIS Jl* 7(4) Dec 1989 : 43-44.

Presents the report of the Rapporteur General of the seminar on management of government libraries and information centres held during 11-13 November 1989 at Goa University, Goa.

Singh, A R 757

Information management in archives and libraries in India, *IM*, 31-37.

Terms information as precious resource. Discusses importance of managing information resources in archives and library/information centres. Explains strategy of information planning from the point of view of users needs, and assessing their needs. Discusses uses of information for decision-making, file management and imagination. Also discusses economic consideration.

Vijaya Sudha, V 758

Information resources management : A case study, *IM*, 74-75.

Gives importance of information as a resource. Describes development of DLRC and its technical Information Centre. Describes that TIC is providing nascent information through various types of services.

Viswanathan, T 759

Information management in library and information centres in India, *IASLIC Bull* 36(4) Dec 1991 : 139-144.

Delivered as Keynote Address at the 18th IASLIC Conference at Kurukshetra, describes the information management for users, acquisition of information, role of IT, technical processing, library automation, networking, electronic media based information, need for indigenous databases, library management, etc.

Vyas, S D 760

Management of technical services in libraries, New Delhi : B R Publishing Corpn, 1990. v, 87p.

Deals with how to manage technical services in a library. Explains bibliographic searching, card preparation, reproduction and maintenance of catalogue, and filing of cards and maintenance of guide cards.

025.1 (1) System Analysis

Rout, R K 761

System approach to university library management, *ULI*, 13-18.

Presents systems view-points for management of libraries. Gives basic notions of a library system. Discusses essential characteristics of a library. States that various library activities are to be executed within the framework of these characteristics. Discusses the premises of systems management as applicable to university libraries in information communication.

025.11 Library Finance. Library Budget

Guruswamy Naidu, N 762

Public library finances, New Delhi : Ess Ess Publications, 1990. 230 p.

Divided into six chapters plus bibliography and appendices. Deals with history, performance, financing, cess etc of public libraries. Gives conclusion and suggestions for public library finances.

Inamdar, N B and **Ramaiah, L S** 763

Norms for allocating funds to university libraries : A review, *CLIS Observer*.

Reviews the recommendations of commissions and committees of the Government of India and UGC which recommended certain norms for allocation of funds to university libraries. Gives the present position in which nobody follows these norms. Suggests that a university library should be allocated 20% of the total university budget.

Kar, Debal C and **Siddiqui, A M** 764

Budgeting techniques used in research/special libraries or documentation and information centres in India, *IASLIC Bull* 35(1) Mar 1990 : 9-15.

Reports the results of a national survey of the budgeting techniques in use in scientific/ special/research libraries and documentation and information centres in India. Discusses some common problems and suggests solutions.

Lahiri, Ramansu 765

Fiscal autonomy in libraries : Is it a myth or reality ?, *SALP*, 54-59.

Attempts to examine the status/authority of some of the university librarians in North eastern region, in the fiscal area of payment procedure in case of journals. Suggests that library manager should be empowered with fiscal authority after the budgetary allotment is over. This would ensure better fiscal administration.

Mishra, Rajeshwar 766

Study of fluctuations in the prices of abstracting and indexing periodicals in the fields of engineering, the sciences and the humanities and social sciences during the period, 1980 to 1989, *Lib Her* 28 (3-4) Oct 1990 – Jan 1990 : 124-164.

Studies fluctuations in prices of 70 abstracting and indexing periodicals subscribed by IIT, Kanpur, Central Library during 1980-89. Analyses and interprets statistical data to discuss patterns of prices rise in different subject categories for determining a systematic and realistic short and long term subscription budget estimates.

Sewa Singh 767

Financing the public library system in India, with reference to the state of Punjab, *Ind Jl Lib Inf & Society* 4(3-4) Sept-Dec 1991 : 269-279.

Gives importance of public libraries and need for library legislation. Describes various sources of finance such as library cess, state government grants, central government grants, and other sources with reference to the situation in Punjab and other states. Offers various suggestions to improve situation of library finance in Punjab.

Sewa Singh 768

Financing the public library system in India; with reference to the state of Punjab, *PLSP*, 78-90.

States the role of UNESCO in the development of public libraries. Discusses various sources of finance. Elucidates problems regarding library cess in the light of experience of other states. Disfavours library cess and suggests 5 per cent to 10 per cent of Education budget for public library development in the state.

Subba Rao, C V 769

Tables and charts on price rise of books and periodicals – columns and juxtaposition : Observations and reforms, *ILA Bull* 25(4) Jan-Mar 1990 : 179-198.

Looks analytically at the tables and charts if they have achieved their purpose of knowing the percentage of increase in prices, air-mail rates, per year increase of books and periodicals. States that methodology may be re-examined.

Tejomurty, A 770

Financial administration of university libraries, *OSUL*, 46-67.

Describes financial administration and its principles. Gives importance of library finance and sources of finance. Deals with university library expenditure and its principles. Discusses financial estimation and budgeting. Gives budgetary standards for university libraries. Deals with accounting, auditing, etc. Concludes that planning for finances is essential.

Tejomurty, A 771

University library finance management : Theory and practice, *ULI*, 140-161.

Discusses sources of finance for university libraries. Compares the finances in 8 university libraries in M.P. Shows various methods of estimating finance in university libraries. Concludes that UGC grants are prominent for improvement of libraries in the states. States that in M P 5.5 per cent of university funds are spent on libraries.

025.12 Reprography

International Council of Archives 772

International Microfilming Programme for developing countries, *INICAE* 10(1) Mar 1991 : 87-89.

Mentions the main decisions taken at the meeting held in 1989. Lists the projects submitted and eligible for immediate funding. Gives materials for microfilmimg.

Kawatra, P S 773

Reprography and reprographic services, *ISL*, 102-132.

Gives origin and development of reprography. Discusses its need and various reprographic processes in detail. Describes reprographic services in India by such centres as INSDOC, DESIDOC, NASSDOC, BARC, NISSAT, SENDOC, etc. Gives the copyright problems. Offers suggestions.

Nagarajan, K S 774

Reprography, micrography and visual communication technology : An outline, *Lib Sci slant Doc & Inf Std* 27(2) June 1990 : 123-128.

Discusses developments in reprography, micrography and visual technology in transfer of information. Identifies value of exact and compact storage. Outlines a course module for library and information professionals at B Lib and M Lib levels.

Rana, Ranjit Singh 775

Role of information technology with special reference to reprography and micrography, *LISE,* 133-142.

Defines IT. Gives its applications. Discusses reprography and micrography as techniques. Mentions legal aspects of reprography. Discusses need for personnel, installations, cost etc. Gives various recommendations in this regard.

Rangra, V K 776

Management of reprographic services in libraries and information centres *AGLIS Jl* 7(4) Dec 1989 : 25-29.

Defines reprography. Explains briefly its broad areas. Describes xerographic process and growth of the industry with reference to plain paper copier. Gives criteria for selection of a PPC. Discusses problems of copyright in photocopying and charging for the service.

025.17 Treatment of Special Materials

025.17(1) Non-book Materials

Goswami, Sajal Kanti 777

Problems of managing non-book information resources, *IM*, 72-73.

Attempts at focussing the problems faced by the National Atlas and Thematic Mapping Organization in managing non-book information resources which form the backbone of its collection.

025.17(1) Grey Literature

John, B 778

Grey literature: The source of information for project financing, *IASLIC Bull* 36(3) Sept 1991 : 125-129.

Outlines the generation, collection and organisation of grey literature that meets the information needs of project financing. Emphasises on developing a network for the organisation and dissemination of this type of information.

025.172 Clipping, Pamphlets, etc

Raghavan, P 779

Press clipping file -its importance in the field of water resources, *Ann Lib Sci & Doc* 37(4) Dec 1990 : 117-120.

Describes the requirement, methodology and importance of the press clipping file organised at Centre for Water Resources Development and Management, Calicut.

Sharma, B K 780

Organisation of pamphlets for use, *Int Lib Move* 12(2) June 1990 : 69-74.

Describes pamphlets, methods of their acquisition. Discusses various methods of filing the pamphlets, their binding, pamphlet boxes, cataloguing, and indexing.

025.1732 Serials . Periodicals

Deo, M S 781

Determination of unit cost of the periodical section of a university library, *IASLIC Bull* 36(1) Mar 1991: 1-8.

Finds out unit cost of the periodical section of Marathawada University Library. Gives the total cost of processing at 172.26 of which about 106.36 belong to variable cost. States that a standard/comparative method to control the costs can be evolved by similar studies by various libraries and information centres.

025.1736 Technical Reports

Kanakachary, M 782

Role of technical report literature in the information world, *Lib Her* 27(3-4) Oct 1988-Jan 1989 : 105-111.

Defines technical report giving characteristics. Gives some important sources of availability of technical reports. Describes methodology to be followed for the process in the libraries/ information centres.

025.177 Audiovisuals

Hemasundar Naidu, G and **Gunjal, S R** 783

Non-conventional literature in the agricultural libraries in India, *IASLIC Bull* 36(1) Mar 1991 : 9-15.

Stresses the dominance of non-conventional literature in agricultural information. Discusses the efforts of agricultural libraries in processing non-conventional literature, based on the data collected from agricultural universities and other ICAR institutions. Suggests measures for effective bibliographic control of non-conventional literature in agriculture.

Kadiri, J A 784

Justification for audio-visual materials in schools and libraries : A review of the literature, *Int Lib Move* 13 (4) Dec 1991 : 195-200.

Defines audio-visual material. Explains the emergence of audio-visual materials. Reviews the literature and explores the importance of new media in the libraries.

025.1794 Microforms

Misra, V N and **Hungar, N C** 785

Micrographic records, *ULI*, 93-99.

Traces importance of micrographic records for university libraries. Defines micrographic record and discusses its various forms. Deals with arrangement, storage and preservation of micrographic records. States that for the organisation and preservation of these records national and international standards should be used.

Padhee, B K and **Choudhury, B K** 786

Microforms : Genesis and utility, *Ind Jl Inf Lib & Society* 3(3-4) Sept-Dec 1990 : 214-226.

Defines microforms. Describes the genesis of microforms. Discusses different types of microforms. Enumerates advantages and disadvantages of each type. Enumerates concrete suggestions.

025.19772 Management of University Libraries

Koner, S S 787

University library management and leadership, *LISE*, 181-190.

Deals with management of organisation and its application to libraries, management through its functions, inputs, outputs. Discusses the university library management and its levels such as top management, middle and lower management. Gives duties of leadership, and importance of leadership.

Verma, L N 788

Place of library committee in the management of university libraries in India, *OSUL*, 1-11.

Makes an effort to survey the university libraries of India on the basis of a sample of 30 university libraries information from which was collected through questionnaire. Discusses about library committee, its composition, functions and functioning.

025.2 ACQUISITION. COLLECTION DEVELOPMENT

Balasubramanian, K and **Neelakantan, K** 789

Rising prices and library acquisitions : An analytical study of Tamil Nadu Agricultural University, *Univ News* 28 (7) Feb 12, 1990 : 5-8, 10.

Aims to provide the required information for a careful development of the acquisition policy of the university library and evolve new policies to purchase books for the library with reference to Tamil Nadu Agricultural University. Finds out rise in the prices of books and their acquisition during 1980-88. Gives suggestions.

Gupta, S R 790

Management of library collections of professional colleges in India, *Lib Her* 28(1-2) Apr- Sept 1989 : 60-69.

Provides a summary of the Ph D theses accepted by the Banaras Hindu University, Varanasi in 1989 under the supervision of Prof P N Kaula.

Hossain, Serwar, Mannen, S M and **Begum, Suraiya** 791

Problems and prospects of library collection in Bangladesh, *ILA Bull* 26(2) July-Sept 1990 : 59-72.

Mentions advent of the concept of public library in Bangladesh. Discusses how library stock is built in Bangladesh. Describes problems of book selection and library stock in detail. Offers some suggestions for improving stock position. Makes a plea for reviewing the acquisition policy.

Inamdar, N B 792

Guidelines for selection and acquisition of materials for State Central Libraries – a case study of Andhra Pradesh, *Granthana* 1(1) Jan 1990 : 40-54.

Describes public library system in AP. Discusses State Central Library, A P and its functions. Reports the philosophy of collection development policy, authority to build library collection, responsibility towards other libraries in the system. Describes selection and scope of library materials. Also gives weeding policy.

Inamdar, N B 793

States Central Library – Andhra Pradesh: Guidelines for framing a policy for selection and acquisition of materials, *CPT*, 82-98.

Mentions briefly public library system in A P. Describes in detail the setting up of State Central Library, its functions, factors in selection, relationship of SCL with other libraries in A P, selection and scope of library materials, selection techniques, allocation on annual fund, weeding policy, handling of complaints, etc.

Meera, B M 794

Publisher, publication and price : Impact on library acquisition – a case study, *Lib Sci slant Doc and Inf Std* 26(4) Dec 1989: 264-272.

Presents a case study of correlation between number of books brought out by different publishers in a particular subject with price escalation and sinking budget. Gives sample of acquisition of books in Statistics in Indian Statistical Institute, Bangalore Library over three years.

Seetharaman, M N and **Gnanasekaran, N** 795

Collection development in libraries and information centres, *AGLIS Jl* 7(4) Dec 1989 : 18-24.

Brings out importance of library collection. Mentions need for a collection development policy. Gives outlines of a collection development policy. Describes principles of book selection and functions of acquisition section. Gives problems in collection development. Explains collection development routines. Points out impact of technology on collection development.

Goyal, S P and **Balbir Singh** 796

University book depot; theory and practice, *ULI*, 41-52.

States the need for a university book depot as it is helpful in procuring books and other reading material for the university library, students, teachers, etc. Discusses how a book depot should be set up, gives its rules, terms and conditions of supply and payment of bills. States the advantages of book depot it terms of discount and savings. Also discusses the working of a University Book Shop of HAU.

025.2 (1) Acquisition – Computerised

Chandrasekaran, G, Venugopal Reddy, Ch D and **Jayaseelan, D** 797

Computerised acquisition system for libraries, *DRTC 1989,* L 1-13.

Presents the requirements, conceptual design of the database and software implementation details about the acquisition system of SHAR Library. States that this package can be used by any other library with minor modifications.

Chudamani, K S and Subhan, V A 798

An integrated library software for acquisition and cataloguing of documents developed at I I Sc Library, *DRTC 1989*, N 1-15.

Mentions advantages of library automation, such as integrating the various activities. Investigates feasibility of integrating both the Acquisition and Cataloguing system at I I Sc Bangalore. Presents the design aspect of integrated system.

025.2 (1) Cooperative Acquisition

Katundu, D R M 799

Cooperative acquisition and collection development in Tanzania, *Int Lib Move* 13 (4) Dec 1991 : 175-181.

Deals with some methods of cooperative acquisition. Explains the current states in Tanzania, Lists problems to cooperative schemes. Stresses the need for cooperative ventures. Mentions some proposals.

025.21 Acquisition Policy

Gupta, R C 800

Factors in formulating an acquisition policy in a research library, *CPT*, 53-59.

States that document acquisition includes selection and procurement. Selection depends on matching of certain characteristics of documents with users interest. Needs to evolve a reliable system for timely and interrupted supply of documents. Discusses formulation of selection and procurement policies based on certain factors that contribute towards taking right decision.

025.216 De-Accessioning

Rajpal, Sital and **Chhotey Lal** 801

De-accessioning for better management of libraries, *ILA Bull*, 26(4) Jan-Mar 1991 : 183-186.

Defines de-accessioning. Gives its importance. Describes what to de-accession. Discusses norms of de-accessioning. Explains methodology of de-accessioning for better management of libraries.

025.21834 Collection Development – Law libraries

Saini, O P 802

Procurement of documents in a law library; with special reference to India, *Lib Her* 28 (3-4) Oct 1989 – Jan 1990 : 165-176.

Points out factors influencing the procurement policy of a law library. Deals with the book selection tools. Defines kinds of materials and suggests various procedures for the procurement of legal documents. Provides annextures containing bibliographical information regarding Indian law journals and foreign law journals.

025.21861 Collection Development – Medical Libraries

Das, Sabita and **Das, G N** 803

Quality selection, core collection, its maintenance and delivery of literature in medical college libraries, *Ind Jl Inf Lib & Society* 3(3-4) Sept-Dec 1990 : 207-213.

Describes the quality selection, core collection of medical literature. Discusses delivery of literature among medical libraries.

025.21877 Collection Development – Academic Libraries

Ebozoje, F 804

Relevance of collection for utilization in academic libraries in Nigeria : Issues, thoughts and views, *Lib Her* 28 (3-4) Oct 1989-Jan 1990 : 177-183.

Emphasises that academic library is the centre of activity of people. Stresses that if library misses this point, then it is nothing but a sophisticated warehouse. Suggests that in these days of financial difficulties an academic library must learn to select materials to avoid unnecessary duplications; must cooperate with others, etc.

025.218771 Collection Development – College Libraries

Bavakutty, M 805

Book collection in college libraries, *CPT*, 60-71.

Assesses the adequacy and quality of book collection based on field study of 51 college libraries in Kerala. Concludes that not even one college satisfies Ranganathan's recommended norm of 2,000 textbooks and 50,000 other subject books; and majority of users reported that books required by them are not available in college libraries.

Goel, Preeti 806

Criteria for building library collections in the college libraries in Chandigarh, *Int Lib Move* 13 (3) Sept 1991 : 132-139.

Defines collection development. Describes college library collection development. States the educational facilities in Chandigarh. Collects data from 17 college libraries through a questionnaire and analyses their collections, budget etc. Suggests a written policy for building collection.

025.218772 Collection Development – University Libraries

Edoka, B Eziukwu 807

Improving access to collections in universities, *Lib Her* 29(1-2) Apr-Sept 1990 : 1-8.

Considers access as a fundamental factor in demand for and setting of branch libraries in academic institutions. Examines some aspects of access to the resources of 46 branch libraries in Nigerian universities. Mentions about barriers hampering access. Stresses need for main library action. Offers ways to improve.

Kankachary, M, Rajagopal, B and **Laxminarayan, B** 808

Role of library and information centres in publication, *Lib Her* 28(1-2) Apr-Sept 1989 : 54-59.

Points out the role of library and information centres in outgrowth of publications. Mentions relationship between libraries and publishers. Suggests that writers and publishers should maintain the standards in their writing and publishing respectively.

Sharma, A K and **Kankachary, M** 809

Book acquisition pattern of Kakatiya University Library, Warangal – a survey, *Int Lib Move* 12 (4) Dec 1990 : 220-228.

Examines the book selection policy adopted by Kakatiya University comparing with the standards quoted by some of the eminent library scientists. Ascertains the opinion of library users by conducting a survey to know their satisfaction with the facilities given by the library, etc.

025.233 Libraries and Book Trade

Lau, Jesus 810

Book industry and libraries in Mexico : A study into their holistic relationship, *CLIS Observer* 7 (1-2) Jan-June 1990 : 16-19.

Discusses status of book industry and libraries and their relationship in Mexico. Reviews problems faced by the book industry. Suggests remedial measures. Stresses role of libraries in the promotion of book industry.

Samuel, Thomas 811

Booking the book importers, *Her Lib Sci* 30 (3-4) July-Oct 1991: 232-234.

Discusses the impact of devaluation of rupee on import of books. Points out less supply of foreign books against heavy charges demanded by importers. Examines the unhelpful role of G O C and exploitation of libraries by book trade. Shows the variance in discount to libraries in Indian publications. Concludes that de-valuation and mark up for foreign books and handling charges would strengthen the libraries for which rethinking is necessary.

025. 2832 Acquisition of Serials and Periodicals

Aina, Joseph O 812

Building a good collection of serial publication for academic libraries : A serials librarian point of view, *Int Lib Move* 13 (2) June 1991 : 102-109.

Finds out what goes into making a good collection of serial publications for the Nigerian academic institution. Gives findings of the data collected through questionnaire. Analyses data in tables.

Choudhury, B K and **Padhee, B K** 813

Price trends in political science and economics journals during 1980-1988, *Ann Lib Sci & Doc* 38(1) Mar 1991 : 30-38.

Discusses importance of serials. Points out constant price rise of journals. Observes increase of 300 per cent and 249 per cent in the prices of journals in political science and economics respectively during 1980-88. Cites some crucial factors responsible for the price rise of journals.

Goud, K Sudhakar 814

Correlation of journal subscription and photocopy/reprint requests data in a technical library, *AGLIS Jl* 8 (1-4) Jan-Dec 1990 : 32-37.

Discusses a method of evolving a journal subscription policy based on photocopy and reprint requests from the library users. Based on the data from PRDH Technical Library, Bombay which is equally applicable to any technical library of a research centre with a moderate subscription of journals.

Isaac, D and **Satyanarayana, I** 815

Escalation of journal prices : An analytical study of Osmania University Library, *Her Lib Sci* 29(3-4) July-Oct 1990 : 247-251.

States problems connected with acquisition of journals. Presents implications of knowledge explosion and rise of interdisciplinary approach. Details the price rise of periodicals during the last five years and increase in budget of Osmania University. Refers to the financial norms for university libraries and on this basis gives comparative figures for Osmania vis-a-vis allocation. Concludes that resource sharing be adopted.

Joseph, Rosamma 816

Direct subscription to periodicals : A case study of the Calicut University Library, *Ind Jl Inf Lib & Society* 3(1-2) Mar-June 1990 : 116-123.

Describes the working of direct subscription to periodicals in Calicut University Library. Deals with the operations and procedures followed. Explains in detail the works involved in connection with invoices, registers, foreign drafts, etc. Deals with the problems of duplicate payments, non-receipt of issues, etc.

Lahiri, Ramansu 817

Serial control system : What does it mean? a study, *Ind Jl Inf Lib & Society* 4(3-4) Sept-Dec 1991 : 187-196.

Enumerates lesser importance given to the organisation of perio-dical section in a library despite the important role it plays for education, research and development. Delineates aspects of development of serial control system defining each concept. Discusses the environment and components of system operators.

Lahiri, Ramansu and **Sangam, S L** 818

Serial control system : A payment factor, *Her Lib Sci* 29(3-4) July-Oct 1990 : 221-226.

Studies 200 cases of payments of serials of Karnataka University, Dharwad and Manipur University Library, Imphal. Discusses administrative machinery of payment operation of two separate regions. Provides comparative account of manpower, authority, decision making, and own finance office.

Mitra, A 819

Challenge of periodicals procurement in university libraries (based on a study of three university libraries in the Orissa state), *ULI*, 53-63.

Discusses various facets of periodicals procurement and related works in a university library. Makes a critical assessment of the qualitative and quantitative aspects of the functioning of periodical sections of three university libraries of Orissa on the basis of data collected for five years through questionnaire. Makes some suggestions.

Mittal, Rekha 820

Acquisition and distribution of primary and secondary serials in information science in India – an analytical study, *Ann Lib Sci & Doc* 37(1) Mar 1990 : 28-34.

Analyses acquisition and distribution pattern of current serials in the field of LIS covered in the secondary periodicals, *LISA, Library Literature*, in libraries located in different zones in India, and participating in NUCSSI database. Reveals that 37.2 per cent of total titles of *LISA* and *Library Literature* are available in participating libraries.

Padhee, B K 821

Trends in rising prices of chemistry and life science journals, *Luck Libn* 22(1-2) Mar-June 1990 : 36-43.

Emphasises the importance of journals in research libraries and discusses the rising prices of journals and their impact on libraries. Analyses rising prices of Chemistry and Life science journals statistically from 1977 to 1988 and traces the causes for such price rise. Gives suggestions to cope with this problem.

Rama Reddy, E, Nagaraja Rao, K and **Burhanuddin, Md** 822

Duplication of periodicals in selected libraries of Hyderabad – an analysis *Ann Lib Sci & Doc* Mar 1990 : 1-19.

Analyses duplication of periodical titles subscribed in Hyderabad with the help of Union List of Current Serials in Hyderabad, 1989, by subject and geographical location. Gives cost of duplication. Suggests creation of a nodal agency for effective cooperation among libraries.

Rama Reddy, E and **Nagi Reddy, Y** 823

Increasing costs of journals and its impact on libraries : A case study, *Her Lib Sci* 30(1-2) Jan-Apr 1991 : 40-45.

Mentions factors influencing the price escalation of scientific journals. Studies the percentage of increase of cost, budget allocation, foreign exchange rates by taking the subscription records of University of Hyderabad. Presents mathematical model for budget estimates. Suggests some ways and means to overcome the problem of increase in price of journals.

Rathore, J M S 824

Rising trends in the subscription rates of periodicals, *Int Lib Move* 12(3) Sept 1990 : 137-142.

Relates problems of the periodical section of a library. Tests the hypotheses whether journal prices have been rising at a rate significantly higher than the general rate of inflation, the rate of devaluation and upvaluation of different currencies.

Rationalization of periodicals acquisition in S & T : Indian effort, *NISSAT Newsletter* 9(3) July-Sept 1990 : 12-13. 825

States the importance of rationalization of periodicals acquisition. Reports some efforts made by NISSAT in some cities like Ahmedabad, Bangalore, Bombay, Hyderabad, Lucknow and Pune. Mentions that NISSAT Sectoral units or local associations can help in this direction.

Singh, J P 826

Rising trends in the subscription rate of military science journals, *ILA Bull* 26(2) July-Sept 1990 : 95-106.

Makes a detailed study of increase in the annual subscription rates of 24 journals subscribed at Defence Science Library during 1981-88. Establishes a relationship between budgetary allocation and fluctuation subscription rates. Discusses factors responsible for increase in subscription rates of military science journals. Recommends a formula to forecast the budget inflating to keep up continuity in subscription.

Tapaswi, M P and **Sainekar, G H** 827

Methodology for discontinuation of journals acquisition, *ILA Bull* 27(1) Apr-June 1991 : 1-7.

Discusses limitations of conventional evaluation methods for finding out the use of subscribed journals in special libraries. Suggests alternatives for evaluation of non-core journals followed in NIO Library. Emphasises the need for cooperative efforts and adoption of modern practices to face the unending problems of financial limitations.

Varun, Vimal Kumar 828

Rationalisation of periodical acquisition in S & T : Survey report, 1990-91, *NISSAT Newsletter* 10(4) Oct-Dec 1991 : 12-18.

Explains the experiment of bringing local libraries in few selected cities together by NISSAT to discuss their acquisitions especially renewal subscriptions and resource sharing possibilities. Reports about the progress of activities.

025.2832(1) Acquisition of Serials and Periodicals – Computerised

Dhanraj, K and **Thulasi, K** 829

Automated Serials Control System (ASCS) at NCSI using dBase III, *DRTC 1989,* D1 -17.

Describes software developed to automate NCSI's Serials Control System to reduce time and complexity of operations involved. Choses dBase III for creation and structuring of database files and quick indexes.

Gupta, R C and **Shiv Dass** 830

Computerisation of serials control a practical approach using a personal computer, *IASLIC Bull* 36(1) Mar 1991: 17-22.

Gives importance of serials publication and professional responsibility. Discusses problems in periodicals receipt. States that for faster and accurate record keeping, issuing timely requests for replacements it may be entrusted to computer. Gives a practical approach alongwith computer program with a PC.

Lalitha, M R and **Ravichandra Rao, I K** 831

A program package for automated serials control, *Lib Sci slant Doc & Inf Std* 26(1) Mar 1989 : 45-68.

Describes a module, automated serials control system that has been developed using dBase III plus software. Highlights the input, processing and output and each modular and file requirements for the system.

Lalitha, M R and **Ravichandra Rao, I K** 832

A program package for automated serials control, *DRTC 1989* VI-31.

Describes a modular automated serials control system developed by using dBase III plus software. Highlights input, processing and output for each module and file requirement for the system.

Natarajan, M 833

Development of software package with special reference to serials control, *DRTC 1989*, K 1-14.

Defines the serials and serials control system. Discusses different software packages developed by OCLC, FAXON, CLASS, EBSCONET, NOTIS, PHILSOM, etc for serials control. Outlines their formats, operational abilities, limitations and special features. Deals with the type of system that should be adopted for different types of libraries.

Paul Pandian, M and **Ravichandra Rao, I K** 834

An automated serial control system - a module, *Lib Sci slant Doc & Inf Std* 26 (4) Dec 1989 : 285-326.

Discusses objectives, various functions, and files requirements of an automated serial control system. Each function is treated as module and its programme is developed. Discusses limitations. Views some of the work done at national and international level.

Rao, Dittakavi Nagasankara 835

Automation of serials development in special libraries, *Luck Libn* 22 (1-2) Mar-June 1990 : 17-27.

Describes the role of special libraries. Points out the need of automation in serials operation. Defines serials. Discusses the overall requirements for an automated serials system including planning, data elements, etc.

Ray Chaudhury, Arup 836

Management of journal information using dBase 3 Plus, *DRTC 1989*, ZA 1-13.

Presents description of the system objectives and approaches followed in developing the program. Discusses the applications of the program and the advantages of using dBase 3 Plus for journals.

Serial Record Division, Library of Congress, Washington, D C 837

Seeking serials with SERLOC, *INICAE* 9(1) Mar 1990 : 96-99.

Describes serial locations (SERLOC) file on MUMS database giving users the record entry. Explains reasons why search SERLOC. Discusses how to interpret SERLOC records. Gives its benefits. Points out the future of SERLOC.

025.29 Collection Development – Area Studies

Saxena, R S 838

Awareness, acquisition and utilisation of Japanese scientific and technical information in USA and Europe, *Ann Lib Sci & Doc* 37(4) Dec 1990 : 125-132.

Discusses current trends in the acquisition and utilisation of Japanese scientific and technical information in USA and Europe, the problems faced by them in its acquisitiron and utilisation, and the role played by Japan in internationalisation of Japanese information. Also gives a brief account of Indian scene of Japanese information.

025.3 BIBLIOGRAPHIC CONTROL

Borchardt, D T 839

Australian commissions of enquiry; their literature and bibliographic control, *CPT*, 22-35.

Concerns mainly with the literature of or on about four types of tribunals set up in Australia disregarding literature on parliamentary committees. Identifies four categories of literature : statutes, commission reports, legal and procedural comments, socio-political comments, but lack and reliable bibliographical control.

Ghosh, Arun 840

Bibliographic control of social science literature in India, *IASLIC Bull* 36(3) Sept 1991 : 111-120.

Defines social sciences and bibliographic control. Surveys the state of art in social science publishing in India. Explains the role of ICSSR in bibliographic control in social sciences literature.

Appends a select list of publications related to social science bibliographic control tools.

Venkatappaiah, V 841

Services for the All Union Book Chamber, *Ind Jl Inf Lib & Society* 3(1-2) Mar-June 1990 : 58-66.

Defines bibliography as in Soviet Union. Traces history of bibliographies in USSR, change in the concept of bibliography after 1917. States that the All-Union Book Chamber since 1920 made responsible for bibliographical control of Soviet book production. Discusses its activities and services.

Vyas, S D 842

Bibliographic control of social science literature in post-independent India, *Lib Her* 29(1-2) Apr-June 1990 : 92-95.

Provides a summary of the Ph D theses accepted by the University of Rajasthan under the supervision of Dr C D Sharma.

025.3 CATALOGUING

Champawat, G S 843

Organisation and management of the cataloguing department of a university library, *OSUL*, 164-175.

Lists tasks of a cataloguing department of a university library. Mentions its location and physical condition. Mentions tools required. States that its staff includes professionals, semi-professionals, and non-professionals. Discusses procedure and work flow in practice. Gives its relation with other departments. Mentions qualities of a cataloguer.

Mohanrajan, P A 844

Steps in cataloguing, Madras : Kalaichelvi Booksellers, 1991. vii, 246 p.

Divided into 64 brief chapters, it deals with all the problems of choice and rendering of all types of documents in cataloguing.

Viswanathan, C G 845

Cataloguing : Theory and practice, 6th rev. ed, New Delhi : Ess Ess Publications, 1990. xiv, 450 p.

Among others, includes two new chapters on computerised

catalogue, and Headings for name entries according to AACR-1988 in this new revised edition.

025.3 (1) Cataloguing – Computerised

Library of Congress, Washington 846

Technology and handling of American memory, *INICAE* 10(1) Mar 1991: 79-84.

Explains the technology and handling of the American Memory, a master catalog on CD-ROM disk regarding reproduction of items, text conversions, etc.

Patnaik, Binayak 847

Computer application in cataloguing for modernising university libraries: A review of the journal literature of 1988, *IASLIC Bull* 35(2) June 1990: 63-71.

Studies the journal literature of 1988 on computerised cataloguing in the university libraries. Aims to build up a comprehensive view of the effects of computer application in cataloguing in modernising university libraries.

025.31 Library Catalogue

Maheswarappa, B S and **Janaki, M S** 848

Use of library catalogue by scientists at CFTRI, Mysore, *CLIS Observe* 7 (3-4) July-Dec 1990 : 84-86.

Surveys the use of library catalogue by the scientists at CFTRI, Mysore on the basis of questionnaire. Concludes that majority of the scientists are in favour of computerization of library catalogue.

Maheswarappa, B S and **Janaki, M S** 849

Use of library catalogue by scientists at CFTRI, Mysore, *CLIS Observer* 8 (3-4) July-Dec 1991 : 23-25.

Surveys the use of the library catalogue by the scientists at CFTRI, Mysore. Concludes that the majority of the scientists are in favour of the computerization of library catalogue.

National Seminar on Modernisation of library catalogue, 5-7 March 1990.: Reading material, Waltair : Dept of Library and Information Science, Andhra University, 1990. Various pagings. 850

Gives reading material on the theme of the Seminar sponsored by the UGC and organised by the Dept of Library and Information Science, Andhra University, Waltair. Programme was divided into 7 Technical Sessions.

025.316 MARC

Hopkinson, Alan 851

A question of formats, *Lib Her* 28 (3-4) Oct 1989 – Jan 1990 : 73-91.

Discusses UNIMARC giving salient features of its manual, technical details including linking techniques and output in AACR form, and its critique. Describes history, use and technical features of the format of UNISIST reference manual. Gives history, and technical aspects as well as evaluates CCF.

Sen, B K 852

From MARC to CCF, *ILA Bull* 27(1) Apr-June 1991 : 22-37.

Mentions how with the automation of the Library of Congress MARC-I format developed and later revised to bring out MARC-II. Also mentions the development of ISBD and ISO-2709. Provides development of CCF, its scope, structure, segments and links. Discusses data elements, and gives their list.

025.316 (1) CCF

Common Communication Format : New phase in development, *MLC*, 1-2. 853

Describes the need for standardisation of the exchange of information and development of several exchange formats. Discusses the application of CCF, computer software and format conversion, extension of the format, and training and promotion.

Format Conversion with the CCF converter, *NISSAT Newsletter* 9(4) Oct-Dec 1990 : 11-12. 854

Discusses the CCF distributed by UNESCO, a program for MS-DOS microcomputers designed to permit the conversion of records from one ISO – 2709-based format to another. Mentions types of conversion, the Conversion Table, running the program, and future development

Hopkinson, Alan 855

The UNESCO Common Communication Format, *MLC*, 1-6.

CCF enables free exchange of bibliographical records within information community. Studies the CCF in relation to other formats like UKMARC, AGRIS, INIS and MEKOF-2.

Katyal, Prem Lata, Vajahat, Abida, Tejpal, Rama and **Gambhir, Sudha** 856

Bibliographic record format, *CALNE*, 129-133.

Defines bibliographic record. Describes main aim of computerization of bibliographic data. Discusses structure and content of exchange format on the basis of bibliographic data definitions. Gives components of records of agencies exchanging data.

National Workshop on CCF : The Common Communication Format, *NISSAT Newsletter* 9(2) Apr-June 1990 : 8-10. 857

Reports about the two-week National Workshop organised by NISSAT, UNESCO and ILA on CCF during 19 Feb -2 March 1990 in New Delhi in which 48 people participated from all over the country. Resource persons included Mr. Alan Hopkinson, Peter Simmons and F J Devadason.

Parekh, Harsha 858

Bibliographic record structure and communication formats, *Luck Libn* 23(1) Jan-Mar 1991 : 1-24.

Describes the concept and logical structure of a bibliographic record. Identifies characteristics of bibliographic entities. Explains content designator such as tags, sub-fields identifiers, record label, etc. Describes prevalent communication formats such as ISO 2709, MARC, UNISIST-Ref Manual, CCF, etc. comparing record labels, directory, etc.

Simmons, Peter 859

A Common Communication Format for bibliographic change, *MLC*, 161-164.

Reproduced from *UNESCO Jl of Inf Sci, Libraries, Archives and Administration*, vol 3, No. 3, 1981, on the UNESCO sponsored symposium to discuss the problems of providing a single communication format for the international exchange of bibliographic information in machine readable form.

Simmons, Peter 860

Using CCF : The Common Communication Format, *MLC*, 285-294.

Describes that CCF is employed as a standard on which biblio-graphic systems are based. CCF differs from MARC. CCF forms the basis for several new formats used in Europe and North and South America. Gives applications.

025.317 Retrospective Conversion

Deogan, M S 861

Retrospective conversion in university libraries, *CALNE*, 124-128.

Defines retrospective conversion of records. Gives nature of collections. Describes determination of total workload to be converted. Mentions need for finances.

025.32 AACR – 2

Gautam, J N 862

AACR II 1988 revision : An appraisal, *ILA Bull* 27(2) July-Sept 1991: 91-95.

States objectives of revision. Mentions guidelines provided for revision. Describes machine processing of bibliographic records, and structure of AACR-II. Explains the description stating features. Discusses important rules.

Mookerjee, B P, Neogi, Deepika and **Banerjee, Ratna** 863

AACR 2 : Main entry vs alternative heading, *IASLIC Bull* 35(3) Sept 1990 : 87-95.

Finds out the merits of Main Entry. Discusses alternative sugges-tions. Stresses the profound changes that are taking place in cataloguing rules and procedures, because of available technologies.

Pulla Reddy, V 864

A proposed evaluative procedure for valuing catalogue entries according to AACR-2, *MLC*, 1-19.

Stresses need for standardisation of evaluative procedures. Develops an evaluative procedure for valuing catalogue entries prepared by AACR – 2. Illustrates the application of formula for valuation. Recommends for standardisation of the formula to achieve uniformity.

025.322 Choice of Entry and Form of Heading

Jayaraman, R 865

Towards a sociological understanding of Hindi personal names and surnames, *Jl Lib & Inf Sci* 14(2) Dec 1989 : 115-127.

Deals with naming practices in India. Provides a sociological account of broad patterns of naming customs among Hindu, Muslims, Sikhs and Jains. Mentions applicability of naming practices over the sub-continent as a whole and for Indians in other parts of the world.

Yahya Haroon, K 866

Cataloguing of Malyali Muslim names according to CCC Ed 5, *CLIS Observer* 8 (1-2) Jan-June 1991 : 18-22.

Discusses various components of Malyali names. Stresses need for standardisation of Malyali Muslim names. Points out the problems as the CCC does not cover the case of Malyali Muslim name in detail.

025.322 (1) Corporate Headings – Government

Choudhury, Bijoy Kumar and **Mishra, Sanjaya** 867

Government as author : Treatment in CCC and AACR 2, 1988 revision, *Her Lib Sci* 30(3-4) July-Oct 1991 : 205 -211.

Discusses various types of government publications. Attempts a critical analysis of the treatment of rules in CCC-Ed 5 and AACR-2, 1988 revision. Brings out similarities in rendering of various types of government publications with examples according to both the codes.

025.322(1) Corporate Heading – Institutions

Choudhury, Bijoy Kumar and **Mohanta, Rabindra Nath** 868

Institution as author : A comparative study of CCC and AACR 2, *Luck Libn* 22(1-2) Mar-June 1990: 6-12.

Enumerates the relevant rules of CCC-5 with amendments and AACR-2 (1988) in the choice of heading and rendering of different types of institutions with suitable examples. Compares the rules to bring out similarities and dissimilarities in the treatment of institutions at the level of its definition and cases of conflict in both the codes.

025.322(1) Pseudonymous Authors

Choudhury, Bijoy Kumar, Raut, B and **Padhee, B K** 869

Pseudonymous works : Comparative study of CCC 5th Edition (with amendments) and AACR 2, 1988 revision, *Her Lib Sci* 29(3-4) July-Oct 1990 : 213-220.

Defines *Pseud* according to CCC and AACR-2, gives its types. Discusses treatment of relevant rules in both the codes. Points out similarities and dissimilarities with regard to rules for choice and rendering of *Pseud*. Suggests that criteria should be the name properly established in literacy world.

025.324 ISBD

Rao, S Sudarshan 870

International Standards for bibliographic description : Brief review, *CALNE,* 134-140.

Defines standardization. Discusses standardization in cataloguing regarding descriptive standards, scope of ISBD, its objectives, ISBD (M), ISBD (G). Concludes that ISBD (G) is the best format available for all libraries.

025.3494 Cataloguing of Microforms

Sabir Hussain, Mohammad 871

Cataloguing of microforms in AACR-2, *ULI*, 135-139.

States that non-book or non-print material is gaining importance and microforms are becoming more important. Defines micro-forms. Discusses cataloguing problems of microforms caused by their peculiar format. Discusses rules for cataloguing for microforms provided in AACR – 2. Gives sample entries to demonstrate the rules.

025.4 Subject Analysis

Gopinath, M A 872

Information processing language and development of knowledge base system, *Lib Sci slant Doc & Inf Std* 26(1) Mar 1989 : 1-11.

Gives importance of information. Information processing language provides a modellar for knowledge based systems. The definition of semantic domain and syntactical featuring of objects, properties, action, space and time will set arrangement of information into knowledge based system. The facet analytic approach provides an analytic synthetic base for the same.

025.4028 Abstracting

Kankachary, M 873

Abstracting and indexing techniques : A critical view, *Ind Jl Lib Inf & Society* 4(2) June 1991 : 122-130.

Gives meaning and species of abstract. Mentions role of abstract in the present information age. Discusses disadvantages of inconsistency in the formats of abstracting and indexing. Points out standardized technique for designing formats for abstracting and indexing journals.

Shukla, B B 874

Information technology transfer : A study of theories in abstracting and their application, *Int Jl Lib Inf & Society* 4(3-4) Sept-Dec 1991 : 290-292.

Delineates the importance of correct abstracting for research work. States that abstract should be the substitute of original. Formulates a set of suitable theories in abstracting. Gives methods of abstracting. Stresses significance of study in existing information.

025.4028(1) Abstracting Periodicals/Services

National Science Library, New Delhi 875

Abstracting and indexing periodicals in India, *Her Lib Sci* 30(3-4) July-Oct 1991 : 242-244.

Makes an analytical study, based on NUCSSI database, to find out the pattern of distribution of some important abstracting/

indexing serials in the fields of agriculture, medicine, engineering, physical and biological sciences.

Suresh Kumar 876

Evaluation of indexing and abstracting services in public administration, *Lib Her* 28 (1-2) Apr-Sept 1989 : 43-53.

Mentions that public administration possesses many of the characteristics of a discipline. Discusses indexing and abstracting services as a source of current information. Evaluates five most relevant indexing and abstracting services in the field of public administration.

025.42 Library Classification

Gopinath, M A 877

Teaching of classifying of document in a library, *Lib Sci slant Doc & Inf Std* 28(1) Mar 1991 : 1-4.

Analyses process involved in classifying a document in a library. Discusses role of Call Number in the arrangement of documents on the shelf. Identifies knowledge and skills for the purpose. Discusses learning and teaching methods that can be adopted for the purpose.

Malla, N 878

Classification of knowledge : A study in the foundation of library science, *Granthana* 2(2) July 1991 : 163-168.

Presents a logical analysis of the concept of classification with special reference to library science. Examines the view that objective of classification adopted in library is not to categories books but knowledge. Points out with regard to classification of knowledge that there are no natural classes and all classification are artificial. Dwells also on the concept of knowledge.

025.42 (1) Classification and Computer

Sarvamangala, G 879

Design and development of a database using CDS/ISIS : An analytico-synthetic classification approach, *Lib Sci slant Doc & Inf Std* 27(3) Sept 1991 : 173-182.

States that CDS/ISIS provides a versatile facility for creation of bibliographic database. Attempts to present instruction for database creation using Dr S R Ranganathan's analytico-synthetic approach.

025.42 (1) Notation

Shabahat Hussain 880

Capacity of notational systems : Some new formulae for calculations, *Lib Sci slant Doc & Inf Std* 28(3) Sept 1991 : 114-123.

Works out certain formulae which may be useful for calculating the capacity of non-faceted and faceted notational system. Analyses data. Reveals a far greater capacity of faceted notation over non-faceted. Concludes that the capacity increases with the addition of digits in a class number.

025.428 Book Number

Mishra, Sanjaya 881

Colon Book Number, *Luck Libn* 22 (3-4) Sept- Dec 1990: 80-88.

Discusses meaning, need, purpose and history of book number Explains Ranganathan's book numbering system. Cites some problems in Colon Book Number with their solutions. Concludes that Colon Book Number is the best.

Satija, M P and **Agrawal, S P** 882

Book numbers : Some Indian methods, New Delhi : Concept Publishing Company, 1990. 96 p.

Divided into four chapters covering Book numbers – what and why; Ranganathan and his system; two other Book Number system; Collection Number and Call number. Also gives two Appendices.

025.428 (1) Collection Number

Mishra, Sanjaya 883

Collection Number, *Her Lib Sci* 30 (1-2) Jan-Apr 1991 : 68-69.

In this Technical Note, defines Collection number and gives its need. Describes the problem as there are clear cut rules for Collection number. Offers solutions as followed in the Sambalpur University Library.

025.43 General Classification Systems

Mandal, Satyananda 884

Geographical area in CC-7 and DDC-20 : Some observations, *Col-*

lege Libn 6 (1-4) 1990 : 3-7.

Discusses area and its problem in classification. Describes salient features and changes concerning geographical areas in CC-7 and DDC-20. Points out some problems and makes suggestions. Stresses the need of revision and cooperation in this regard.

025.431 Dewey Decimal Classification (DDC)

Comaromi, John P and **Satija, M P** 885

Dewey Decimal Classification : International and Indian aspects, *DLIS*, 381-396.

Discusses DDC, its expansion, influence, limitation, translation, worldwide use. Covers also its international and Indian aspects including use in bibliographical works.

Comaromi, John P and **Satija, M P** 886

Exercises in the 20th Edition of the Dewey Decimal Classification, New Delhi : Sterling Publishers, 1990. xiv, 127 p.

Includes 14 chapters on various aspects of the DDC-20. Provides introduction to the text of 4 volumes, salient features of DDC-20. Explains practical number building according to DDC-20.

Gangadhar Rao, P and **Ramesh Babu, B** 887

20th edition of Dewey Decimal Classification (DDC) : A review, *CLIS Observer* 7(1-2) Jan-June 1990 : 25-29.

Reviews salient features of 20th edition of DDC, comparing the schedules with the previous editions, especially the 19th. Discusses the changes newly incorporated. Concludes that 20th edition is an improvement over all the previous editions.

Krishan Kumar and **Sharma, Jaideep** 888

Dewey Decimal Classification (Edition 20) : A review, *Lib Her* 29 (3-4) Oct 1990 Jan 1991 : 105-113.

Describes general format, major changes, important areas of revision in Tables and Schedules. Mentions changes in Relative Index. Describes revision policy, its use in libraries and glossary. Concludes that new edition is better organised and more convenient to handle.

Kumar, P S G 889

Practical guide to DDC 20 (Dewey Decimal Classification, Edition 20), Nagpur : Dattsons, 1990. 247 p.

Divided into 7 parts : Part A includes introductory material, while Part B gives summaries. Schedules are given in Part C, and Part D includes synthesis. In Part E are given the Seven Auxiliary Tables, in Part F the Schedules, and Part G covers the End Matter.

Satija, M P 890

Dewey Decimal Classification for schools, *Ind Jl Inf Lib & Society* 3 (3-4) Sept-Dec 1990 : 285-290; Also in *ILA Bull* 26 (4) Jan-Mar 1991 : 179-182.

Provides information about the use of DDC all over. Discusses the use of its 4th Edition in School libraries.

Sen, Bharati 891

Data processing and computer science in DDC 20th edition-some applications, *ILA Bull* 27(3) Oct-Dec 1991 : 130-134.

Examines the difference in the ability of DDC 19 and DDC 20 in classifying the documents falling in the field of 'Data Processing and Computer Science' in view of its rapid developments. Finds the phonixing of DDC 20 to be satisfactory for the present.

025.432 Universal Decimal Classification (UDC)

Raju, A A N 892

Universal Decimal Classification (IME, 1985) : A practical and self instructional manual, Madras : T R Publishers, 1991. xiv, 234 p.

Divided into two blocks each consisting of four units. The first block deals with genesis and development of the UDC, salient features of 1961 Edition and IME, 1985. The second block deals with practical classification with IME. Gives also exercises for practice.

Sharma, Jaideep 893

Special auxiliaries in UDC : A critical valuation, *Lib Her* 29 (3-4) Oct 1990-Jan 1991 : 114-124.

After giving background discusses the structure of UDC. Explains concepts of principal divisions and special auxiliaries. Mentions cases of inappropriate allocation of concepts to special auxiliaries. Discusses their types and gives suggestions for improvement.

025.435 Colon Classification (CC)

Gopinath, M A 894

General systems theory *vis-a-vis* classification theory of Ranganathan, *CPT*, 114-121.

Discusses general systems theory and its laws. Highlights application of these laws to the development of a theory of classification. Evaluates research done in classification in India and Britain. Re-defines PMEST in terms of systems theory. Formulates rules on the basis of principles derived from system law, for the development of schedules for classification and procedures for classifying of documents for collection formation.

Navaneethan, R 895

Implementation of COBOL program for index to the Colon Classification, Edition 7, *DRTC 1989,* S1-12.

Explains briefly the data structure, organisation, and program development of CC INDEX program for preparing index to CC-7 using COBOL. Explains development of screen using COBOL screen manager utility.

Satija, M P 896

Colon Classification 7th Edition, *ULI*, 123-134.

States that CC-7 has drastic changes. Examines these changes critically. Mentions features of new edition such as simplification of rules, identification of more basic subjects, increase in number and variety of common isolates. Points out demerits. States that 17 Indian universities and 16 colleges use CC. Says it should be kept alive.

Sewa Singh 897

A practical manual of Colon Classification : Edition 7, Bombay: Jaico Publishing House, 1990. xii, 305 p.

Includes 49 brief chapters on the practices and theory of Colon Classification. Part I includes 38 chapters on practical examples, analysis of titles, rules etc. Part II includes 11 chapters on the theory of CC-7; while in Part III are given answers to Exercises for practice given in Part I.

Soma Raju, P 898

Colon Classification on the march : An overview of Edition 7, *DLIS*, 297-408.

Describes the development of CC through its various editions, particularly its Ed 7. Presents the features of CC-7 in conceptual and notational aspects. Points out shortcomings in the Schedules. Makes suggestions to improve it further.

025.435 (1) Fundamental Categories

Shabahat Hussain and **Khan, M Tariq Mustafa** 899

Conceptual changes in the fundamental categories in CC 7, *Her Lib Sci* 29(1-2) Jan-Apr 1990 : 45-50.

Makes an evaluation of the many conceptual changes with regard to fundamental categories (FC) in CC-7. Traces development of (FC) explaining each of the concepts with examples. Discusses Matter Material, Matter Property, and Matter Method category introduced in the new edition of CC.

025.46608 Classification – Patents

Ramachandran, R 900

Patent classification system in India, Japan, United Kingdom and USA, *Lib Sci slant Doc & Inf Std* 26(4) Dec 1989 : 245-263.

Discusses need for patent retrieval system and systematisation of patent documents for effective utilization. Compares the scope of existing library classification with patent classification. Traces emergence of patent classification systems and their use in India, Japan, UK and USA. Describes their structure and principles. Gives efforts of International Patent Classification.

025.48 Subject Indexing

Bakewell, K G B 901

Humour in indexing, *Ind Jl Inf Lib & Society* 4(1) Jan-Mar 1991: 1-4.

Describes humour in indexing to books, etc by giving examples from a large variety of sources.

Chakraborthy, A R 902

Indexes to secondary periodicals in science and technology, Calcutta: Asiatic Books Agency, 1990. xvi, 328 p.

Discusses as to how indexes to various secondary periodicals in science and technology are to be prepared for the easy retrieval of information from them.

Chowdhury, G G and **Mahapatra, M** 903

Scope of relation analysis in studying the concept of interrelationship in subject literature, *INICAE* 10(1) Mar 1991 : 67-74.

Makes a study of the various relational situations displayed by a given relational operator in a subject literature. Presents ideas about nature of the subject literature. Provides stages of relational analysis of a subject statement as an example with a brief note on scope of each relational operator as proposed by Farradane.

Gopinath, M N 904

Chain index and its impact on subject indexing, *Lib Sci slant Doc & Inf Std* 26(3) Sep 1989 : 167-185.

Analyses the bases of Ranganathan's chain indexing and its value in the systematic subject index to information retrieval. Discusses impact of hierarchical chain in the formation of chain in POPSI and PRECIS. The current approach to on-line search strategies stimulate the formation of chain in subject heading formulation.

Riggs, Fred W 905

Indigenous concepts : A problems for social and information science, *Lib Sci slant Doc & Inf Std* 28(2) June 1991 : 43-57.

Mentions that development of indigenous terms to denote indigenous concept is a phenomena which occurs in societal space of many Third World countries. Shows several such illustrations. Advocates for a universal onomatic approach wherein concept-term relation is governed by intellectual categorical system. Advocates INTERCOCTA as an international programme to assist the development and internationalization of indigenous concepts.

Riggs, Fred W 906

Delphic language : A problem for authors and indexes, *Lib Sci slant Doc & Inf Std* 28(1) Mar 1991: 18-30.

Presents a new approach to naming of terms known as *Onomatic* approach. Provides detailed structure of this approach and its application in the field of information science and sociology. Suggests further study in these areas.

Sharma, S K 907

Role of indexing in scientific communication particularly in the field of superconductivity, *INICAE* 10(2) Sept 1991 : 198-203.

States the essential operators of indexing and categories of the information sources. Gives a modern list of journals in superconductivity and its evaluation countrywise, ranking them based on current contents and research productivity. Discusses advantages of computerised method of indexing.

Tyagi, K G, Manohar Lal and **Mahabir Singh** 908

Indexing of Indian newspapers : Brief survey, *IASLIC Bull* 35(1) Mar 1990 : 17-23.

Mentions purpose of index and objectives of newspaper index. Traces brief history of press in India. Describes indexing scene in India based on English press. Describes some foreign and Indian documentation tools. States that documentation service is not supported by document delivery. Points out need to coordinate indexing activities in India.

025.48 (1) Book Indexes

Ramesh Babu, B 909

An investigation into the treatment of personal names in book indexes, *IASLIC Bull* 36(2) June 1991 : 77-80.

As a short communication explains exhaustively of an index to a book. Examines indexing of personal names and their treatment in books from India, Britain and America. Observes different practices in indexing personal names and typographical distribution. Makes use of standards for evaluation.

025.48 (1) Bibliometrics
Bibliometric Studies

Bavakutty, M and **Taher, Mohamed** 910

Flow of Islamic information through journal articles : A bibliometric analysis, *Luck Libn* 22(3-4) Sept-Dec 1990 : 75-80.

Attempts to quantitatively analyse the Islamic literature published in journals and as covered by 'Index Islamics' for a period of five years (1970-74).

Bose, Ranjana, Upadhyay, J L, Ghosh, B N, Mukhopadhyay, Shyamal and **Sengupta, I N** 911

Ranking of cancer periodicals in the field of virology, *Ind Jl Inf Lib & Society* 4(1) Jan-Mar 1991 : 69-86.

Estimates qualitatively the growth of cancer literature on one of its basic aspects, virology. Identifies international communication channel of virology literature pertaining to cancer. Prepares an international ranking list of periodicals on virology.

Gupta, Davendra K 912

AIDS : Development and growth of a newly emerging research speciality in medical sciences, *Int Lib Move* 13(2) June 1991 : 78-88.

Gives definition and concept of AIDS. Conducts bibliometric study of AIDS literature giving size and growth of literature, forms of literature, subject dispersion, journal literature, etc.

Kannappanavar, B U and **Nulvi, C N** 913

Authorship trend and solo research in rural transformation : A bibliometric study, *ILA Bull* 27 (1) Apr-June 1991 : 38-41.

Attempts to know the authorship pattern in rural transformation literature based on a comprehensive bibliography on rural transformation, by National Institute of Rural Development analysing 1145 entries. Concludes that the solo research is more favourable than the collaborative research.

Karisiddappa, C R, Maheswarappa, B S and **Shirol, M V** 914

Authorship pattern and collaborative research in psychology, *IASLIC Bull* 35(2) June 1990 : 73-78.

Studies the authorship pattern and collaborative research in psychology based on data collected from 'Psychological Abstracts' for 1988. Indicates trend towards multiple authorship, though it varies from one subject field to another.

Lalita Kumari and **Sengupta, I N** 915

Bibliometric evaluation of biochemical research in India : Part II, *Ind Jl Inf Lib & Society* 3(1-2) Mar-June 1990 : 16-28.

Describes the publication pattern and citation of Prof Jangannath

Ganguly who has done extensive research in Vitamin A metabolism. Analyses on the basis of citations collected from 1955 to 1982.

Lalita Kumari and **Sengupta, I N** 916

Bibliometric evaluation of biochemical research in India-Part III, *Lib Her* 27 (3-4) Oct 1988-Jan 1989 : 77-85.

Makes out a case for the evaluation and assessment of the productivity and quality of research work done by Indian scientists. Evaluates the work of Prof M Kanungo, using bibliometric techniques. Concludes that his ideas have been simulated scientists in different countries.

Lalita Kumari and **Sengupta, I N** 917

Bibliometric evaluation of biochemical research in India – Part IV, *Ind Jl Inf Lib & Society* 3 (3-4) Sept-Dec 1990 : 185-196.

Evaluates the scientific contribution of Prof Birendra Bijoy Biswas, one of the prominent biochemist of India. Collects data from *Science Citation Index,* 1960-86. The scientist received 795 citations for his 87 contributions. Calculates the impact factor of his main author and co-author articles.

Maheswarappa, B S, Karisiddappa, C R and **Mathias, S A** 918

Collaborative research in science and technology in India : A comparative study of different disciplines, *INICAE* 9(1) Mar 1990 : 35-44.

Mentions interdisciplinary nature of modern science and need for collaborative research. Examines the data collected from the *Indian Science Abstract* relating to science and technology as a whole and its different disciplines. Shows, based on tables, that the extent of collaboration varies from on discipline to another, and from time to time. Reveals that 3/4th of papers in S & T were the result of collaborative research.

Maheswarappa, B S and **Mathias, S A** 919

Multiple authorship an collaborative research in biological sciences in India : A bibliometric study, *Lib Her* 27(3-4) Oct 1988-Jan 1989 : 86-94.

Investigates trends in multiple authorship, authorship patterns, collaborative research in biological sciences based on data taken from *Indian Science Abstracts* with 1965, 1970, 1975, 1980 and 1983 as sample years. Mentions that while single authorship papers declined, two authors were maximum.

Maheswarappa, B S and **Savadatti, S G** 920

Authorship pattern and collaborative research in plant breeding (1934-1989), *IASLIC Bull* 35 (3) Sept 1990 : 119-123.

Studies authorship pattern and collaborative research in the field of plant breeding based on the data collected from *Plant Breeding Abstracts*, 1934-89. Points out that single author papers were maximum upto 1974, while in 1989 they are only one-fourth, indicating gradual increase in collaborative research.

Mishra, Sanjaya and **Mohanta, Rabindra Nath** 921

IASLIC Bulletin : A bibliometric study, *IASLIC Bull* 35(3) Sept 1990 : 125-128.

Analyses numerically the yearwise distribution and break up of papers published in *IASLIC Bull* for 1984-88 in respect of country and type of organisation to which authors belong, authorship pattern, subject areas, references and average length of articles.

Munshi, U M, Karanjai, A and **Sen, B K** 922

Indian medical journals and Science Citation Index, *IASLIC Bull* 35(1) Mar 1990 : 43-46.

Studies the impact factor of Indian medical journals. Points out on the basis of the impact factor that some of the Indian journals which are not being covered by Science Citation Index deserve coverage.

Ray, Dilip Kumar 923

Development of bioscience research system with a reference to BA on CD and CC on diskette TM : An analytical study, *Ind Jl Info Lib & Society* 4(2) June 1991 : 162-166.

Discusses various aspects of bio-research, the core titles of journals, present Indian science and other related topics in Biological Abstracts and Current Contents. Makes special reference to Biological Abstracts on Compact Disk and Current Contents on Diskette TM.

Sangam, S L and **Biradar, B S** 924

A bibliometric analysis of fluid mechanic literature, *CLIS Observer* 7(3-4) July-Dec 1990 : 103-112.

Makes bibliometric analysis of references collected from the 'Journal of Fluid Mechanics' covering period 1985-87 to determine the characteristics of fluid mechanic literature and to test whether the data fits into Bradford's Law of Distribution or not.

Sarojam, N 925

Bibliometric analysis of Indian forest entomology literature, *Lib Sci slant Doc & Inf Std* 26(3) Sept 1991 : 228-244.

Gives a quantitative analysis of literature on forest entomology in India from 1877 to 1988 in Kerala Forest Research Institute library. A computerised data base on this subject is developed by using CDS/ISIS software at the library and is subjected for analysis.

Sen, B K and **Lakshmi, V V** 926

Bibliometrics in India – 1988 : A review, *ILA Bull* 26(4) Jan-Mar 1991 : 198-206.

Reviews literature reported in India on bibliometrics in 1988 particularly presented at the Workshop of Scientific Communication and Bibliometrics during 15-26 Feb 1988 at Calcutta and Seventh Annual Convention and Conference of the SIS held during 18-20 Jan 1988 at Calcutta.

Sen, Subir K and **Chatterjee, Sunil Kumar** 927

An introduction to researches in bibliometrics. Part 1. Background and perspective, *IASLIC Bull* 35(3) Sept 1990 : 105-117.

Indicates unorganised and unstable situation of bibliometrics studies. Sketches scientific status of information science and growth of quantitative studies in bibliometrics. Discusses position of bibliometrics, librametrics, scientometrics, informetrics. Mentions activities in bibliometrics.

Sen, Subir K and **Chatterjee, Sunil Kumar** 928

An introduction to researches in bibliometrics : Part II. Glossary, *IASLIC Bull* 35(4) Dec 1990 : 155-170.

Provides definition and description of single word items, hyphenated terms, phrases, named effects, etc., which have appeared in the literature of bibliometrics. Includes in the glossary both colloquial and non-colloquial terms.

Sen, Subir K and **Gan, S K** 929

Bio-bibliometrics : Concepts and application in the study of productivity of scientists, *Int Forum Inf & Docum* 15(3) 1990 : 13-21.

Deals with the concepts and application of bio-bibliometrics in the study of productivity in science and technology of 28 Fellows of the INSA. States that persons attaining high positions in R & D or academic establishments early in life tend to be more productive and collaborative.

Sengupta, I N 930

Bibliometrics and identification of core periodicals : Kaula Endowment Lecture, *Her Lib Sci* 29 (3-4) July-Oct 1990 : 226-247.

Lecture delivered on the occasion of the Ranganathan-Kaula Gold Medal and Citation awarded to the author. Provides conceptual development of bibliometrics. Stresses how core periodicals of a particular discipline can be identified by applying bibliometrics techniques.

Sengupta, I N 931

Bibliometrics and its application, *ISL*, 254-263.

Explains what is bibliometrics. Gives its origin and development. Discusses its fundamental laws, models and applications.

Sengupta, I N 932

Four measuring techniques in library and information science, *Ind Jl Inf Lib & Society* 4(3-4) Sept-Dec 1991 : 197-228.

Discusses four analogous or rather synonymous terms, namely bibliometric, informetrics, scientometrics and librametrics. Discusses also their genesis, scope, application, development and potentiality in solving various library problems.

Sengupta, I N 933

General introduction to librametrics and bibliometrics, *INICAE* 9(2) Sept 1990 : 191-205.

Elucidates librametry and bibliometry – two analogous and synonymous terms coined by Ranganathan and Pritchard. Discusses scope, application and development in India and abroad. Points out reasons for universal and restricted acceptance of the two concepts. Presents general connotation and differences in their growth. Suggests ways and means to boost librametrics research in India.

Sinha, S C 934

A bibliometric analysis of a research field, *CPT*, 239-250.

Analyses articles on building science published during 1972-75 in the form of abstracts in *Building Science Abstracts*, and plots a graph based on Bradford's Law-Zipf Law of scattering. Identifies most important journals called core and their citations which could be considered for inclusion in *Science Citation Index* to improve coverage in building science.

Taher, Mohamed 935

A bibliometric analysis of the literature in the field of Islamic studies, *Lib Her* 29 (1-2) Apr-Sept 1990 : 96-98.

Gives a summary of the Ph D thesis accepted by Calicut University under the supervision of Dr M Bavakutty. States the reasons, hypothesis, methodology, bibliometric analysis and findings of the study.

Upadhyay, J L, Ghosh, B N and **Sengupta, I N** 936

International channel of communication for breast cancer literature, *INICAE* 10(1) Mar 1991 : 48-59.

Discusses present day growth of cancer literature, its basic and clinical research areas. Mentions difficulties in bibliographic control because of scattering and seepage. Analyses data taken from CANCERNET for 1968-78 that covers nearly 80 per cent of world's cancer literature from nearly 1150 journals.

Upadhyay, J L, Mukhopadhyay, S K and **Sengupta, I N** 937

Study of scatter and seepage in breast cancer literature, *Ind Jl Inf Lib & Society* 3(3-4) Sept-Dec 1990 : 261-278.

Elucidates scatter and seepage from different angles and their impact on breast cancer literature. States that only 34 per cent of total literature on the subject comes out in journals of peripheral areas, the remaining 10.5 per cent are published in unanticipated discipline journals causing seepage of information.

Vaishnav, A A 938

Journal of Marketing – A bibliographic study, *CLIS Observer* 8(1-2) Jan-June 1991 : 3-5.

Analyses the contents of the *Jl of Marketing* to determine the extent of its coverage. Discusses broader as well as specific objectives of the Journal. Identifies the emerging and decaying subjects dealt within the Journal. Evaluates authoritativeness of the authors and highlights the findings of the study.

025.48 (1) Bradford's Law

Gupta, D K 939

Application of Bradford's Law to citation data of Ethiopian Medical Journal, *Ann Lib Sci & Doc* 38(3) Sept 1991 : 85-98.

Makes a citation analysis of items published in EMJ during 1977-87. Makes a rank list of journals based on number of citations. Shows wide scattering of citations in journals. Tests the Bradford's Law and finds satisfactory to both data sets.

Gupta, D K 940

Productivity trends of in-vitra fertilisation and embryo transfer research, 1978-1983 : Application of Bradford's Law and Lotka's Law *INICAE* 9(2) Sept 1990 : 175-190.

Studies productivity trends of journals and authors for in-vitra fertilization and embryo transfer literature for 1978-83. Compares these productivity distribution against standard bibliometric distribution and application of Bradford and Lotka's laws. Reveals that bibliography is over represented by about 35 per cent of journals and 11 of journals items. Points out that Lotka's Law did not apply in the original form. Concludes that IVF-ET is still a dynamic research speciality.

025.48 (1) Citation Analysis/Indexing

Alafiatayo, Benjamin O and **Kadiri, Jasiliu A** 941

The periodical literature of health economics, *Jl Lib & Inf Sci* 15(1) June 1990 : 74-86.

Covers the literature of health economics published in English sources from 1914 to 1982. Makes citation study to find out that journals are mostly used followed by books/monographs. Gives core journals and other characteristics of literature.

Anand, H R and **Taher Ahmed** 942

Methodology for mapping information needs of research scientists in the field of powder metallurgy, *Ann Lib Sci & Doc* 37(3) Sept 1990 : 96-101.

Analyses cited literature to gauge information needs of R & D personnel in powder metallurgy. States that most significant literature are monographs, serials, conference proceedings, books and patents. Mentions that non-journal literature has lower-half life.

Anand, J K 943

CLIS Observer, 1984-1989 : An analytical study, *CLIS Observer* 8(3-4) July-Dec 1991 :7-17.

Gives importance of learned journals. Mentions India's position among LIS journals in the world. Describes and evaluates sources, contributions, authorship and citation patterns of papers published in *CLIS Observer* during 1984-89. Reveals collaborative authorship, leading contribution, geographical location, subjects, referencing patterns and cited journals, etc. Brings out unique features of this journal.

Anand, J K 944

Journal of Documentation, 1980-1989 : An analytical study, *Lib Her* 30(2-4) July 1991-Jan 1992 : 181-215.

Discusses the importance of learned journals. Identifies various studies that have analysed literature published in professional journals in LIS. Surveys and analyses literature both published and cited in the *Journal of Documentation,* 1980-89. Makes out various features of the journal such as institutional affiliation, collaborative authorship, sexwise distribution, etc. Describes various topics discussed, referencing patterns, most cited journals, etc.

Anand, J K 945

Journal of Library and Information Science, 1976-89 : An analytical study *Jl Lib & Inf Sci* 15(2) Dec 1990 : 101-128.

Discusses importance of learned journals. Highlights India's position among LIS journals producing countries. Describes and evaluates source contributions, authorship, citation patterns of papers published in the *JLIS*, 1976-89. Brings forth leading contributors, foreign contributors, subjects, most cited journals, heavy reliance on foreign literature. Compares the findings of this study with the results of similar studies of various subjects.

Aravinda, P and **Pulla Reddy, V** 946

Citation analysis of socio-cultural anthropology literature, *Luck Libn* 22 (3-4) Sept-Dec 1990 : 51-57.

Analyses 3807 citations appended to the review articles in

'Annual Review of Anthropology' for 1980-82. Reveals that most of the socio-cultural anthropology literature is published in book form. Gives the citations by single author, two and three authors. Makes a list of core journals.

Arjun Lal 947

Ranking of periodicals in the field of soil science, *Ann Lib Sci & Doc* 37(2) June 1990 : 67-73.

Analyses 4361 citations appearing in 22 Ph D theses in soil science received by Rajendra Agricultural University, Pusa, Bihar during 1980 81 – 1987-88. Identifies major forms of literature used. Prepares a ranked list of 38 most cited journals representing 84.40 per cent to total citations out of 261 titles cited. Gives geographical distribution of journals.

Arjun Lal and **Ray, P K** 948

Pattern of research contribution in leading horticulture journals of the world : A comparative study, *IASLIC Bull* 36(3) Sept 1991 : 95-102.

Analyses 511 papers published in four leading horticulture journals during 1987-88. Reveals that contribution of Indian scientists largely appears in domestic journals. Mentions USA as leading contributor of research papers in international journals. Gives countrywise break up of research papers, authorship pattern, etc.

Arunachalam, Subbiah and **Singh, Udai N** 949

Places of "Sankhya" in the literature of statistics, *INICAE* 10(1) Mar 1991 : 5-17.

Compiles the citing journal packages of series A & B of *Sankhya* (1984), and compares them with those of many core journals of statistics. Examines international impact of *Sankhya* by finding out the number of times it has been cited in several core journals of statistics during 1977-83 from Journal Citation Reports. Reveals that proportion of reference to literature less than three years old is very low. Shows that it is international in its authorship.

Begum, Khaiser Jahan and **Rajendra, N** 950

Research collaboration on zoological sciences, *IASLIC Bull* 35 (2) June 1990 : 79-82.

Analyses Indian zoological science literature for 1975-84 to study the authorship pattern and collaborative research trend indicating the trend of multiple authorship in the field. Compares the results with the findings on authorship in other scientific fields.

Chandel, A S, Binwal, J C and **Saraf, Veena** 951

Characteristics of social science literature : A study of bibliographic citations of dissertations submitted in universities of North East Region, *SSI*, 212-223.

Ascertains the information needs of social science scholars in the three universities of North-Eastern region engaged in area studies of North East India to find out type and forms of literature in use, age and language of documents, distribution by country of origin.

Deo, V N 952

Citation study of the Marathawada University Journal – A case study of the use pattern by scholars, *Ann Lib Sci & Doc* 38(4) Dec 1991 : 131-147.

Analyses 1906 citations collected from Marathawada University Journal during 1975-84 to determine the use pattern of the literature by the scholars in zoology. Gives analysis of bibliographic forms, journals used and their distribution according to countries of origin, and language. Studies the half-citation pattern, obsolescene, productivity, chronological distribution, etc.

Gopinath, M A and **Patil, M D** 953

Interdisciplinary nature of information science and technology (IST) : A quantitative analysis, *Lib Sci slant Doc & Inf Std* 28 (3) Sept 1991 : 87-95.

Studies literature published in IST. Identifies different types of bonding. Uses review articles published in the *ARIST*, 1985-89. Studies rate of incidence of different disciplines associated with IST. The quantitative analysis indicates that the transaction concepts IST are provided by the fields of computer technology, telecommunication technology, information science technology, and AI.

Gupta, Sushma and **Tsadik, Degife Gabar** 954

An analytical study of doctoral dissertations on West and Central Africa submitted to United States and Canadian universities for the period 1970-1980, *INICAE* 9(1) Mar 1990 : 45-54.

Analyses characteristics of doctoral dissertations of West and

Central Africa produced in US and Canadian universities during 1979-80 indexed in *Dissertation International.* Reveals that dissertations have grown exponentially during 1970-80. Shows that 63.73% dissertations were on Nigeria and Ghana, 6.7 per cent on West and Central Africa, and the rest on other 14 countries.

Humayoon Kabir, S 955

Citations in Indian agricultural research – an analysis, *Ann Lib Sci & Doc* 37(3) Sept 1990 : 102-109.

Analyses 7049 citations from doctoral dissertations in agriculture from 1981 to 1988 in order to determine the Indian journals most frequently used by researchers. Identifies more important Indian journals as Journal Indian Society of Soil Science, Indian Journal of Agricultural Science, Indian Journal of Agronomy, etc.

Humayoon Kabir, S 956

Growth and development of Indian agricultural dissertations, *Lib Her* 29 (3-4) Oct 1990-Jan 1991 : 137-152.

Analyses growth and development of Indian agricultural doctoral dissertations using data taken from 'Bibliography of doctoral dissertations', covering the years 1979-85. Analyses data yearwise, subjectwise, geographical distribution, etc.

Humayoon Kabir, S 957

Utilization of periodical literature in ship technology : A survey, *Lib Sci slant Doc & Inf Std* 28 (3) Sept 1991 :100-108.

Analyses 102 answers on the basis of a questionnaire circulated to 122 members of the Dept of Ship Technology, Cochin University of S & T. Determines the most used periodicals in ship technology. Discusses problems and solutions regarding display, binding, photocopying, transfer, etc. Provides a gradation list of primary journals.

Ijari, S R and **Kannappanavar, B U** 958

Information use pattern of Indian clinical psychologists : A citation study, *Jl Lib & Inf Sci* 15(2) Dec 1990 : 179-189.

Analyses all the citations appended to 155 articles published in *Indian Jl of Clinical Psychology,* vol 9-11 for 1982-84 to identify the most cited journals. Gives a ranked list of journals most frequently cited. Also gives the geographical distribution.

Karisiddappa, C R and **Sangam, S L** 959

Citation patterns in social sciences : A case study, *SSI*, 206-211.

Finds out the characteristics of the sources of literature used by social science scholars of Karnataka University in their Ph D theses in respect of average number of citations, multiple authorship, distribution by form of literature, distribution by place of publication, distribution by language, and availability in Karnataka University Library.

Kundu, A K 960

Comparative study of published papers in pure sciences, humanities and social sciences : Citation analysis, *DLIS*, 273-278.

Makes a comparative analysis of papers in science, social science and humanities based on citations. Studies the citation analyses of 153 articles published in *Annals of Library Science and Documentation*, 1955-75. States that low utilization of citations in social science is apparent.

Maheswarappa, B S and **Surya Rao, K** 961

Information use pattern of American, British and Indian food scientists as indicated by citations in journals: A comparative study, *Lib Her* 28(1-2) Apr-Sept 1989 : 32-42.

Identifies and compares the information use pattern of American, British and Indian food scientists as indicated by citations from three representative journals, as to form, subject and country of literature cited, journals most cited, journals most frequently used, and obsolescene of literature.

Mujoo-Munshi, Usha, Karanjai, Aruna and **Sen, B K** 962

Citation behaviour of chemical scientists : A case study, *ILA Bull* 27(2) July-Sept 1991 : 47-53.

Analyses references cited by scientists of chemistry and chemical technology of India, USA, UK and Canada to evaluate effectiveness of information system of these countries, how the availability of journals affect the citation practice. Finds that Indian authors generally cite older references, whereas Americans cite more recent literature, and those of UK and Canada in between the two.

Nweke, Ken M C 963

Citation analysis study of authors of the literature used by research scholars in zoology at the Ibadan University, Nigeria, *Ann Lib Sci & Doc* 36(4) Dec 1989 : 139-147.

Identifies 1055 authors cited 1376 times in zoological theses submitted to Ibadan University between 1970-75. Mentions 154 core. authors cited above 35 per cent of all citations. Uses graph of R(n) and Bradford parameters.

Parekh, Harsha 964

Characteristics and types of literature used by social scientists in India, *SSI*, 165-183.

Defines social science, social scientists, and literature use. Presents an overview of thc findings of a few empirical studies which give some indications of the characteristics and types of literature used by social scientists in India. States that these studies fall in two broad groups : citation analysis and user surveys.

Pichappan, P 965

Indian agricultural science journals : A comparative study of the ranking list of journals by citations, impact factor and discipline influence score, *IASLIC Bull* 35(2) June 1990 : 83-86.

Reports inferences drawn from a study conducted by using three citation measures viz ranking of journals, impact factor, and discipline influence score. Finds the extent of association of the influences obtained in the three methods.

Pichappan, P 966

National network for the transfer of citation data: A proposal, *CALNE*, 250-252.

Makes a proposal for transferring citation data from *Science Citation Index* and from records of citation data of Indian journals to scientists working in various regions.

Pichappan, P and **Ponnudurai, R** 967

Influential life science journals, *IASLIC Bull* 36(2) June 1991 : 81-84.

States that study of citations to the papers immediately after the publication is an important factor in measuring significance of journals. Calculates two year citations of life science journals and listed by most cited papers. Finds that general journals supercede the speciality journals in all respects.

Sangam, S L and **Biradar, B S** 968

Pattern of information use by Indian surgical scientists – a citation study, *Ann Lib Sci & Doc* 37(4) Dec 1990 : 133-142.

Discusses pattern of information use by researchers in surgery as indicated by citations in the M S dissertations submitted to the Gulbarga University during 1982-89. Identifies use of different sources of information, their languages, countries of origin, and subjects. States the obsolescene of literature, and applies Bradford's law of Scattering.

Sen, Subir K 969

A theoretical glance at citation process, *Int Forum Inf & Docum* 15(1) 1990 : 3-7.

Analyses citation process. Contrasts citational linkages and cognitive linkages of documents. Discusses Kochen's approach, a theorem with two corollaries. States two more theorems without derivation.

Sethi, A R and **Sharma, S K** 970

Information search by historians, *SSI*, 324-332.

Makes a content analysis of the dissertation/theses submitted to the Centre of Historical Studies, Jawaharlal Nehru University during 1972-86 to know the channels and sources that the history scholars refer to in search of their information.

Sharada, B A 971

Multiple-authorship pattern in linguists, *Lib Sci slant Doc & Inf Std* 28(3) Sept 1991 : 96-99.

States that multiple-authorship in journals and papers is increasing especially in science and technology. Attempts to study the authorship pattern in the field of linguistics. Observes hat though single authorship continues to be predominant, multiple-authorship is also on the increase.

Sharada, B A and **Devaki, L** 972

Contribution of journal articles by Indian linguists at the international scene, *Ann Lib Sci & Doc* 37(1) Mar 1990 : 35-52.

Analyses articles abstracted in 'Linguistic and Language Behaviour Abstracts'(LLBA), 1977-87 to identify authorship pattern, topics covered in linguistics and related fields, geographical distribution of authors, chronological distribution, most preferred periodicals.

Sinha, S C 973

Indian contribution on the literature of building science : A quantitative analysis, *Int Lib Move* 13(1) Mar 1991 : 10-26.

Studies the literature on building research in India produced by Indian scientists in the form of original papers published in Indian and foreign journals scientists by *Building Science Abstracts,* 1972-76. Evaluates data form *Science Citation Index* through citation analysis.

Sinha, S C and **Furqan Ullah** 974

Citation profile of Dr. V S Ramachandran : A bibliometric analysis of his highly cited articles and books in cement and concrete science, *Ind Jl Info Lib & Society* 4(3-4) Sept-Dec 1991 : 237-257.

Analyses 49 articles, out of 161, published in foreign journals. Examines in detail two articles and two books highly cited by other scientists evidenced by *Science Citation Index.* States that his two papers and two books were highly cited because the books were first of their kinds and papers discussed applications of a novel technique in cement sciences.

Thaty, Rajendra Kumar and **Mishra, Sanjaya** 975

Periodicals cited most frequently by Indian agricultural economists, *ILA Bull* 26 (1) Apr-June 1990: 45-50.

Analyses citations appended to 170 articles published in *Indian Jl of Agricultural Economics*, vol 40-44, 1985-89 to identify periodicals most frequently cited by Indian agricultural economists. Gives a list of 20 periodicals cited at least five times.

Vaishnav, A A and **Dharmapurikar, R G** 976

Citation analysis of the 'Herald of Library Science', *Her Lib Sci* 29(3-4) July-Oct 1990 : 252-260.

Analyses the citations provided in articles in the journal *Herald of Library Science* for the period 1977-1986, vol 16-25. Underlines the objectives, methodology and highlights the findings of the study.

025.48 (1) Informetrics

Gopinath, M A and **Meera, B M** 977

Informetrics and its use in library management as an area of specialization, *Lib Sci slant Doc & Inf Std* 28(3) Sept 1991 : 109-113.

Presents case studies of application of quantitative techniques in different operation of library management. Based on current development in the area, the need for recognition of *Informetrics* as specialised course in Advanced Courses in LIS is suggested.

Sen, B K and **Taneja, Ram D** 978

Conference on informetrics heralds Dr S R Ranganathan centenary year, *NISSAT Newsletter* 10(3) July- Sept 1991 : 20-21.

Reports about the Third International Conference on Informetrics held in Bangalore during 9-12 August 1991. Discusses Technical sessions and panel discussion held at the Conference.

025.48 (1) Librametrics

Sengupta, I N 979

Librametrics vis-a-vis bibliometrics, *Ind Jl Lib Inf & Society* 4(1) Jan-Mar 1991 : 41-68.

Discusses two analogous or rather synonymous terms, librametry and bibliometry coined by Ranganathan and Pritchard respectively. Describes their scope, application and development including the reasons for the restricted/universal acceptance of these two terms.

Subba Rao, C V 980

Librametry : A statement of limitations an values, *Her Lib Sci* 30(3-4) July-Oct 1991 : 216-221.

States the need for a second check on data after defining and illustrating studies. Points to human limitations and human values in work-standards. Examines human values in filing cards, books, periodicals, tickets, kardex and preparation of bibliography etc. Explains the effect of age, height, shelf position, team work, floor planning, physical location. Observes variations in classifications, cataloguing, indexing, etc. Emphasises that librametry is essential for development of profession

025.48 (1) Lotka's Law

Gupta, Davendra K and **Gupta, Sushma** 981

Conference literature : International Conferences on Ethiopian Studies, 1959-1988 : Application of Lotka's Law, *INICAE* 10(2) Sept 1991 : 177-184.

Analyses cumulative index of International Conference on Ethiopian Studies, 1959-88 containing 865 papers presented by 520 authors to test the applicability of Lotka's Law and Negative Binomial distribution model to author productivity distribution patterns. Observes that negative Binomial distribution was found fitting very well.

Kannappanavar, B U 982

Productivity pattern of authors in rural development in India during 1983-84, *Ind Jl Inf Lib & Society* 4(2) June 1991 :131-136.

Analyses database consisting of 746 items on rural development literature for the period between 1983-84 to study author productivity pattern and to test the applicability of Lotka's Law. Shows that Lotka's Law in its original form does not fit for present day.

025.48 (1) Scientometrics

Kalyane, V L and **Kalyane, S V** 983

Scientometrics dimensions of innovation communication productivity system *Ann Lib Sci & Doc* 38(1) Mar 1991 : 8-29.

Analyses communication activities of Sugarcane Breeding Institute, Coimbatore during the years 1912-87 for general characteristics, collaborations core channel, creativity of researchers. Gives communicator's productivity and distribution of paper to a number of domains as Botany, breeding, genetics, mutations Tissue culture, etc.

025.49 Subject Headings

Rajagopal, B and **Kanakachary, M** 984

Subject heading in the humanities : Some problems and solutions, *Ind Jl Inf Lib & Society* 4(2) June 1991 : 139-146.

Gives importance of subject headings. Discusses the difficult task in deriving the subject indexing terms in humanities. Explains need of uniformity and standardization in determination of subject headings. Gives suggestions.

025.49 (1) Thesaurus

Chatterjee, Amitabha 985

Thesaurus-an information retrieval aid, *ISL*, 43-65.

Traces the origin of thesaurus. Gives its definition and related concepts. Discusses need, functions, types. Gives its internal structure. Describes various relationships between terms. Mentions its complication. States how computer application can help it.

Humphreys, Betsy 986

Metathesaurus and semantic network, *INICAE* 10 (1) Mar 1991 : 104-106.

Describes the two new initial versions of Metathesaurus and the Semantic Network as machine readable 'knowledge sources' developed as part of Unified Medical Language System (UMLS).

Rousseau, R 987

Use of an existing thesaurus in a knowledge based indexing and retrieval system, *Ann Lib Sci & Doc* 38 (4) Dec 1991 : 127-130.

Describes a thesaurus, and its use in weighted retrieval. Proposes a simple heuristic method to use an existing thesauri for weighted indexing.

Ruge, Gerda 988

A spreading activation network for automatic generation of thesaurus relationships, *Lib Sci slant Doc & Inf Std* 28(4) Dec 1991 : 125-130.

Presents a spreading-activation-network for the generation of semantically-related terminology to obtain an output terminology such as synonyms. States that the network is automatically developed.

Srikanthaluxmi, A and **Ravichandra Rao, I K** 989

CDS/ISIS PASCAL Interface for thesaurus construction : Procedures involved, *DRTC 1989*, U 1-31.

Describes the operations of THES program mainly designed to generate a thesaurus using CDS/ISIS. Explains the procedure for using the program. Includes a brief description of this program.

Vandana Ranjan

990

Role of thesaurus in online information retrieval system, *CALNE*, 141-144.

Gives aim of information retrieval. Discusses that online IRS make use of thesaurus as the language normalisation tool. Describes types of thesaurus, major purposes of thesaurus. Lists merits of such a retrieval system.

025.5 SERVICE TO USERS

Shukla, B B

991

An evaluation of the planning of library services in India with special reference to Orissa : A study, *Ind Jl Inf Lib & Society* 3(3-4) Sept-Dec 1990 : 197-206.

Determines aims of library services. Describes planning of library services with regard to educational, social and economic aspects of our country. States that the study was conducted in 1974 and research results so obtained give a very sorrowful picture of planning of library services in Orissa.

Thakur, Ranjeet S

992

Information for executive's desk, *Lib Her* 28 (3-4) Oct 1989-Jan 1990 : 191-192.

Discusses ways to fulfil the need for information of executives which helps them in decision-making. Calls for such a service as IFED (Information for Executive's Desk) and suggests the preparation of an IFED Service Bulletin.

025.52 REFERENCE AND INFORMATION SERVICES

Abraham, Alexander

993

Information services for Third World countries with special reference to India, *NIPP*, 125-129.

Explains various information services and impediments to the use of information services by developing countries, Mentions briefly the information services in India as NISSAT and other computer-based information services.

Bhattacharyya, Amarendra Nath

994

Reference service : Its neglected potential to promote higher education, *College Libn* 6 (1-4) 1990 : 15-20.

Defines reference service and reference work. Explains librarian's role in information society to help the readers particularly in a college library. Discusses new role of reference service and library staff in the present day academic libraries with new technology. Explains importance of reference service in larger knowledge system. Describes the scene in Indian college libraries.

Foskett, D J 995

Information services in libraries, New Delhi : Akashdeep Publishing House, 1990. 142 p.

Describes in 11 chapters the origins of information services in libraries, the role of information officer, selection, acquisition, arrangement, dissemination of information. Explains reference service and other services. Describes the future developments in information services, and training and qualification for information work.

Gessesse, K and **Mbwana, S S** 996

Scientific literature service in Tanzania – historical account, *Ann Lib Sci & Doc* 37 (4) Dec 1990 : 121-124.

Gives historical background of Tanzania Literature Service and the types of information services it offers to the research scientists engaged in various agricultural and veterinary establishments in Tanzania. Also highlights requirements of funds for continuation of the service.

Kaula, P N 997

White House Conference on Library and Information Services : Role of libraries and information services for literacy, productivity and democracy, *Her Lib Sci* 30 (3-4) July-Oct 1991 : 222-229.

Mentions genesis of WHCLIS. Gives brief account of the Pre-Conference International Symposium held in May 1991. Puts forth the highlights of the second WHCLIS, held in July 1991, including excerpts from speeches of President Bush, Mrs Bush who opened the Conference, Mrs Quayle, and others. Records the deliberations of the 'Great Debate', views at the 'Open Forum', recommendations. States some other features and observations.

Pilsk, Suzanne C 998

Information Resource Centre and its services, *Her Lib Sci* 30 (1-2) Jan-Apr 1990 : 65-67.

Describes the increased usage of the Information Resource Centre of SLA in 1989 when more people turned to its services. Discusses services of IRC, its topics of interest, and archives database.

Prafulla Chandra, T V 999

Improving library and information services, *Lib Today* 12 (1) Jan 1990 : 2-5.

States that efficient and effective communication system coupled with advanced library and information science techniques will give quick and easy information about the location of needed documents. Explains the efforts made in this regard, particularly the INFLIBNET of the UGC.

Srivastava, A P 1000

Teacher-librarian academic team, *Univ News* 28 (53) Dec 31, 1990 : 1, 3.

Makes a case for the teacher-librarian team as the modern approach integrates them in academic life in measuring and disseminating knowledge.

025.52(1) Reference and Information Services – Computerised

Sathyanarayana, N V 1001

EASYNET : An electronic reference librarian, *MLSUL,* 109-114.

Identifies troubles with databases. Mentions problems with online systems. States that the solution lies in electronic reference librarian who is interactive and user-friendly. Proposes EASYNET as an intelligent gateway.

Shekhawat, R S et al 1002

ISDN-an integrated approach to information services, *OIPMC,* 65-88.

Describes the concept of Integrated Services Digital Network (ISDN), factors responsible for ISDN. Attempts to bring out various forces which have played major role in bringing about change in thinking and led to the CCITT guidelines and specifications. Gives present efforts to implement ISDN in different countries.

1991 : 87-103.

Discusses the nature of current awareness bulletins. Explains about the cooperation in the publication of the bulletins. Highlights importance of information bulletins in national and regional languages. Provides suggestions for their improvements.

Baradol, A K 1012

Routing of journals in science and technology libraries, *CPT,* 160-165.

Explains meaning of 'routing of journals'. States it as one of the methods of CAS. Describes utility of routing. Highlights methodology of routing. Explains advantages and disadvantages of routing journals in S & T libraries.

Lalita Kumari and **Sengupta, I N** 1013

Dissemination of current information in a biomedical research library, *Ind Jl Inf Lib & Society* 3 (3-4) Sept-Dec 1990 : 252-260.

Defines documentation. Gives emergence of scientific research, and growth of research activities, particularly biomedical sciences. Outlines methodology to meet the demand of dissemination of current information through manual process. Concludes that it can efficiently meet the information needs of the users.

Nagaraja Rao, K and **Burhanuddin, Md** 1014

A comparative analysis of subscription lists of periodicals – a case study of libraries in Hyderabad, *Ind Jl Inf Lib & Society* 2 (3-4) Sept-Dec 1990 : 161-170.

Analyses lists of periodicals of 30 libraries in Hyderabad and Secunderabad. Compares similarities and differences between them. Highlights internal and external formats of the lists. Suggests the ways to make the lists more user oriented.

025.5276 Reference and Information Services – Special Libraries

Muddumoolya, S and **Koganurmath, M M** 1015

Interaction between institutions and industries : Information programmes and service in KREC Library, *NIPP,* 92-96.

Explains the organisational and functional infrastructure of information service to industries. Describes the various steps taken by Karnataka Regional Engineering College Library in planning information programmes and resource sharing services.

Sampatha Chary, K 1016

A study of information services in nutrition science with special reference to India, *Luck Libn* 22 (1-2) Mar-June 1990 : 28-35.

Presents information transfer activities in human nutrition and its allied sciences in India and abroad. Describes information dissemination activities of NIN Library. Proposes for upgrading the present Library of NIN and for establishment of the 'National Information Facilities for Nutrition and Allied Sciences'.

025.5277 Reference and Information Services – Academic Libraries

Ogundipe, O O 1017

The subject specialist and readers services in academic libraries, *Lib Her* 29(1-2) Apr-Sept 1990 : 51-62.

Gives definition of subject specialist, his qualification and function. Discusses academic nature of readers service. Explains image and job satisfaction of a subject librarian, his role in automation of services. Concludes that he can contribute to the qualitative improvement in academic libraries.

Venkateswarlu, Tadiboyina 1018

Philosophy and reference service in academic libraries : A model, *IASLIC Bull* 36 (3) Sept 1991 : 121-124.

States that declining budgets are compelling libraries to reformulate their strategies for providing high quality service to users within meagre resources. Makes an attempt to outline a working model of reference service to users, particularly the academic community.

025.52772 Reference and Information Services – University Libraries

Malhan, I V 1019

Reference Division of a university library, *ULI,* 64-74.

States functions of a reference division in a library. Discusses impact of centralisation and decentralisation of the library on the organisation of reference services. Discusses organisation of reference collection to suit the convenience of users. Deals with reference staff and its strength. Mentions necessary furniture and equipments.

Sabir Hussain, Md 1020

Dimensions of extension service in university libraries, *OSUL,* 125-132.

Describes importance of libraries in university set-up. Discusses role and functions of university libraries. Defines extension service. Gives its main aim and purposes. Lists extension services useful and suitable for university libraries.

Sewa Singh 1021

Information services in university libraries, *OSUL,* 86-98.

Describes objectives of university library. Discusses services in order to achieve the objectives. Gives the concept of information services. Describes in detail such information services as abstracting and indexing service, CAS, bibliographical and documentation services, ILL and resource sharing, reprographic services, referral services, translations services. Offers various suggestions. Gives also future developments.

Sewa Singh 1022

Information services in university libraries in India, *Int Lib Move* 12 (1) Mar 1990 : 1-11.

Gives objectives of university libraries to achieve which lists some services. Explains the concept of information services. Describes such information services as abstracting and indexing services, ILL, bibliographical, documentation, resource sharing, reprographic, referral and translation services. Offers some suggestions for improving information services. Discusses future developments also.

Sewa Singh 1023

Reference services in a university library, *ULI,* 75-83.

States that reference service is not a priority item in the university libraries of India. Discusses the organization of reference service, user education and information services. Suggests the bibliographical and documentation services the university libraries should bring out. Deals with bringing out of document delivery service, reprographic service, indexing and abstracting service. States the new forms of reference and information sources and points out emergence of computer in information communication. Gives requirements of manpower for organising reference service and recording queries. Deals with evaluation of reference and information services.

025.56 User Education. Library Orientation

Balasubramanian, K and Neelakantan, K 1024

User education : Universities and research centres, *Univ News* 29 (30) 29 July 1991 : 14-16.

Deals with the user education in universities and research centres for the benefit of the users.

Fjallbrant, Nancy 1025

Why user education and how can information technology help?, *Jl Lib & Inf Sci* 15 (1) June 1990: 62-73.

Emphasises usefulness of user education (UE) programmes in libraries. Discusses in detail about usefulness of IT in database creation and for storage and servicing of information. Emphasises need for UE in the context of IT.

Subramoni, T K 1026

Library communication, *IASLIC Bull* 36 (1) Mar 1991 : 29-36.

Describes importance of communication in library. Discusses two types of communication in library – between library staff and user; and management and staff. Explains some of the methods followed like brochure, user orientation, signs, and guiding, etc in improving the efficiency of the library services.

025.5665 User Education – Scientific Libraries

Malhan, I V 1027

Users' education and training in scientific and technical libraries in India, *DLIS,* 429-436.

Describes the overview of user education and training programmes conducted in scientific and technical libraries in India. Gives suggestions for providing user education and training in order to utilize the information resources and services.

025.5677 User Education – Academic Libraries

Sewa Singh 1028

User education in academic libraries : Workshop report, *Her Lib Sci* 30 (1-2) Jan- Apr 1991 : 91-94.

Reports about the inaugural session of the Workshop held at the Guru Nanak Dev University, Amritsar during May 20-June 1, 1989. Highlights discussion about the Session I, lectures delivered on various aspects by various scholars on different days. Mentions about the Concluding Session.

025.56772 User Education – University Libraries

Nagi Reddy, Y and **Rama Reddy, E** 1029

User education in university libraries : Need for introducing library science as part of curriculum, *Ind Jl Inf Lib & Society* 4 (2) June 1991 : 153-161.

Discusses importance of UE programme and role of libraries in implementing such programme. States that for augmenting such programme, document collection storing, processing, etc. should be done by libraries. States importance of UE programme and introduction of information science as a part of such programme.

Sain, Chittaranjan 1030

Importance of user education in university libraries, *LISE,* 207-214.

Discusses need for user education. Lists objectives of UE. Identifies two groups of users and their three levels. Describes methods of instruction, courses offered. Enumerates UE programmes in India. Concludes that UE is essential to face new challenges.

Sood, S P 1031

User education in university libraries, *OSUL*, 99-109.

Gives meaning and definition of UE. Differentiates between UE, orientation and initiation. Identifies need of UE and its objectives. Discusses various methods of UE. Gives user education for teachers, agencies for UE. Describes user educational programmes in university libraries in India.

Zaki, Magaji M 1032

User education in Nigerian universities : The need for new approaches, *Int Lib Move* 13(1) Mar 1991 : 27-43.

Gives importance end value of UE. Discusses need for effective UE programme in academic community. Explains types of UE. Gives advantages and disadvantages of library orientation, library instruction course. Mentions present provision for UE programme in Nigerian universities. Gives curriculum for library use instruction.

025.56778 User Education – School Libraries

Shaibu, Samaila 1033

Information handling skills instruction across the school curriculum : The teacher-librarian's input, *Int Lib Move* 13(4) Dec 1991 : 182-188.

Explains the need of information skills in libraries. Discusses value of library skills instruction to students. Describes in detail the teacher-librarian's role in the library skills instruction programme.

025.56 (1) Information Needs
User Needs

Abbas Ibrahim and **Shajahan, Abbas Ibrahim** 1034

Information resources in electronic media in India : Needs-fulfilment-gap, *NIPP*, 51-56.

Studies in detail the information needs of Indian user community. Gives two major categories of information needs. Discusses availability and gap in these categories of information needs in various subject areas. Makes recommendation to policy makers to fill this gap.

Aziagba, P C 1035

Stock evaluation and user needs, *Ann Lib Sci & Doc* 38(3) Sept 1991 : 99-107.

Shows how the selection of core journals could be made from users requests. Gives in detail the mode of meeting the requirements of the staff and the students in the university library under different conditions. Indicates areas of low use of library. Makes suggestions.

Dutt, Suchitra 1036

Assessment of user needs for effective utilization of information systems, *CPT*, 366-370.

Deals with the user needs and their assessment. Discusses marketing of information services. Mentions the need for identification of groups of potential users. Stresses on the need of making user survey, through various methods, to make assessment of their needs and library use.

Girja Kumar 1037

Defining the concept of information needs, *SSI*, 253-274.

Defines user studies and information seeking behaviours. Explains data, information, knowledge, information need and information gathering habits in India. Describes the use of information by social scientists in India based on three independent studies conducted at New Delhi, Varanasi and Bombay with similar results.

Girja Kumar and **Jayaswal, P K** 1038

Case studies in information gathering habits, *SSI*, 275-294.

Defines information gathering behaviours. Undertakes a case study of nine research scholars enrolled for their Ph D degree with the Centre for the Study of Social Systems, Jawaharlal Nehru University, New Delhi for comprehending the pattern involved in establishing channels for access to information but limiting only to library use.

Girja Kumar and **Jayaswal, P K** 1039

Utilization of periodicals literature by Indian economists, *SSI*, 230-249.

Uses citation analysis method to study the pattern of utilization of periodicals literature by Indian economists. Takes sample of three Indian periodicals to find out categories of documents cited, use of foreign journals, comparative foreign and Indian situation analysis of ranking. Identifies areas of further research.

Kankachary, M 1040

Planning for the users in the library and information centres with a special reference to the university libraries, *Ind Jl Inf Lib & Society* 3(3-4) Sept-Dec 1990 : 279-284.

Identifies different groups of users and their articulated needs in various species of library and information centres. Suggests the planning strategy for the users with a special reference to the university libraries.

Kashyap, M M 1041

Bibliographic information services in social sciences and information needs of social scientists, *SSI*, 417-426.

Outlines the development and growing complexity of social sciences. Discusses information needs of social scientists. Describes the development of primary and secondary information sources. Gives the rate of growth of Indian abstracting and indexing services. Describes that the future of bibliographic information services is towards the online services.

Krishan Kumar 1042

Information seeking behaviour of sociologists, *SSI*, 295-309.

Studies the information seeking behaviour of sociologists of University of Delhi and Jawaharlal Nehru University through a questionnaire and unstructured interview. Describes various steps involved in conducting research such as compilation of bibliography, sources of information, forms of literature, citation of journals, use of other libraries, etc.

Maheswarappa, B S and **Nagappa, B** 1043

Information needs of social scientists, *CPT*, 357-365.

Points out need for user studies. Mentions major objectives of the study. Gives methodology and sample. Analyses data collected from the representative social scientists from different parts of the country in July 1987. Identifies use of different sources of information, usefulness of various methods in locating information, difficulties faced by them. Suggests that a nation wide study should be made in this area.

Manda, Paul A 1044

Informations seeking behaviour of sociologists : A case study, *INICAE* 10(1) Mar 1991 : 18-28.

Investigates information needs and information seeking behaviour of sociologists at the University of Dar-es-Salam in Tanzania based on the data collected through a questionnaire. Evaluates the findings.

Musib, S K 1045

Information needs of the cottage industries : A survey report, *CLIS Observer* 8(1-2) Jan-June 1991 : 14-17.

Attempts to find out major information needs and sources of information of persons engaged in cottage industries of wooden and bamboo products in the rural areas of Burdwan district. Reveals main sources of information on production, marketing, etc are the self, family members, relatives and local market. Respondents express willingness to use public library services.

Naidu, M K R 1046

Information needs of social scientists in India : UGC Information Centre for social scientists, *SSI*, 346-353.

Traces setting up of the UGC Information Centre at the SNDT Women's University Library. Describes its goal setting, service goals, resources management goals, collection, facilities, staff, services, etc. Gives its planning for development of services, computerization, indexing work, etc.

Sengupta, I N 1047

Information needs of scientists : An overview, *CLIS Observer* 7(3-4) July- Dec 1990 : 73-78.

States that with information revolution information scientist is in a pivotal position for assessing and providing information needs of scientists. Calls for cooperation between researchers and information scientists in the creation and maintenance of information files. Mentions that information files should help the scientists to know not only monographs and serials but instruments, their sources of supply, scientific news, etc.

Sridhar, M S 1048

Information requirements of the Indian space technologists, *Lib Her* 29 (3-4) Oct 1990 – Jan 1991 : 125-136.

Explains scope of information requirements. Gives typology of information needs, Suggests probing nature and type of information required by scientists, engineers, technologists. Describes overlapping classification of nature and type of information required by Indian space technologists based on a survey.

Vij, Rajeev 1049

Information needs of research scientists, *AGLIS Jl* 8(1-4) Jan- Dec 1990 : 23-31.

Attempts to study and survey the information needs of Indian R & D scientists after making review of existing literature. States that for the effective management of library and information centres and to provide pin pointed information service to library clientele, an essential prerequisite is to conduct use study.

Vij, Rajeev 1050

Survey of users information needs : A key to effective library management, *AGLIS Jl* 7(4) Dec 1989 : 30-33.

Points out the need of users study for improvement of existing library and information services in India and their future planning in conformity with the nation's educational, social and economic needs. Attempts to study information needs with a methodology, giving Indian scene and implications.

025.58 User Studies/Surveys
Library Use Studies

Ahanene, E M 1051

Use of library and information services in development planning – case of local government decision-makers in Imo state, Nigeria, *Ann Lib Sci & Doc* 38(2) June 1991 : 74-78.

Describes importance of libraries and information centres in decision making by administrators and managers. Reports a survey conducted to study the use of libraries and information centres of IMO. Makes suggestions to establish libraries in various government departments, etc.

Ghosh, Arun 1052

Types and characteristics of literature used by social scientists : Some observations, *SSI*, 224-229.

Defines social sciences. Explains that social science research is becoming inter and multi-disciplinary. Identifies sources material used by social scientists in India; classifies them according to their content and form. Gives some recent examples to show inter and multi-disciplinary approach.

Lahiri, Ramansu and **Choudhuri, G C** 1053

Knowing the social science user : Some preliminaries for the investigation, *SSI*, 336-345.

Discusses what and why of user studies. Discusses variety of users and their behaviour pattern in a university. Describes method of user study with behavioural approach. Concludes that user studies be conducted on the basis of the principles mentioned herein.

Musib, S K 1054

Information seeking pattern in the rural areas of West Bengal, India : A survey report on cottage industries, *IASLIC Bull* 36(4) Dec 1991 : 177-186.

Attempts to find out principle information needs and sources utilised for obtaining information by persons engaged in cottage industries in the rural areas of Burdwan district. Shows that the main sources of information regarding production, marketing etc., are self, family members, fellow professionals, friends, neighbours, relatives, shop keepers etc. States that they showed willingness to receive public library services.

Rana, M S 1055

Information use pattern of Wildlife managers, *Lib Her* 30(2-4) July 1991-Jan 1992 : 264-266.

Presents analysis of 4,698 references cited in the articles of Wildlife Management published in the *Jl of Wildlife Management* for 1989. Concludes that the major source of information used by scientists in wildlife management was journals, followed by books, proceedings, conference, theses, reports.

Saraf, Veena, Binwal, J C and **Misra, R** 1056

Information seeking behaviour of research scholars in North Eastern India : Case study of North East Hill University and Manipur University, *SSI*, 354-362.

Attempts to investigate the types of information sources consulted by research scholars, frequency of use of different types of literature, modes of information gathering, and frequently consulted journals by researchers. Collects data through questionnaire. Concludes that they depend more upon their supervisors.

Satish, N G 1057

Attitude-behaviour relations in information use : A study of social scientists, *CPT*, 340-356.

Gives brief history of user studies. States that user studies has been a neglected area. Presents findings of a study of 262 social scientists for knowing the magnitude of their attitude towards information and its relation with source use behaviour. Suggests that such studies should be made to ascertain the information use behaviour.

Sengupta, I N 1058

Assessing information requirements of scientists in a research institute *Ind Jl Inf Lib & Society* 3(1-2) Mar-June 1990 :1-15.

Discusses information revolution brought about by development of computer and ancillary techniques, places the information scientist in a pivotal position for assessing and providing information needs of scientists in a research institute. Assessment and provision of information requires cooperation between research and information workers. Stresses limitation of information science in promoting, creating research and stresses need to encourage scientists to read widely.

Sethi, A R 1059

Information seeking behaviour of social scientists : An Indian conspectus, Delhi: Hindustan Publishing House, 1990. xv, 238 p.

Deals with the behaviour of the social scientists in their respective organisations in India. Describes how they seek information from a variety of sources in a library.

025.585 User Studies – Scientific Libraries

Sridhar, M S 1060

Studies on use of library collections by scientists, engineers and technicians, *AGLIS Jl* 7(4) Dec 1989 : 9-17.

Stresses the need for user-research and use studies at the individual library level. Defines concept like user, use, need, want, demand, requirement. Reviews some important studies on use of library collections. Enumerates relationship found in past studies between characteristics of users and their use of library collections . Points out lack of sound use studies.

Sridhar, M S 1061

Users' research : A review of information behaviour studies in science and technology, Bangalore : Biblio Infon Services, 1990. 174 p.

Discusses users research studies conducted thus far. Makes a comprehensive review of information behaviour studies made particularly in the field of science and technology. Gives the information seeking patterns of scientists.

025.586 Use Studies – Special Libraries

Korah, Accamma C and **Devarajan, G** 1062

Information needs and use pattern of rubber scientists, *IASLIC Bull* 36(3) Sept 1991 : 89-94.

Reports the study conducted on information needs and use pattern of scientists utilising literature on rubber at RRII by questionnaire method. Examines use pattern of different types of materials, adequacy of library collection and services, information strategy, etc. Indicates the need to expand library services in procuring foreign language journals, bridging gaps, user education, etc.

Sridhar, M S 1063

Information seeking behaviour of the Indian space technologists, *Lib Sci slant Doc & Inf Std* 26(2) June 1989 : 127-166.

States the objectives, hypotheses, scope, limitations, research design, data collection tools of the study. Enumerates its significant findings. Examines various aspects of information seeking behaviour. Compares the results with similar other studies.

Sridhar, M S 1064

Patterns of user visit, movement and length of stay in a special library: a case study, *Ann Lib Sci & Doc* 36(4) Dec 1989 : 134-138.

Presents a case study based on observations of patterns of library visits, library traffic, user movement, and length of stay of Indian space technologists at ISRO Library. Depicts the relative use of different services.

025.5863 User Studies – Agricultural Libraries

Malhotra, Harpal Kaur 1065

Faculty participation and library use at post graduate level in agricultural universities, *Lib Her* 28 (1-2) Apr-Sept 1989 : 10-16.

Studies the role faculty plays in promoting library use by the PG students. Takes two independent samples from Haryana Agricultural University and Panjab Agricultural University, and identifies and ranks statistically a total of nine variables used to predict that method of instruction of teachers is library based or not.

Malhotra, Harpal Kaur 1066

Meeting the information requirements of postgraduate students in agricultural universities, *Lib Her* 29(1-2) Apr-Sept 1990 : 44-50.

Studies the relationship of adequacy of library collection and quantum of daily library use based on two samples taken from Haryana Agricultural University and Panjab Agricultural University. Calculates Spearman's Rank Correlation Co-efficient for two different sample groups and their results compared.

Malhotra, Harpal Kaur 1067

User studies in libraries of agricultural universities, 1 : Faculty participation and library use at post-graduate level, *Ann Lib Sci & Doc* 37(2) June 1990 : 53-58.

Studies role of faculty in promoting library use by the P G Students, based on two independent samples from Haryana Agricultural University and Panjab Agricultural University. Identifies and ranks nine variables used to predict whether method of instruction of teachers is library based or not.

Malhotra, Harpal Kaur 1068

User studies in libraries of agricultural universities, 2: Meeting of the information requirements of postgraduate students, *Ann Lib Sci & Doc* 37(2) June 1990 : 59-62.

Studies the relationship between adequacy of library collections and quantum of daily library use based on two samples taken from Haryana Agricultural University and Panjab Agricultural University. Calculates Spearman's Rank Correlation Co-efficient for two different sample groups and compares the results.

Shinde, P A and **Karande, A G** 1069

Use of CAB international abstracting periodicals in Mahatma Phule Agricultural University Library. Rahuri – a survey, *Ann Lib Sci & Doc* 38(2) June 1991 : 69-73.

Aims at reviewing the use of *CAB International* abstracting periodicals subscribed by this University Library. Conducts the study through questionnaire and interviews of teachers, researchers, students, Ph D students, selected at random.

025.5877 User Studies – Academic Libraries

Daniel, James O 1070

Predictive factors of academic library usage, *Int Lib Move* 13(2) June 1991 : 71-77.

Gives value of university libraries in developing countries. Studies the library use of Ahmadu Bello University at Samaru, Zaria by undergraduate and graduate students through questionnaire. Analyses records on the basis of 20 variables to facilitate library usage in academic libraries.

Obokoh, N P 1071

Library socialization of summer students : A case study from a developing country, *Lib Progress (Int)* 9-10 (1-2) Jan-Dec 1989-90 : 1-10.

States the need for socialization of part-time students in academic library as they find themselves helpless in well-organised libraries because of lack of previous experience of use of library. Based on a questionnaire discusses the rationale, need and how to start this socialization process.

025.58772 User Studies – University Libraries

Kapoor, A L 1072

Use pattern of the periodicals and strategy of research scholars in geography : A case study of Delhi School of Economics, *SSI*, 310-323.

Studies the use pattern of the periodicals and the information seeking behaviour of the scholars in geography in the Delhi School of Economics. Ascertains the periodicals mostly used, gaps in periodicals, research strategy of scholars, dependence on libraries, steps to improve services and materials.

Rajagopal, B 1073

User survey of Srikrishna Devaraya University Library, *Lib Her* 28(1-2) Apr- Sept 1989 : 17-25.

Reports about the survey of the Library conducted through a questionnaire. Gives information about users background, their views regarding catalogues, use of library and types of publications needed, kinds of services given and their usefulness. Gives some recommendations.

025.6 Circulation Services

Burrell, Quentin L 1074

Correlation structure of library circulation data : A case study : Part 1 – the empirical view, *Lib Sci slant Doc & Inf Std* 27(4) Dec 1990 : 213-236.

Reconsiders the 11-year period data for library circulation collected at the University of Saskatchewan using alternative simple regression analysis to more clearly reveal the regression structure. Continues in Part 2.

Burrell, Quentin L 1075

Correlation structure of library circulation data : A case study: Part 2 – the theoretical aspects, *Lib Sci slant Doc & Inf Std* 27(4) Dec 1990 : 237-252.

Uses theory of mixers of point processors to provide models for library circulation data. Investigates extent to which such models are able to mimic the observed correlation structure making use of so-called Poisson regression ratio with reference to the data given in Part 1.

025.6 (1) Circulation and Computer

Annapurna, T S 1076

Computerised circulation system at work in MECON – a case study, *DRTC 1989*, ZB 1-6.

Discusses briefly the Automated Circulation System in practice at the TIC of Metallurgical & Engineering Consultation (India) Ltd (MECON), Bangalore.

Gupta, R C and **Shiv Dass** 1077

A simple way to computerise circulation activity in a research library, *CALNE*, 78-84.

Discusses the need of computerising the circulation activity. Outlines the research environment regarding circulation activity. Gives the program in BASIC, its structure, file structure, external files. Describes specification and features of computerised circulation activity.

ISX/CIRC circulation program for CDS/ISIS, *NISSAT Newsletter* 10(2) Apr-June 1991 : 12-14. 1078

Explains the ISX/CIRC as a program written in CDS/ISIS Pascal to automate the loan and return of library materials. Mentions its special features.

Jambhekar, Ashok and **Mehta, Neelam** 1079

Online circulation system :VSL experience, *Lib Sci slant Doc & Inf Std* 28 (4) Dec 1991 : 160-166.

Discusses the factors that led to adoption of automated circulation system in Indian Institute of Management, Ahmedabad. Presents in detail system design and output features of the system.

Kuppuswamy, S 1080

Library software for personal computer based information retrieval and circulation systems, *DRTC 1989*, Z 1-11.

Explains the development of dBase modules for PC-based information retrieval and circulation system at the Design Library, H A L, Bangalore.

Murthy, T A V, Dasgupta, Kalpana, Kumarappa, G and **Sarkar, Sukruti** 1081

Corporate database for circulation system, *CPT*, 270-278.

Mentions reasons for modernisation of library and information services. Defines a database. States how to design a database by DBMS. Explains circulation system and designing a database for it having data structure, file design, random and indexed files, etc.

Pulkeshi, D and **Jahangirdar, I H** 1082

PC-based circulation system using dBase III, *DRTC 1989*, F 1-7.

Develops a module based dBase III for circulation control, and gives its implementation. It is a PC-based system and works satisfactorily.

Sarvamangla, G and **Ravichandra Rao, I K** 1083

dBase III + modules for library circulation control, *Lib Sci slant Doc & Inf Std* 26(1) Mar 1989 : 69-96.

Discusses various functions of automated circulation control developed using dBase III plus. Gives various files required, their structure and index files. Describes input, processing, output, etc. for each of the functions of the circulation system.

Sarvamangla, G and **Ravichandra Rao, I K** 1084

dBase III + modules for library circulation control, *DRTC 1989,* W 1-31.

Discusses various functions of automated circulation control developed by using dBase III plus. Gives various files, their structure, and index. Describes input, processing, output etc for each of the functions of circulation system.

Shalini, R and **Harinarayana, N S** 1085

A microcomputer based circulation system for a university library : An experiment using COBOL, *Lib Sci slant Doc & Inf Std* 26(3) Sept 1989 : 217-227.

Discusses computer application to circulation control. Describes objectives of circulation system, inventory v/s absence system, etc. Gives data files and record structures. Mentions circulation system functions.

025.62 Interlibrary Loans (ILL)

Bourkoff, Vivienne 1086

Making books available to readers : Interlibrary loan at the Library of Congress, *Her Lib Sci* 29(1-2) Jan- Apr 1990 : 64-67.

Describes the beginning of ILL at Library of Congress in the beginning of 20th century. Discusses its purposes as stated by Putnam, impact of new technology, clients from several countries. Mentions type of material loaned and borrowed, and staff involved.

Murthy, S Radhakrishna 1087

Need for standardization in resource sharing of inter-library loan and photocopying facilities, *Luck Libn* 22(1-2) Mar-June 1990 : 45-48.

States that standards promote the efforts in information handling and documentation services. Describes few important aspects and the need for standardization in resources sharing of ILL and photocopying facilities. Describes some important sources, basic standards and terminology.

Sengupta, I N 1088

Bibliographical facilities for research and inter library cooperation : Indian scenario, *Ind Jl Inf Lib & Society* 4(1) Jan-Mar 1991 : 5-40.

Traces history of medical bibliography. Discusses tools for the compilation of medical bibliography. Describes need for sharing of resources of various medical libraries in India. Gives current trends of Indian medical research. Discusses role of INSDOC, DGHS, NISSAT, British Council in India, etc. Stresses on the need for coordination.

025.62 (1) Document Delivery/Supply System

Krishnaswamy Rao, V, Ramanna, B and **Chennakesava Das, S B** 1089

Document delivery system at the National Information Centre for Food Science and Technology (NICFOS) – a case study, *Lib Sci slant Doc & Inf Std* 25(2) June 1988 : 65-77.

Presents analysis of the document delivery services by NICFOS, Mysore during 1987. Indicates that there is need for translated articles from non-English languages. Document delivery services help in setting priority for selection of periodical publication and other documents.

Navjot Kaur 1090

Document delivery in microform, *ULI*, 100-105.

Mentions the document delivery services available all over the world which are costly. States that COM, CAR, etc be introduced in India in view of its advantages. Makes a case for the setting up of Job Service Bureaus for providing this service.

Otike, J N 1091

Document reproduction and supply in East Africa, *Int Lib Move* 13(1) Mar 1991 : 1-9.

Explains information systems in East Africa divided into six main divisions Describes photocopying services in Uganda, Tanzania, Kenya. Discusses microfilming services, document reproduction. Discusses the future of cooperation in document reproduction and supply in East Africa.

Swain, Leigh and **Cleveland, Gary** 1092

Electronic document delivery and libraries : Technologies, strategies and issues, *Jl Lib & Inf Sci* 16(1) June 1991 : 70-84.

States that using IT access to bibliographic information has greatly improved but delivery of documents to end users remains dependent on traditional methods which can be overcome through electronic document delivery. Describes a number of covering technologies for electronic document generation, storage, transfer to create electronic document delivery systems. Gives strategies for their coordinated use. Explains some relevant issues.

025.62 (1) Universal Availability of Publications (UAP)

Omoniwa, Moses A 1093

Barriers to UAP in the underdeveloped countries, *Int Lib Move* 13(2) June 1991 : 61-70.

Defines UAP. Traces history of UAP. Gives its current status. Describes why UAP programme is needed. Discusses essential features and principles of UAP. Gives its elements also. Describes various barriers to UAP, and how these apply to Nigeria as an underdeveloped country. Offers solutions.

025.81 Access to Collections

Mahapatra, P K 1094

Access to non-bibliographic data in social sciences, *SSI*, 443-449.

Discusses role of information in new set up : Describes problems of accessibility of information in view of structure of the social sciences. States that as a result of technological development in our country non-bibliographic data management has assumed importance. Concludes that machine readable database has advantages.

025.82 Theft, Losses, Mutilation, etc

Rajagopal, B 1095

Loss of books and the role of the librarian, *ILA Bull* 27(3) Oct-Dec 1991 : 111-114.

Considers the changing role of library since the days of preservation of books and also the responsibilities of the librarian. Discusses methods, both preventive and curative, for saving books from damage, loss, and vandalism.

025.82 (1) Stock Verification. Stock Taking

Gupta, S R 1096

Stock verification in libraries : Problems and solutions, Delhi : Ken Publications, 1990. 260 p.

Based on a Ph D thesis, studies the data collected from 220 colleges from the country regarding the conceptual framework of stock verification in libraries. Examines the existing norms and suggests modifications. Gives the operational aspects of the work in second part giving different methods.

Sridhar, M S 1097

Library stock verification : A ritual and an occupational hazard, *IASLIC Bull* 36(3) Sept 1991 : 103-110.

Explains stock verification as one of the occupational hazards. Emphasises need for clarity of objectives and procedures regarding stock verification. Points out that its cost far exceeds the benefits. Highlights norms and procedures for Govt of India institutions. Discusses some advantages and methods. Puts forth precautionary measures against loss and mutilation. Analyses issue of responsibility of loss. Gives procedure for write off. Stresses need for rational and updated rules and procedures about stock verification.

025.84 Preservation and Conservation

Fadayomi, J A 1098

Preservation of materials in Nigerian academic libraries – a survey, *Int Lib Move* 13(2) June 1991 : 110-112.

Gives importance of preservation of library materials. Explains causes of deterioration of books etc. Describes various house keeping methods of preservation.

Fadayomi, J A 1099

Preservation of materials in Nigerian academic libraries, *Int Lib Move* 13(3) Sept 1991 : 113-122.

Identifies methods of preservation of materials such as shelving, preservation against insects. Gives environmental standards of preservation for humidity, temperature, air pollution, light. Mentions chemicals used, problems of book theft, mutilation, deterioration. Gives suggestions and recommendations.

Gupta, B M 1100

National research laboratory for conservation of cultural property, *HLAICI*, v 9, Pt 1, 44-52.

Discusses the aims and activities of the National Research laboratory for conservation of cultural property. Discusses various conservation projects. Explains library and documentation activities.

International Council of Archives 1101

Seminar on archival conservation, *INICAE* 9(1) Mar 1990 : 108-109.

Reports about the seminar. Discusses problems of conservation. Mentions about training course on conservation held in Feb 1988 in Harare.

Kalina, Charles R 1102

National policy on acid-free paper use, *INICAE* 10 (1) Mar 1991 : 86-87.

States that deterioration of acid paper threatens the future survival of literary works, while acid-free paper lasts for centuries. Gives brief about the adoption of acid-free paper for preservation through a Public Law 101-423 to establish national policy.

Kapoor, A L 1103

Preservation of library materials in India; proposals and plans, *HLAICI*, v 9, Pt 2, 422-428.

Ascertains the steps taken by official and non-official agencies, government to ensure location and preservation of rare books and Mss, facilities available in leading libraries for preservation, and plans and proposals of Govt of India. Gives the present position. Reports the findings of the survey in the light of the above. Gives some national plans and proposals.

Mukhopadhyay, K K and **Guha, P** 1104

Library conservation, Calcutta : Information Research Academy, 1990. xvi, 328 p.

Discusses in detail about the need and importance of conservation. Describes various methods available for conservation of library materials for present as well as future use.

National Seminar on Preservation of cultural heritage : Manuscripts and their future, *Granthana* 1(2) July 1990 : 63-66. 1105

Reports the proceedings of the National Seminar on Preservation of Cultural Heritage : Manuscripts and their Future, organised by Raja Rammohun Roy Library Foundation, and Asiatic Society, Calcutta in collaboration with Ramakrishna Mission Institute of Culture, Calcutta during March 8-10, 1990 in Calcutta.

Ramesh Babu, B 1106

Towards the programme for preservation of information materials in a college library : Librarian's view, *RILISAR Bull* 7(1-4) Jan-Dec 1991 : 8-13.

Mentions main activities of a library. Gives genesis of paper as a material. Describes situation in college libraries towards preservation of materials in Tamil Nadu. Suggests measures for ensuring preservation of library materials. Gives also some barriers to the preservation programme.

Tiwari, P C 1107

Essential measures in conservation and preservation of library reading materials, *Her Lib Sci* 30(3-4) July-Oct 1991 : 212-215.

Defines conservation. Explains the need of preservation. Discusses causes of deterioration of reading materials. Suggests various preventive measures like insecticides, fumigants, etc. States general preservation rules. Concludes that preservation techniques provide longevity to documents for future use.

026 SPECIAL LIBRARIES

026.000954 Special Libraries – India

026.000954 (1) Adyar Library

Anjaneyelu, D 1108

The Adyar Library is 100 years old, *HLAICI*, v 9, Pt I, 220-227.

Describes the richness and value of the significant Mss on oriental studies in this old library. Mentions about research series, research journals, etc. States that it is gaining popularity among scholars. Appends a list of its publications.

026.070172 Newspaper Libraries

Chatterjee, Amitabha 1109

Information resource management in newspaper libraries, *IM*, 25-29.

Defines newspaper library. Gives its characteristics. Points out information need of newspaper. States that efficient management of information resources involves timely collection of information resources for present and anticipated future use and their effective organisation for speedy and pin-pointed retrieval. Requires planning, role of new technology, etc.

Joseph, Rosamma 1110

Changes in the news information environment, *SALP*, 78.

Gives one page abstract highlighting the importance of newspaper libraries where more staff is needed for organisation and management of information. States that the new electronic devices will help in transferring the library and librarian which will enhance their status.

Joseph, Rosamma 1111

Information network in newspapers in India, *ILA Bull* 27(2) July-Sept 1991 : 58-62.

Discusses importance of newspapers in modern society and role of library in newspaper organisations. Discusses uses of information in a newspaper industry and their information requirements. Proposes the setting up of an information network in newspapers in India.

Savanur, S K 1112

Organizing photographs in newspaper libraries, *CPT*, 122-127.

Aims at focussing on the problems of organizing photographs in newspaper libraries. Gives reasons to use photographs and photographs as source of information. Makes observation at *The Hindu*, *The Statesman* and *The Times of India*. Presents findings without reference to any specific newspaper.

026.42 (1) CIEFL Library

Prabhakar, S S 1113

Computerization of Ramesh Mohan Library database : Analysis and review, *CALNE*, 9-13.

Discusses importance of databases in academic and research work. States that the Ramesh Mohan Library of CIEFL caters to the needs of the staff and research scholars in linguistics, literature and language teaching. Suggests that this manual database be converted into computerized one to save time of the reader.

Ramaiah, L S 1114

The Central Institute of English and Foreign Languages; library and documentation services, *HLAICI*, v 9, Pt 1, 9-17.

Discusses in detail the library and documentation services of the CIEFL, Hyderabad. Includes information on collection development, databank, bibliographies, document delivery service. Serves as nodal centre for foreign languages.

026.6 Technical Libraries

Saxena, R S 1115

Research and technical libraries : Their role and problems, *DLIS*, 59-79.

Explains role of technical libraries in the era of information explosion, devices for meeting the challenge. Describes three basic elements of research and technical libraries. Discusses staff, gadgets, tools and equipments, etc.

026.61 Medical Libraries. Health Science Libraries

Kumbar, Mallinath 1116

Library services in the medical colleges in Karnataka, *Lib Her* 28(1-2) Apr-Sept 1989 : 26-31.

Explains present position of medical libraries in Karnataka. Describes the staff, finance, existing library facilities of M R Medical College Library Gulbarga. Points out that the services are unsatisfactory due to inadequate library staff and inadequate finance. Offers suggestions.

Mishra, B N 1117

Common Indian literature in medical and veterinary sciences : Health professional point of view, *Lib Progress (Int)* 9-10 (1-2) Jan-Dec 1989-90 : 32-46.

Gives the similarity of medical and veterinary sciences. Narrates importance of library. Gives in detail technical and documentation activities in the library for users. Suggests main points to develop efficiency of the library professional. Indicates Indian documents in the field of veterinary and medical sciences. Mentions sponsoring agencies, subject wise coverage of Indian science journals. Makes also citation analysis.

Perkins, Miriam L and **Spann, Melvin L** 1118

TOXLEARN : Microcomputer-based training for TOXLINE, *IN-ICAE* 9(2) Sept 1990 : 227-228.

Describes the TOXLEARN – a microcomputer based training program for TOXLINE of NLM. Discusses that it is organised into 7 chapters. Describes features of this training programme. Also gives specifications.

Varalakshmi, R S R 1119

Regional Health Information System – a proposal, *IASLIC Bull* 36 (1) Mar 1991 : 23-28.

Identifies limitations prevailing in medical college libraries in AP in retrieving health information. Traces advantages of networking and resource sharing at the regional level. Proposes a Regional Health Information System in A P. Examines the infrastructural requirements necessary.

026.62 Engineering Libraries

Kar, D C and **Siddiqui, A M** 1120

Periodical section of TERI Library (1985-1989) : Growth and development, *Ann Lib Sci & Doc* 36(4) Dec 1989: 125-133.

Points out services provided by the periodical section of TERI Library. Analyses showing the trend of growth of journals received and expenditure during 1985-89.

Nivedita 1121

Tata Energy Research Institute Information System and Services,

HLAICI, v 7, 176-180.

Deals with the setting up of TERI, its objectives, and TERI Information System including library, documentation and information centre, mycorrhiza information centre, and the publication unit.

026.63 Agricultural Libraries

Chakraborty, Arun Kumar 1122

National policy for agricultural library in the perspective of information base for agricultural library, *NIPP*, 103-112.

Stresses the need for building a network of documentation and information services in agriculture and allied areas. Delineates an information base for agriculture policy. Enumerates categories of information and data requirements, information collecting agencies, important documents as sources of information. Mentions briefly what should be a national policy for agriculture.

Naidu, Hemasunder and **Gunjal, S R** 1123

Contribution of Indian agricultural libraries to AGRIS, *Luck Libn* 22(3-4) Sept-Dec 1990 : 89-92.

Stresses importance of agricultural literature and the effects in cooperative information handling in agriculture. Mentions about AGRIS and reviews the contribution of Indian agricultural libraries to AGRIS. Suggests effective role of agricultural university libraries and ICAR libraries in this regard.

027 GENERAL LIBRARIES

Narinder Kumar 1124

Indological libraries : New dimensions, *DLIS*, 93-105.

Describes briefly library with indological subjects in new technology with new dimensions. Discusses indological Mss libraries in Indian scene. Clarifies dimensions of science of Mss, manuscriptology and its offshoots. Gives their purpose, goals and objectives, services, staffing pattern, problems. Offers solutions. Proposes INMALIS – an Integrated National Mss Library and Information System.

Varadan, V K S 1125

Libraries and holistic approach: Needs, roles, opportunities – a global view with special reference to India, *IASLIC Bull* 35(2) June 1990 : 47-54.

Delivered as Special Annual Lecture of IASLIC for 1990. Shares his thoughts on the needs, roles and opportunities of libraries taking a global view with special reference to India where responsibility of library development lies with the national government.

027 (1) Archives

Chakravarti, Adhir 1126

The State Archives of West Bengal, *HLAICI*, v 9, Pt 2, 354-359.

Traces historical development. Describes the holdings spread over 19 kms of shelf-space. Lists important series of pre-1858-records, post-1859 records. Mentions the private papers it acquired. Gives publication, and other activities.

Chowdhury, Shuba 1127

Archives and Research Centre for Ethnomusicology, *HLAICI*, v 9, Pt 2, 439-447.

States aims and objectives, the primary sources materials. Describes activities as acquisition, cataloguing, preservation, research and publication. Gives a descriptive report of ARCE database on computer. Gives two appendices.

Dash, M P 1128

Role of Orissa State Archives, *HLAICI*, v 9, Pt 2, 386-397.

States the duties and responsibilities. Describes collection and preservation, finding aids. Gives survey of records in private possession. Mentions role of oral archives. Presents a note on main series of records. Describes private records and their role in politico-history of the state. Gives a list of publications in Appendix.

Desai, Sanjiv P 1129

Maharashtra State Archives, *HLAICI*, v 9, Pt, 2, 334-346.

Gives development of Bombay Archives with variety of records. Explains Pune Archives from its beginning to the present. Discusses Kolhapur Archives having various records.

Jain, J K 1130

Rajasthan State Archives, *HLAICI* v 9, Pt 2, 375-381.

Gives development since 1955. Explains the earliest records, the Jaipur State Records, Kota State Records, Bikaner State Records, etc. Deals also with private records. Gives a list of publications.

Mandanjit Kaur 1131

The Sikh archives : Need for its re-organisation, *HLAICI*, v 9, Pt 2, 454-465.

Deals with the different times faced by Sikhs and development of sense of history and desire to preserve their heritage, which led to the establishment of the Sikh Reference Library and other agencies. Describes in detail the Sikh Reference Library, its development, holdings, their significance, etc. Adds Appendices.

Mundell, Sue 1132

Archival survey project, *INICAE* 10(1) Mar 1991 : 77-79.

Gives genesis of the Archival Survey Project and the preparation of a *Guide* to documents photoreproduced in Spain and available in US institutions. Presents the results of the survey conducted in 1987-88.

Muniswamy, R 1133

Karnataka State Archives, *HLAICI*, v 9, Pt 2, 365-370.

Gives objectives, main functions, and staff. Discusses general records and space copies wing. Describes historical records and integrated records wing, private papers wing, reprography wing. Discusses preservation and intermediate repositories.

Nair, R Madhudevan 1134

That State Archives of Kerala, *HLAICI*, v 9, Pt 2, 328-333.

Describes various record offices at Trivandrum, Ernakulam, and Calicut. Discusses various stages of development. Gives training programme. Explains record holdings including rare collections of bamboo splits. Gives other activities also.

Pal, S.S 1135

Status of archives in the university system, *Her Lib Sci* 30(3-4) July-Oct 1991 : 190-195.

Explains that universities create, collect and use documentary resources to support higher education though their acquisition programme is vastly directed at the external intellectual sources for storage and dissemination of information. Points out that university records have received inadequate attention as a valuable primary resource for planning in universities. Surveys the need and state of archival material in the university information system.

Pal, S S

1136

University archival programme in India, *HLAICI*, v 9, Pt 2, 416-421.

Describes record creation process, historical development of academic archives in universities. Explains university archives as research material, archives cells, UGC guidelines. Gives contents of archives of textual, cartographic, and pictorial nature. Mentions library-archives relationship.

Rangamani, Thiru S

1137

Tamil Nadu Archives, *HLAICI*, v 9, Pt 2, 347-353.

Describes the beginning, holdings, district records centre, information services, conservation and preservation, training, library, publication, facilities, district gazetteers, regional committee for survey of historical research. Gives Tamil Nadu Council of Historical Research.

Sharma, V K

1138

Delhi Archives, *HLAICI*, v 9, pt 2, 323-327.

Gives establishment in 1972. Describes its records, reference media, microfilming and photo duplication, library, research facilities, repairs of records, oral history programme, acquisition of records. Mentions holdings of Delhi State Archives.

Shirodkar, P P

1139

Historical Archives of Goa, *HLAICI*, v 9, Pt 2, 371-374.

Traces origin and development of this Archives. States that its expansions is now being done on a large scale, has a full-fledged microfilming section, bindery, a rich reference library and a modern building. Mentions that it is one of the oldest in the country having very important records in its holdings.

Sinha, S N 1140

U P State Archives, *HLAICI*, v 9, Pt 2, 398-415.

Traces history. Gives duties, aims and objectives. Discusses holdings since its establishment. Gives origin of Divisional Commissioners and creation of district collectors to collect records. Describes growth of the Secretariat, regional archives, Mss library, private archives. Includes two Appendices.

Srivastava, Anurag 1141

Haryana State Archives, *HLAICI*, v 9, Pt 2, 360-364.

Mentions creation of this Archives. Gives its main function. Discusses activities of the Department. Provides research facilities to bonafide researchers. Mentions some of its publications. Gives the Headquarters holdings.

Sudarshan Rao, S, Reddy, Y Yadgiri and **Krishnamurthy, P** 1142

State Archives of Andhra Pradesh : an overview, *HLAICI*, v 9, Pt 2, 315-322.

Describes about the State Archives of Andhra Pradesh having various records of different categories belonging to Deccan Sultans, Mughal documents, Asafia records, etc. Discusses about the library and documentation activities, reprographic section, archival museum, publication, preservation and binding, information services. Gives future programme.

Tshering, Gyatsho 1143

A report of Tibetan culture, *HLAICI*, v 9, Pt 2, 429-438.

Gives origin and development of the Library of Tibetan Works and Archives. Mentions objectives. Explains various facilities and services available in the library, the courses held, publication programme, research facilities, etc. Gives a list of publications.

Walia, Jagjiwan Mohan 1144

Punjab State Archives, Patiala, *HLAICI,* v 9, Pt 2, 382-385.

Deals with the records in its holding such as PEPSU records, the chamber of Princes, Khalsa Durbar records, district records, copies of orders, instructions and letters. Also gives private collections. Describes reference library having books, Mss, maps, etc. Gives the preservation and archival gallery.

027.006 Archives – Associations

Kapoor, Rammi 1145

Association of Indian Archivists, *HLAICI*, v 10, 28-30.

Gives its origin in 1977. Mentions aims and objectives. Discusses its structure, membership, and nature of professional issues it takes up. Describes some of its activities.

Mishra, Nisha 1146

National Committee of Archivists, *HLAICI*, v 10, 130-135.

Points out origin and development of the NCA. Discusses various meetings and their important recommendations from the first meeting held in 1954 to 35th meeting held in 1986.

027.00902 Libraries – Medieval Period

Sharma, A K and **Kalpana** 1147

Historical survey of libraries during medieval period in India, *Lib Progress (Int)* 9-10 (1-2) Jan-Dec 1989-90 : 24-31.

Makes a brief survey regarding the development of libraries during the medieval India by the Muslims, Hindus, and Mughals in the form of private libraries and imperial library.

027.00903 Libraries – Mughal Period

Serwar Hossain 1148

Glimpses of the Mughal libraries, *CPT*, 184-198.

Explains in detail the love for and establishment of libraries by Mughal Emperors such as Babur, Humayun, Akbar, Jahangir, Shahjahan, Auranzeb. Describes their collections, location of library, cataloguing, classification, Mss illustration, preservation, reading hours, book loss and punishment, etc.

027.047 Libraries – Russia

Grikhanov, G A 1149

Soviet libraries : Perspectives and reflections, *DLIS*, 323-330.

Describes the development of Soviet libraries based on the culture of Soviet society. Describes the literary activities and programme of library development in the USSR originally initiated, planned and worked out by V I Lenin. Points out increasing role of libraries.

027.054 Libraries – India

Serwar Hossain 1150

Akbar – the great library administrator, *HLAICI*, v 9, Pt 1, 209-212.

Deals with the classification, cataloguing, organisation, management, storage of books in the Imperial Library of Akbar. States that he provided suitable administration for libraries.

027.05412 Library Development – Bihar

Esperanza, M 1151

Situation of libraries in Bihar : BILSA Seminar, *Her Lib Sci* 29(1-2) Jan-Apr 1990 : 95-99.

Describes the inauguration and addresses of Seminar of 'Situation of Libraries in Bihar' on 12 August 1989 to mark the 97th Birthday of Ranganathan. It was organised by Bihar Library Service Association.

027.05414 Library Development – Bengal

Sharma, Ajay Kumar 1152

Origin and development of libraries in Bengal during 1800-1947 A D, *Int Lib Move* 13(3) Sept 1991 : 156-161.

Deals with the origin and development of libraries during the 19th and the first half of the 20th century.

027.0544 Library Development – Rajasthan

027.0544 (1) Pothikhana of Jaipur

Sahai, Yaduendra 1153

Pothikhana of Jaipur, *HLAICI*, v 9, Pt 1, 108-111.

Traces its origin. Describes its growth and valuable Manuscripts preserved in this Pothikhana, i.e. library.

027.054792 Library Development – Maharashtra

027.054792 (1) The Royal Library of Bijapur

Quraishi, S 1154

The Royal Library of Bijapur, *HLAICI*, v 9, Pt 1, 165-173.

Traces history. Deals with the rich and rare collection of this Royal Library developed over the years by the Sultans. Mentions about the use of the collection after publication of the catalogues.

027.05484 Library Development – Andhra Pradesh

Venkatappaiah, V 1155

Gautmi Granthalayam, Rajahmundry, *HLAICI*, v 9, Pt 1, 138-141.

Gives history of Gautmi Granthalayam and its aims and objectives. Describes various articles, construction of library building, total stock, Manuscripts, etc. States that the Andhra Pradesh Government has taken over the management since 1979.

027.05487 Library Development – Karnataka

027.05487 (1) Saraswati Mahal Library

Narinder Kumar 1156

Thanjavur Maharaja Serfoji's Saraswati Mahal Library, *HLAICI*, v 9, Pt 1, 98-107.

Traces history of this library. Gives its holdings on palm leaf in various languages. Mentions publications. Explains service to researchers, conservation and preservation, binding section, microfilming unit, finance, etc.

027.0678 Library Development – Tanzania

Bgoya, Walter 1157

Libraries in Tanzania, *DLIS*, 339-345.

Gives an account of libraries in Tanzania describing rural libraries, university and special libraries, children's libraries, and work of Tanzania Library Association.

027.1 Private Libraries
Personal Libraries

Allauddin, Shaikh and **Rout, R K** 1158

Personal library of Adbul-Rahim-Khan-i-Khanan, *Granthana* 2(2) July 1991 : 179-182.

Presents a short treatise on collection and staffing of personal library of Khan-i-Khanan, son of the Governor of Gujarat under Akbar's regime. States that great names and work of scholarship are associated with this library.

Kodiyan, Cicily 1159

V I Lenin's personal library, *Lib Her* 28(3-4) Oct 1989-Jan 1990 : 184-190.

Describes the use of different libraries in Europe and Russia by V I Lenin. Discusses the reading interests of Lenin. Analyses his personal collection, indicating the subjects, languages and authors of special interest to him. Mentions the way the collection has been organised.

027.4 PUBLIC LIBRARIES

Krishan Kumar 1160

Role of public libraries in the promotion of literacy, *Lib Her* 30(2-4) July 1991 – Jan 1992: 155-161.

Points out that National Policy on L & I System document gives great importance to literacy programmes. Mentions that public libraries provide extension services to a certain extent. Emphasises the need to drive ways and means to reach out to the weaker sections and agencies involved in the promotion of literacy. Gives suggestions about network of public libraries.

Mitra, Tarun Kumar 1161

Development of public library : Its meaning and evaluation, *Granthana* 1(2) July 1990 : 45-58.

Discusses significance of education and drawbacks of formal education. Defines ideal of adult education. Discusses place of public library in promoting education. Describes how public library can serve as a centre of culture transmission. Proposes à theory and method of evaluation of the development of public library in educational terms.

Palanivelu, C and **Raghavan, K S,** *Eds* 1162

Education through public libraries : A practical approach, Madras : Directorate of Public Libraries, Tamil Nadu, 1991. 410 p.

Contains 47 papers by specialists presented at the National Seminar on Public Library Movement : Concepts and Strategies from 19-21 April 1991 at Madras. The papers cover various aspects of library movement. Includes three appendices regarding programmes of the Directorate of Public Libraries, Tables and figures, and officers working for the movement.

Riswadkar, M R 1163

Public library as knowledge situation, *CPT*, 99-103.

Explains what it means by library as a knowledge situation. Discusses briefly various factors contributing to its success. Concludes that a library, for it to be a true knowledge situation, should have appropriate an adequate literature, efficient services, and well trained and motivated staff.

Shukla, B B and **Behuria, R K** 1164

The role of public libraries in adult literacy programmes, *Ind Jl Inf Lib & Society* 3(1-2) Mar-June 1990 : 149-152.

Considers public library as a social service centre. States that an integrated network of public libraries is essential to raise the literacy rate in Orissa. Gives service to be rendered to adults. Concludes that public libraries are necessary for liquidation of illiteracy and promote mass education.

Yourkov, S V 1165

End result of library activities as a variable of all round analysis of public library functioning, *Jl Lib & Inf Sci* 15(1) June 1990 : 51-61.

Discusses the role of evaluation in public library functioning. Emphasises that end result of such an evaluation should be useful to how an overall understanding of such a library.

027.4 (1) Mobile Libraries. Book Mobiles

Siitonen, Leena 1166

Mobile library services as a functional unit in public library systems : The United States/Context, *Jl Lib & Inf Sci* 15(1) July 1990 : 28-50.

Gives purpose of public libraries and mobile libraries. Discusses development of public libraries in the US giving their services, budget, planning, collections and standards. Discusses the provision of mobile library services, its planning as units of public library system made possible by corporate efforts. Discusses types of bookmobiles and their status.

027.4 (1) Rural Libraries

Jagtar Singh 1167

Rural public library : The bastion of democracy, *PLSP,* 31-43.

Emphasises that government should provide library service under the mandate of law. Flays the faulty composition and functioning of the Central Library Committee, administrative control without professional leadership. Does not favour levying of cess and funds be arranged by the state.

Kempson, Elaine 1168

Rural community information services : Guidelines for researching need, setting up services and evaluating performance, *Jl Lib & Inf Sci* 15(2) Dec 1990 : 139-152.

Summarises the guidelines, on the development of rural community information services on the basis of 1987 IFLA Conference, in three main areas : (i) analysing community needs, (ii) establishing appropriate services, and (iii) monitoring and evaluating performance.

Khan, H A 1169

Role of rural libraries in the promotion of literacy and adult education, *Granthana* 2(2) July 1991 : 135-145.

Studies role of public libraries in relation to national problems of literacy and adult education. Examines reasons for viewing libraries not helping in resolving these problems. Describes role of rural libraries in literacy and adult education, information service programmes, educational and cultural function.

Oyesiku, F A 1170

Developing rural libraries in Nigeria, *Int Lib Move* 12(1) Mar 1990 : 48-53.

Provides historical background of public library development in Nigeria. Gives rationale for development of libraries in rural

Nigeria. Gives strategy for development which include public lectures, posters and leaflets, library exhibitions, etc.

Ramanayya, Iyyanki Venkata 1171

The rural library movement in India, *Her Lib Sci* 30(1-2) Jan- Apr 1991 : 31-34.

Narrated the activities of Iyyanki on rural library movement. Mentions his activities in Bhimavaram Taluk and for the promotion of libraries in Andhra Pradesh. Describes the pattern of library movement involving library pilgrimages. Pays tribute to the association and work of the two library field workers.

Thakar, G S and **Pawar, S S** 1172

Rural library network for Amb tehsil of Una district, Himachal Pradesh : A project plan, *Ind Jl Inf Lib & Society* 3(1-2) Mar-June 1990 : 124-138.

Proposes a network of rural public libraries in Amb tehsil of Una district (HP) to promote desire for books, to facilitate access to resources, to use library as a means for encouraging rural people to make use of untapped resources. Gives budget estimates also.

027.442 Public Libraries – UK

Saiful Islam, K M 1173

Public library system and services in Great Britain and Bangladesh, *Her Lib Sci* 29(3-4) July-Oct 1990 : 163-172.

Studies the outcome of a survey research project carried out in Great Britain in 1989. Delineates current status and structure of public library system and services in Great Britain and Bangladesh. Describes working of the public library system main difference between British and Bangladeshi public libraries. Lists some recommendations.

027.444 Public Libraries – France

Wiele, Nic Van De 1174

Public libraries, *Jl Lib & Inf Sci* 16(1) June 1991 : 48-59.

Discusses historical development of public libraries in France since 1789. Mentions different types of libraries such as city libraries, rural libraries giving their collection, role etc. Discusses current trends in the development of public libraries including such important issues as their role as multimedia libraries, decentralisation, cooperation and application of new technology.

027.454 Public Libraries – India

All India Public Library Conference, 1989 1175

Proceedings of All Indian Public Library Conference on Eighth Plan Perspective of Public Library Development, New Delhi, February 24-25, 1989, *Granthana* 1 (1) Jan 1990 : 73-81.

Reports about the Conference of Eighth Plan perspective of public library development organised by RRRLF, Calcutta. The deliberations of the Conference took place in six sessions.

Augustine, C A and **Devarajan, G,** *Eds* 1176

Public library system in India, New Delhi : Ess Ess Publications, 1990 xii, 135 p.

Includes 13 articles on various aspects of public library system contributed by various scholars. Brought out as a falicitation volume in honour of Prof M N Ramakrishnan Nayar of University of Kerala, Trivandrum.

Barua, B P 1177

Universal accessibility of information – role of a public library in Indian context, *Granthana* 1(1) Jan 1990 : 19-24.

Emphasises the importance of information and accessibility to information. Describes the need for public library and need for national information system. Discusses national library and information system in India and public library and information system in India which help in UAP or UAI.

Gopinath, M A 1178

Information policy perspectives for public library system, *NIPP*, 220-228.

States that public library system in India is still in the mould of 19th century scholarship and has been slow to respond to the contemporary needs. Mentions that information policy perspectives have to be put into this. Analyses a case study for developing community information services in public library system. Presents in detail the inputs needed to be included into information policy perspectives.

Kalia, D R , Biswas, S C, Krishan Kumar and **Barua, B P** 1179

Guidelines for public library systems and services, *Granthana* 2(1) Jan 1991 : 31-84.

Mentions need for guidelines, definitions, library standards, Indian public library through the plans. Discusses objectives and functions of public library, categories of public libraries. Explains public library system, its need, model, role of SCL and other libraries. Discusses structure and administration of public library services, library finance, public library service, reading material, library personnel, physical facilities. Organisation of materials, library records and statistics, application of IT, planning public library system at various levels.

Khan, H A 1180

Public libraries and the contemporary Indian society, *CPT*, 166-172.

Outlines growth features of public libraries since Independence in India. Explains needs of contemporary Indian society such as information needs, educational needs, recreational or cultural needs. States that public libraries have not developed in relation to the needs of society. Describes the future role of public libraries they should play in the socio-economic development of the country in which library and society have a responsibility.

Khomdon Singh, Th 1181

Public library system, a necessity for the success of democracy; with special reference to India, *NIPP*, 229-232.

States that democracy is the most popular form of government success of which depends upon people's understanding for which right dose of information is needed. Describes that public library system is the righteous institution for the right information to right people at right time. Discusses that a national programme for public libraries is required to make Indian democracy successful.

Palanivelu, C 1182

National seminar on public library movement, *Her Lib Sci* 30(3-4) July-Oct 1991 : 255-259.

Reports about the Seminar held during 19-21 April 1991 in Madras. The Vice-Chancellor, University of Madras delivered the Keynote Address. In all 47 papers were received for presentation in 8 sessions. Gives the resolutions adopted at the Seminar.

Raman Nair, R 1183

Public library system : A modern outlook on its principles and practice, *NIPP*, 233-242.

Defines public library and public library system. Discusses need for public library system. Explains the role of public library system in maintaining democracy, economic development, social well being, mass education, etc. Gives the development of public library system concept mentioning possibilities support for Indian thought, right to information, recent trends, etc. Suggests a plan for public library system in India.

Ravindran, K 1184

Public libraries in India, *PLSI*, 1-7.

Traces development of public libraries since pre-independence period to the present. Describes the situation of library legislation in India. Points out some problems which need attention.

Viswanathan, C G 1185

Public library organisation, with special reference to India, 4th rev edition New Delhi: Ess Ess Publications, 1990. xxi, 218 p.

Divided into 15 chapters it deals with library and community, public library service, legal basis, public library laws of India, finance, personnel, building, furniture, collection, rules and regulation, the future of library service in India.

027.45412 Public Libraries – Bihar

Gupta, B M 1186

Khuda Baksh Oriental Public Library, *HLAICI* v 9, Pt 1, 88-94.

Relates its story of development from 1891. Describes its rich collections from various countries of the world on various subjects in different languages. States that its library now functions in five different areas : Reference service, acquisition, preservation, dissemination, and research.

Singh, R S P 1187

Public library development in Bihar, *Granthana* 2(2) July 1991 : 193-203.

Discusses in detail position of public libraries from state to village level. Deals briefly with activities of library associations in

Bihar, training in librarianship, financing of library service, administrative structure of library service etc. Mentions reasons for poor performance as low literacy rate and dearth of funds.

027.45415 Public Libraries – Tripura

Roy, Kanu Ranjan and **Binwal, J C** 1188

Public libraries in Tripura, *Lib Her* 30 (2-4) July 1991-Jan 1992 : 232-236.

Provides an overview of the land and the people. Describes development of public libraries in historical perspective. Gives library structure. Describes financial resources, collections, services and qualifications of library personnel. Points out the problems faced by public libraries.

027.454162 Public Libraries – Assam

Bharali, Bhriguram and **Binwal, J C** 1189

Public library services in Assam, *Lib Her* 30(2-4) July 1991-Jan 1992 : 226-231.

Gives background about the state. Describes developments leading to the present state of public libraries. Enumerates existing structure. Discusses the finance, manpower, book purchase policy, services and readership. Points out that low literacy rate and some economic factors have contributed to unsatisfactory state of public libraries.

027.454163 Public Libraries – Arunachal Pradesh

Adhikari, A K and **Binwal, J C** 1190

Public library services in Arunachal Pradesh, *Lib Her* 30(2-4) July 1991-Jan 1992 : 249-256.

Describes in brief the land and people. Describes various developments in historical perspective, leading to the present situation. Discusses administration, financial resources, collection, staff, services of the SCL. Describes briefly district, subdivisional, block, and circle libraries. Concludes that the public libraries have a long way to go.

027.454164 Public Libraries – Meghalaya

Lanong, Bibi Diana and **Binwal, J C** 1191

Public library services in Meghalaya, *Lib Her* (3-4) July 1991-Jan 1992 : 239-242.

Gives background about the state. Mentions developments leading to present state of public libraries. Describes the existing resources and services rendered by the SCL. Gives data regarding collection, budget, expenditure on books, staff, building and services of district libraries. Enumerates suggestions for evolving an integrated library services in the state.

027.454165 Public Libraries – Nagaland

Naga, Moses M and **Binwal, J C** 1192

Public library services in Nagaland, *Lib Her* 30(2-4) July 1991 – Jan 1992 : 243-248.

Provides a brief view of the land and people of the state. Describes developments in the field of public libraries in the historical perspective. Gives existing structure. Describes staff, financial resources, collection, book selection policy and services of the SCL. Discusses the state of district and rural libraries. Makes out a case for library legislation.

027.45455 Public Libraries – Punjab

Davinder Kaur 1193

Builder of tomorrow and the wisdom house, *PLSP*, 165-180.

Mentions need of public libraries in providing material to children. Identifies neglect of public libraries in Punjab and gives factors responsible for it. Stresses on the need to provide library facilities to children who are builders of tomorrow.

Janak Raj and **Singla, Romi** 1194

Public library system in Punjab and its financing, *PLSP*, 91-116.

Studies present status of public library system in Punjab. Discusses drawbacks of library cess. Suggests that funds raised through various sources be credited direct to the State library authority which in turn may allocate to all libraries according to their needs.

Jasmer Singh 1195

Public library and information network in Punjab : A suggested model, *PLSP*, 44-67.

Describes the role of public libraries as disseminator and retrievers of information. Points out present state of public libraries in Punjab. Proposes public library and information network. Suggests provisions of 8 per cent of state budget for proposed network and matching grant from the Central Govt. Stresses on immediate need for enacting a public library law.

Katyal, H R 1196

Public libraries in Punjab : A critique, *PLSP*, 68-76.

Provides a brief about the state of Punjab and importance of public libraries. Identifies libraries providing library services in the absence of a library law. Discusses some provision in the Model bill. States that trend is against the library cess.

Navalani, K 1197

Public library system in Punjab : A comment, *PLSP*, 1-13.

Discusses need for public library system. Describes public library services in Punjab. Pleads for library legislation in the state for providing public library system. Makes some suggestions in this regard.

Punjab Library Association, Patiala 1198

Seminar on Public Library System in Punjab, at Punjabi University, Patiala from November 22-23, 1991, *Seminar Papers*, Patiala : Punjab Library Association, 1991. vi, 184 p.

Includes 13 papers in the bound volume which deal with various aspects of public libraries in Punjab such as legislation, finance, role of library associations (PLA), role of libraries and continuing education, libraries for children, etc. The papers were presented at the two day Seminar held at the Punjabi University, Patiala during Nov 22-23, 1991.

Sethi, Sudarshan Kaur 1199

Central State Library Punjab : A review, *PLSP*, 127-143.

Examines the functioning of Masafir Memorial Central State Library, Patiala. Evaluates the extent to which it is performing the functions of CSL. Compares its services with that of TS Central

State Library, Chandigarh to show its relative position with regard to the development of public libraries of Punjab.

1200

Sewa Singh

Public library development in Punjab, *Granthana* 2(2) July 1991 : 147-154.

Provides brief introduction about Punjab. Traces history of libraries in ancient Punjab. Describes library scene in Punjab during 19th and 20th centuries. Discusses library development in post-independent period. Discusses establishment and role of district libraries, municipal libraries, block and village libraries with a critical book at such facilities as building, collection, services, finance. Mentions role of voluntary organisations and Punjab Library Association in library development. Concludes that library development was lopsided. Offers various suggestions for improvement of library services in Punjab

027.45456 Public Libraries – Delhi

1201

Kalia, D R

The role of Delhi Public Library in adult education : A recapitulation, *CLIS Observer* 8(3-4) July-Dec 1991 : 33-42.

Mentions setting up of the Delhi Public Library (DPL). Gives an appraisal of programmes of DPL for production of reading material for the new reading public and its contribution in the organisation of cultural activities.

1202

Taneja, Ram D

American Centre Library : 45th anniversary lecture, *NISSAT Newsletter* 10(4) Oct-Dec 1991 : 9.

Gives a brief report about the special lecture delivered by Prof F W Lancaster on the occasion of the 45th Anniversary celebration of the American Centre Library on 29 Nov 1991 in New Delhi.

027.4546 Public Libraries – Jammu & Kashmir

1203

Shafi, S M and **Rufai, Reyaz**

Public libraries in Jammu & Kashmir : An appraisal, *Granthana* 2(2) July 1991 : 169-177.

Discusses briefly history of public libraries in Jammu & Kashmir.

Surveys their present status in terms of collection, finance, and personnel with regard to last three years. Gauges the prominent features and shortcomings of the public library system. Concludes with suggestions for improving the system.

027.45475 Public Libraries – Gujarat

Upadhyay, H J

1204

Gujarat and its libraries, *Granthana* 2(2) July 1991 : 123-133.

Discusses the administrative set up of public libraries and various kinds of assistance given by it for its promotion. Deals briefly with procedure of starting a new library. Dwells fairly on public library system in Gujarat. Suggests to have trained librarians and library extension programme.

027.454792 Public Libraries – Maharashtra

Chahande, M S

1205

Development of public libraries in Maharashtra, *Granthana* 2(2) July 1991 : 183-192.

Traces growth of public libraries in Maharashtra from the pre-independence era to date. Deals comprehensively with public, library system currently prevalent in Maharashtra, staffing pattern, financing, training, etc. Touches briefly on impact of RRRLF assistance on development of public libraries in Maharashtra.

027.454799 Public Libraries – Goa

Rodgrigues, Pia De Menezes

1206

Central Library, Panaji, Goa : Brief sketch with special reference to local history collection, *HLAICI*, v 8, 199-209.

Gives brief history (pre-liberation period) of the Central Library. Gives post-liberation period of its development of this Library. Discusses financial resources and budget, staffing pattern, collection, lending section, reference section, children section, local history and rare book collection, books on Goa and Indo-Portuguese history, official correspondence and documents, ecclesiastical documents and history, bound newspapers and journals published in Goa, books received under the 1867 Act, services, uses, future planning, etc.

027.4548 Public Libraries – South India

Raman Nair, R 1207

Public library system in ancient South India, *ILA Bull* 27(2) July-Sept 1991 : 68-75.

States that the concept of free public library service goes back to ancient times. Mentions that government of those times were aware of their role. Evaluates free library service system that existed in South India. Evaluates the collection, access, service, professional status of librarians and the laws relating to them.

027.45482 Public Libraries – Tamil Nadu

Seethapathy, R K and **Ramesh Babu, B** 1208

New challenges to the public library systems in Tamil Nadu, *NIPP*, 243-248.

Highlights significance of an effective public library system (PLS). Enumerates factors demanding change in the existing PLS in Tamil Nadu. Describes the challenges to develop existing PLS in Tamil Nadu such as application of IT, impact of distance education, creation of networks, mobilisation of financial resources, man-power development, bibliographic organisation, etc.

027.45483 Public Libraries – Kerala

Abraham, Thomas 1209

Kottayam Public Library : A citadel of learning, *HLAICI*, v 8, 189-191.

Traces the history of the Kottayam Public Library through the last hundred years. Describes the activities of this Library, donations received, collections built, children library project, financed through members subscription being a private library, extension project of KPL Cultural Society.

Devarajan, G 1210

Changing concept of public library development in Kerala, *PLSI*, 34-42.

Defines public library. Describes historical development of public library in Kerala since 19th century through plan periods. Gives contribution of Raja Rammohun Roy Library Foundation. Discusses enactment of library legislation in Kerala.

Thomas, Kurian K 1211

Trivandrum Public Library, Kottayam : Archana Printers and Publishers, 1989. 144 p.

Relates the genesis of Trivandrum Public Library, its early history, major events, State Central Library, library movement, and its development in 7 chapters. Includes 12 appendices, and many tables.

027.45484 Public Libraries – Andhra Pradesh

Burhanuddin, Mohamed and **Taher, Mohamed** 1212

States Central Library, Andhra Pradesh : A centennial review (1891-1990), *HLAICI*, v 9, Pt 1, 154-164.

Mentions development of public libraries in India and the SCL, Andhra Pradesh. Describes its collection of all types, staff, acquisition, processing, finance. Gives a plan for action and the strategy for future.

Dutta, T C 1213

Library pilgrimage to Andhra, *Her Lib Sci* 30(1-2) Jan-Apr 1991: 34-35.

Pays rich tributes to the inspiration and guidance of I V R in laying the foundation of library movement in Bengal and public library movement in India. Describes tour of Andhra Pradesh guided by I V R and its impact.

Raju, A A N 1214

Constraints on the public library services in Andhra Pradesh, *CLIS Observer* 7(3-4) July-Dec 1990 : 69-72.

Evaluates the working of the A P Public Libraries Act and its contribution towards the development of public library services in the state. States that the achievements of the Act have been much below the expectations and the results not commensurate with the public funds being incurred.

027.463 Public Libraries – Ethiopia

Job, M M 1215

Public libraries in Ethiopia, *Her Lib Sci* 29(3-4) July-Oct 1990 : 173-179.

Surveys historical development of public libraries in Ethiopia.

Mentions activities of the National Library and Archives, etc. Examines total intake of books in public libraries, reading rooms. Brings out state of affairs of reading materials and rural newspapers. Gives general set up of Ethiopian Library Association. Mentions need for local initiative for improvement of public libraries.

027.466 Public Libraries – West Africa

Aina, Joseph O 1216

Public libraries in West Africa : A case study in an investigation into time of opening, *Int Lib Move* 12(4) Dec 1990 : 213-219.

Describes the state of public libraries in West Africa, particularly Nigeria, based on a questionnaire-based study of 19 states in Nigeria, receiving 50 responds from only ten states. States that public library development here leaves much to be desired. Gives suggestions.

027.4669 Public Libraries – Nigeria

Apeji, Adeche 1217

Libraries, information and democracy : A synthesis, *Int Lib Move* 12(3) Sept 1990 : 161-168.

Provides historical background of public library movement in general and in Nigeria in particular. Deals with the problems of actualizing the concept of democratised library services to serve the rural population, the non-literate, the female, the adolescent, the handicapped, etc.

Oyesiku, F A 1218

Setting up libraries in rural areas in Nigeria : A practical approach, *Int Lib Move* 13 (4) Dec 1991 : 189-194.

Deals with the state of the art of public libraries in Nigeria. Explains the ways with which the idea for need of the library can be sown in the minds of people. Mentions actual development of the library.

027.5 NATIONAL LIBRARIES

027.554 National Libraries – India

Barua, B P 1219

National library system for India – a policy perspective, *Granthana* 2(2) July 1991 : 103-121.

Defines national library. Enumerates function of National Library. Discusses a brief history of National Library from 1835 to the passing of National Library of India Act, 1976. Stresses on rationalization of deposit collection laws. Makes reference to organisation of British Library, Library of Congress, Lenin State Library. Discusses deficiencies of National Library. Makes recommendations to the development of a National Library System for India for preserving cultural heritage.

Dasgupta, Kalpana 1220

Personal papers in India's National Library, *HLAICI*, v 9, Pt 2, 448-453.

Gives brief history of National Library. Describes the private archives received in the National Library from various individuals. Explains Sapru papers, Ramananda Chatterjee collection, Tagore letters, Bose family correspondence. Gives conservation and preservation of rare materials.

Joseph, A and **Ramani, C M** 1221

National Science library – its place in S & T information set up in the country, *NIPP*, 97-102.

Examines scope and objective by the National Science Library. Traces its development. Examines its acquisition policy relating to monographs, conference proceedings, reports, theses and periodicals. Makes suggestions for strengthening its collections to meet users needs and to provide quick and efficient document back up service.

027.573 National Libraries – USA

Crawford, John C 1222

The Library of Congress Office, New Delhi, *HLAICI*, v 8, 143-148.

Narrates the establishment of the Library of Congress Office in the name of American Libraries Book Procurement Centre in 1954. Lists participating libraries getting the Indian materials in the US which is also catalogued here. Describes the development of this office and switching to AACR – 2, use of computer, MARC. Mentions other services of the Office also.

MACRO-organization concept for the Library of Congress : Fact sheet, *Her Lib Sci* 29(1-2) Jan-Apr 1990 : 104-106. 1223

Explains the new macro-organizational concept of Library of Congress operations as given by its Librarian James H Billington for measuring the Library of Congress.

National Institute of Health, Maryland (US) 1224

AIDS information resources, *INICAE* 10 (1) Mar 1991 : 101-103.

Describes about the National Library of Medicine (US) and its resources developed on AIDS, such as AIDSLINE, DIRLINE, AIDS Biblio, etc.

027.6 LIBRARIES/LIBRARY SERVICES FOR SPECIAL GROUPS

Janardana Rao, S S 1225

Library services for professional groups, *ILA Bull* 26(4) Jan-Mar 1991 : 207-210.

Defines characteristics of public libraries on the basis of various definitions. States that public library definition should also include services to the disadvantaged reader. Explains such disadvantaged groups as illiterates, patients in hospitals, prisoners, blind women and children, minorities, etc who need greater attention.

027.652 Libraries for Children

Mudhok, M V 1226

Children's libraries : A study, New Delhi : Ashish Publishing House, 1990. vi, 84 p.

Deals with the provision of library services to children through separate libraries for them. Explains in different chapters various procedures followed and services given in children libraries which are essential for their all round development.

027.63 (1) Libraries for Women

Baradol, A K 1227

Separate libraries for the women in Karnataka, *PL*, 98-104.

Stresses need for separate libraries for women for such reasons as adult education, women's need for information, etc. Mentions agencies which can take up responsibilities. Presents scene in other states in India discussing existing facilities in Karnataka. Makes suggestions.

027.65 Parliament Libraries

Kashyap, Subhash C 1228

Information service in the Parliament of India, *HLAICI*, v 8, 130-142.

Gives importance of parliamentary information. Mentions the establishment of a library of the Indian legislature in 1921 which started expanding after 1950. Describes the Library Division, Parliament Library Information System (PARLIS), Reference and Documentation Division, Research & Information Division, Press and Public Relations Divisions, Parliamentary Museum and Archives Division, Research and Information Services in Hindi.

Robinson, William H 1229

Building a parliamentary research capability, *Jl Lib & Inf Sci* 16(1) June 1991 : 34-47.

Discusses some linkages connecting information, legislatures and democracy. Considers some fundamental design issues. Gives more detailed choices in terms of size and make up of staff, internal organisation. Describes operating styles including institutional culture and values, and ways of relating to the outside world of clients. Concludes with a case study tracing the modes of operation of the Congressional Research Service of the Library of Congress.

027.662 Hospital Libraries

National Library of Medicine, USA 1230

Information services for hospitals, *INICAE* 10 (2) Sept 1991 : 237-238.

Describes about the Conference held on 17 November 1990 at

the American National Library of Medicine. Discusses about the current and future N L M activities. Offers various recommendations.

027.663 Libraries for Blind
Libraries for Visually Handicapped

Arora, Madhuri 1231

National Library for the Print Handicapped : Unique service centre for the blinds who are keen to read and study, *Aryan Heritage* Aug 1990 : 28-29.

Describes its establishment, library building, equipments, studios, and recording, library collection that includes talking books, brailles magazines, etc, braille press, publications, membership of this National Library. Also discusses special features and future plans.

Karisiddappa, C R 1232

Information services in visual disabilities : Seminar report, *Her Lib Sci* 30 (1-2) Jan-Apr 1991 : 89-90.

Reports about the National Seminar on 'Information Services in Visual Disabilities' at the National Institute for the Visually Handicapped, Dehradun from 3-5 Sept 1990. Describes about the papers presented, discussion held, and resolutions passed.

027.663 (1) NIMH Library

Reddy, S H R 1233

National Institute for the Mentally Handicapped : Library & documentation activities, *HLAICI*, v 8, 175-179.

Mentions the setting up of the Institute. Enumerates its objectives, service programmes, extension services, training programmes, and research activities. Explains library and documentation activities of NIMH such as collection development, information services, answering the technical queries.

027.68 Libraries for Non-Profit Organizations
Libraries for Learned Societies

027.68 (1) American Institute of Indian Studies

Gupta, B M 1234

American Institute of Indian Studies, *HLAICI*, v 9, Pt 1, 53-61.

Describes the establishment of American Institute of Indian Studies, its organisation, research programmes, programme activities. Discusses about its library, photographic archives, and publications.

027.68 (1) American Studies Research Centre Library

Taher, Mohamed and **Gupta, B M** 1235

American Studies Research Centre : Library & information services, *HLAICI*, v 8, 165-174.

Mentions setting up of American Studies Research Centre, Hyderabad. Gives its establishment and activities. Describes the various activities of ASRC's library such as collection development, special collections, information services and products.

027.68(1) Arabic and Persian Research Institute, Library

Khan, Shaukat Ali 1236

Arabic and Persian Research Institute, Tonk, *HLAICI*, v 9, Pt 2, 243-250.

Gives aims and objectives, academic and cultural activities of the Institute. Describes the source material in its reference library, the new building, school of oriental studies, etc. Mentions about translation work, exhibition and publication work.

027.68 (1) Asiatic Society Library

Joshi, V 1237

Asiatic Society Library, Bombay, *HLAICI*, v 9, Pt 1, 85-87.

Describes the birth of the Society in 1804, its library collection, special collections, classifications system, dissemination of information, particularly through its *Transactions*.

Kabir, A F M Fazle 1238

Asiatic Society Library of Bengal, *HLAICI*, v 9, Pt. 1, 177-194.

Traces origin and development of the Asiatic Society and its Library. Describes the collection development over the years with two distinct divisions of European books and Oriental library. Gives a partial list of publications in Appendix.

027.68 (1) CIBS Library

Dolma, Tsewang 1239

Central Institute of Buddhist Studies, *HLAICI*, v 9, Pt 2, 301-302.

Mentions the establishment of the Institute in 1959 which also imparts traditional education to students. Describes the library collection of about 20,000 manuscripts, books, reports, journals related to Buddhist studies. Appends a list of publications.

027.68 (1) CIIL Library

Murty, Sulochana S 1240

Central Institute of Indian Languages; library, documentation and information activities, *HLACI*, v 9, Pt 1, 18-30.

Provides objectives of CIIL. Deals with its library, information processing, information services, membership, current projects, future plans. Explains the need for National Information Centre for Indian Languages and computerised database for Indian languages.

027.68 (1) Guru Nanak Foundation Library

Rajwant Singh and **Lamba, Navneet** 1241

Guru Nanak Foundation and information sources on Sikh studies, *HLAICI*, v 9, Pt 1, 213-219.

Gives a brief history of the Foundation and its aims and objectives. Mentions its academic programmes. Relates its library and information services. Gives its value as research and reference library. Mentions its publications, and Information sources in sikh studies.

027.68 (1) Historical Research Libraries

de Souza, Teotonio R 1242

Xavier Centre of Historical Research, *HLAICI*, v 9, Pt 2, 239-242.

Set up in 1977, it has developed a research library having good collection of books, rare atlases, government reports, seminar papers, dissertations, bibliographies, etc. States that the Centre holds seminars, Portuguese language courses, etc.

Gupta, B M 1243

Bharat Itihasa Samshodhaka Mandala, Pune, *HLAICI*, v 9, Pt 2, 293-300.

Explains the need of such an Institute. Discusses its management and finance. Gives the aims and objectives. Mentions the achievements of the Mandala. Describes the archival repository. Lists the publications.

Janaki, S S 1244

The Kuppuswami Sastri Research Institute, Madras, *HLAICI*, v 9, Pt 2, 258-260.

Describes about the collection of books, journals, etc of the library of this Institute, the projects taken, research done, seminars organised, and publications.

027.68 (1) Indian Association for the Study of Conservation of Cultural Property

Bist, A S 1245

Indian Association for the Study of Conservation of Cultural Property, *HLAICI*, v 10, 72-75.

States the aims and objectives of the Association. Gives its management, finances and membership. Describes its activities including seminars, lectures, publications, etc. Mentions nature of professional issues taken up. Gives international relations.

027.68 (1) ICPR Library

Mukherjee, A 1246

Indian Council of Philosophical Research, *HLAICI*, v 9, Pt 1, 62-64.

Gives its origin and major areas of activities. Describes its activities such as fellowship scheme, seminars, conferences, publications. Explains the library and information services of the Council.

027.68 (1) IIIS Library

Ali, S A 1247

Indian Institute of Islamic Studies; archival, library and publication activities, *HLAICI*, v 9, Pt 2, 251-253.

Discusses about this important Institute meant for study and research of Islamic religion, culture and civilization. Describes various sections of the library. Mentions important research publications.

027.68 (1) IIM Library

Raina, Roshan 1248

Indian Institute of Management Lucknow (IIML) and its library, *HLAICI*, v 8, 244-255.

States the objectives of the IIM of Lucknow. Describes a diverse range of academic activities aimed at creation, dissemination and application of management knowledge and know-how. Gives objectives of the Library. Discusses such activities as resources, facilities, library computerization, and services. Appends a list of projects undertaken, and a list of backfiles of periodicals in microforms.

027.68 (1) IIMC Library

Prasad, B K 1249

Indian Institute of Mass Communication; library and documentation activities, *HLAICI*, v 8, 43-46.

Identifies main functions of the Institute. Describes its academic activities. Discusses the library and information activities of the IIMC. Gives its future programmes.

027.68 (1) IIPA Library

Ragavan, M C 1250

Indian Institute of Public Administration : Library and information services, *HLAICI*, v 8, 180-188.

Discusses public administration as a discipline. Describes the objectives of Library of the IIPA established in 1954. Explains activities of the Library such as collection development, database, information services including CAS, documentation, press clippings service, literature search and bibliography, reference and referral service, etc, Appends a list of publication of IIPA.

027.68 (1) IGNCA Library

Indira Gandhi National Centre for the Arts (IGNCA), *HLAICI*, v 9 Pt 2, 474-482. 1251

States the aims of IGNCA. Mentions its divisions : Kalanidhi, Kalakeva, etc. Describes the library having multilingual printed material comprising various collections, microfilm, visual library and slide collection. States that it is being developed as National Information System and Databank on art, humanities and cultural heritage. Describes cultural archives on literature, music, dance, theatre, etc.

027.68 (1) NCAER Library

Sebaston, N J 1252

National Council of Applied Economic Research : Library and information activities, *HLAICI*, v 8, 161-164.

Describes the library and information activities of the NCAER including its collection, computerisation, database, services. Appends a list of NCAER publications.

027.68 (1) NCERT Library

Alag, Polly 1253

National Council of Educational Research and Training: Library and information activities, *HLAICI*, v 8, 47-54.

Gives objectives and programmes of the NCERT. Discusses the setting up of its Library, Documentation & Information, place of library, its collection, sequences. Mentions recommendations of various committees. Describes objectives of DLDI, collection development, library and information services, in-service training programme. Also gives future plans.

Malhotra, Nirmal 1254

The National Institute of Educational Planning and Administration; library and information services, *HLAICI*, v 8, 55-59.

Lists main functions of NIEPA, its activities like research, training, publications. Describes activities of its library as collection development, documentation services, etc, its role as sub-national documentation unit.

027.68 (1) NIDRC Library

Majumdar, Swadha 1255

National Institute of Design Resource Centre, *HLAICI*, v 9, Pt 1, 31-35.

Lists main objectives of the Institute, professional education programmes. Describes its resource centre (library) and information services. Gives a list a publications.

27.68(1) NSD Library

Sivaramayya, B Leela 1256

National School of Drama; library and information services, *HLAICI*, v 9, Pt 1, 36-45.

Describes the library of the National School of Drama (NSD), its resources on drama and plays, classification schemes, cataloguing system, etc. Also gives the proposed documentation services.

027.68 (1) Oriental Research Libraries

Ahmad, K Md 1257

Abul Kalam Azad Oriental Research Institute, *HLAICI*, v 9, Pt 2, 279-284.

Deals with the research work done and publications brought out by the Institute, particularly the Urdu Encyclopaedia. Mentions about the seminars, conferences, lectures organised. States that its library is well developed with literature on Indian culture. Has other collection also. Includes a list of publications.

Bhaskaran, T 1258

The Oriental Research Institute and Manuscript Library, *HLAICI*, v 9, Pt 2, 285-288.

Gives history of the Institute. Describes the Manuscript collection of its library and its preservation. Explains about the publications including the Index of about 28,000 Mss. Also has palm-leaf Mss.

Bhatia, K C 1259

Vrindaban Research Institute; archival, library and publication activities, *HLAICI* v 9, Pt 2, 254-257.

Explains that the Institute has four departments : Manuscripts and Reference Library, Conservation, Microfilming and Office. Discusses about the rich collection of Mss, their conservation and preservation, reprography, and publications.

Chaubey, B B 1260

Vishveshvaranand Vishva Bandhu Institute of Sanskrit & Indological Studies, *HLAICI*, v 9, Pt, 2, 266-272.

Traces history of VVRI. Describes collection development of Mss in the library. Gives account of other activities as postgraduate oriental teaching section, research section. Includes a list of its publications.

Johnson, Donald Clay 1261

On the origin of the Bhandarkar Oriental Research Institute Library – Part I : The initiation of the searches for Sanskrit Manuscripts in Bombay, *HLAICI*, v 9, Pt 1, 195-205.

Traces development of this Library with government support after extensive searches for manuscript collection. States that it proved very valuable to scholars in India and abroad.

Ladu, S D 1262

Bhandarkar Oriental Research Institute; archival, library and publication activities, *HLAICI*, v 9, Pt 2, 306-314.

Explains that the Institute works through its five main departments : Postgraduate teaching and research, Mahabharata and research unit, Prakrit dictionary project, Publication, and Mss. Discusses about the library and archival activity, Govt. Mss library with some unique Mss. Appends a list of publications.

Pathak, P D 1263

Rajasthan Oriental Research Institute, Jodhpur, *HLAICI*, v 9 (Pt 2, 273-278.

Spells out aims and objectives of the Institute. Describes the Manuscripts collection in the Institute library and their catalogues for the use of scholars. Mentions about its publication. Appends a list of the publications.

Sood, H R 1264

Rampura Raza Library : past and present activities, *HLAICI*, v 9, Pt 1, 95-97.

Deals with this well known oriental library of Rampur possessing printed books, Manuscripts and rare paintings (including Bhoj-patras) in various languages.

Venkatappaiah, V 1265

Andhra Pradesh Governmental Oriental Manuscript Library and Research Institute, Hyderabad, *HLAICI*, v 9, Pt 2, 261-265.

Describes the collection development of Manuscripts of this library since its establishment, the catalogues prepared, publications, research scholarships. Also gives future plans. Appends a list publications.

Venkatappaiah, V 1266

Shri Venkateshwara Oriental Research Institute, Tirupati, *HLAICI*, v 9, Pt 2, 289-292.

Describes the activities of the Institute after its reorganisation. Describes the treasure of books and manuscripts it has in its possession.

027.68 (1) PID Library

Nathan, S S 1267

Publications and Information Directorate (PID), *HLAICI*, v 7, 103-113.

Mentions basic objectives of PID. Gives its organizational structure, staff and budget. Provides information about research and popular periodicals, Wealth of India project, planning and research, S & T information services division, MAPIS, infrastructural facilities, and other activities.

027.68 (1) Saraswati Niketanam Library

Venkatappaiah, V 1268

Saraswati Niketanam, Vetapalem, *HLAICI*, v 9, Pt 1, 228-231.

Mentions aims and objectives of this Institute. Describes its books and periodicals, library services and other activities.

027.68 (1) Shri Krishan Devarya Andhra Bhasha Nilayam

Venkatappaiah, V 1269

Shri Krishna Devarya Andhra Bhasha Nilayam, Hyderabad, *HLAICI*, v 9, Pt 1, 174-176.

Deals with this Library as the Centre of all activities of Telugu people. Mentions aims and objectives. Describes reading material, other activities, and the impact of the library.

027.68 (1) Tibetology Libraries

Chonpal, Ngwang 1270

Central Institute of Higher Tibetan Studies (Shantarakshita Library-collections and services), *HLAICI*, v 9, Pt 1, 65-72.

Deals with the Library of the Institute giving its collections, etc. Lists publications of the Institute in Appendix.

1271

Sikkim Research Institute of Tibetology, *HLAICI*, v 9, Pt 2, 303-305.

States aims and objectives of this Institute. Discusses research activities. Describes the library collections of wrappers, treatises and tracts, books of all sects, etc. Has a museum also. Mentions some of its publications.

027.68 (1) Museum Libraries

Khan, Rahmat Ali 1272

Salar Jung Museum and Library, *HLAICI*, v 9, Pt 1, 73-76.

Deals with the activities of the museum and the library containing about 10,000 rare and illustrated Manuscripts from Arabia, Turkey, Iran, India, etc.

Mukherjee, D T 1273

Indian Museum, Calcutta (library, documentation and information activities), *HLAICI*, v 9, Pt 1, 77-84.

Gives description of the museum objects, its activities. Discusses the library and information activities also. Mentions its publications in Appendix.

Verma, Kanwal 1274

Nehru Memorial Museum and Library, *HLAICI*, v 8, 149-160.

Mentions the setting up and objectives of the Nehru Memorial Museum and Library which is divided into different divisions. Describes the activities of Museum, Library, Manuscript division, Oral history division, Research and Publications division, Reprography and Preservation division. Appends a list of publications of this Institute.

0.27.69 Industrial Libraries.
Business Libraries

Industrial Information system in private sector, *RILISAR Bull* 7(1-4) Jan-Dec 1991 : 1-5. 1275

States that industrial information systems are in primitive stage in developing countries. Makes a case for industrial information system with the participation of private sector to develop an INDNET. Gives also the strategy.

Seetharama, S 1276

Information services to small scale industry, *ISL*, 66-92.

Discusses recent developments in small scale industries and varieties of services that could be rendered by the Documentation Unit of an Industrial Information Centre.

Sinha, S C 1277

Forty-five years of a specialist library in the area of building research in Indian context : A case study of CBRI, Roorkee, *Ind Jl Inf Lib & Society* 4 (3-4) Sept-Dec 1991 : 292-293.

Traces the history of establishment of CBRI, Roorkee. Discusses development of the library during 1947-91. Analyses data about library holdings. Discusses procurement of documents, their processing till they are placed on the shelf. Gives suggestions.

027.7 ACADEMIC LIBRARIES

Chandel, A S and **Saraf, Veena** 1278

Teaching role of academic libraries : Fact or assumption, *DLIS*, 43-50.

Underlines that library profession and services are not given due recognition and status even in academic circles, status dilemma and semi-professional activities. Looks critically at the library instruction, staff inadequacy, faculty attitude, etc. Concludes that profession has to meet the challenge to improve higher education by integrating it with library work.

Esperanza, M (Sister) 1279

Academic libraries as viewed by readers, *Ind Jl Inf Lib & Society* 3(1-2) Mar-June 1990 : 67-75.

Relates the evaluation of libraries given by the various readers from academic institution and in this view discusses importance of libraries and their functioning. Describes expectations of readers. Points out ills libraries are afflicted with.

Meera, B M 1280

Utility factors in research support services of academic library, *Lib Sci slant Doc & Inf Std* 28(1) Mar 1991 : 36-41.

Discusses utility analysis, its importance and need for such a study in a library particularly in ISI, Central Library Bangalore. Measures its benefits or the effectiveness in terms of research publications of the users of the library and evaluates against the cost structure of the system.

027.7 (1) Academic Libraries and NEP

Kemparaju, T D 1281

New Education Policy and academic libraries : Need for revitalisation, *LISE*, 197-206.

Discusses NEP of 1986 giving its objectives. Makes review of education commissions and academic library. Describes various problems faced by the academic libraries in the country.

027. 70954 Academic Libraries – India

Sahai, S N 1282

Academic Library system, New Delhi : Allied Publishers, 1990. xi, 324 p.

Includes 8 chapters on library in academic system, library governance, library finance, library building and furniture, library collection, organization and administration, library staff and library services. Develops as comprehensive text discussing academic library system, addressed to, besides librarians, university and government administrators and faculty.

Sewa Singh 1283

Academic librarianship in India : A literature survey, *LISE*, 155-165.

Analyses contributions to academic librarianship in India as reported in LIS journals, books, monographs, etc. up to 1985. Studies data on chronological scatter, subject scatter, article scatter, etc. Makes some suggestions in this area.

027.71 College Libraries

Bavakutty, M 1284

The college library, *LISE*, 166-172.

Lists objectives of a library in higher educational institutions. Discusses college libraries in India. Describes importance of libraries in higher education on the basis of the recommendations of various commissions.

Sharma, H D and **Singh, B N** 1285

Manual for college libraries, Varanasi : Indian Bibliographic Centre, 1990. 325 p.

Divided into 22 chapters on such aspects of college librarianship as collection development, classification, cataloguing, reference service, circulation, public relations, etc. Also discusses administrative problems of librarians. Includes appendices.

027.7154 College Libraries – India

Boonlia, Naresh 1286

National information programme for college libraries : A crying need, *NIPP,* 253-257.

Evaluates critically the present state of college libraries in India. Discusses the underlying factors such as attitude of the management, and teachers, and their impacts. Suggests the essential programmes to develop college libraries.

University Grants Commission (India), Library Committee (Ranganathan Committee (1957) 1287

Recommendations, *OSUL*, 243-255.

Includes 63 recommendations of the UGC Library Committee (1957) on grant, library fund, book selection and book purchase, promotion of reading habits, weeding out, documentation, library staff, department of library science, library buildings, etc in Appendix II.

027.715414 College Libraries – West Bengal

Chatterjee, Sunil Kumar 1288

Carey Library, Serampore College; a national heritage, *HLAICI*, v 9, Pt 1, 126-137.

Traces history since 1800. Describes the collections and their richness in content. Also gives microfilm and microfiche collections. Describes facilities and services. Mentions users, fields of study, academic activities, and support.

Mukhopadhyay, Bijayanath 1289

Sanskrit College Library, Calcutta, *HLAICI*, v 9, Pt 1 142-153.

Deals with establishment and development of this college library. Describes the Manuscripts collection and its catalogues. Discusses the Mss section, printed book section. Explains space problem, which was solved. Mentions other facilities and services of this old library.

027.7154 College Libraries – Delhi

Krishan Kumar and **Datta, N** 1290

Delhi University college libraries : An overview, *CPT*, 72-81.

Discusses objectives of a college library. Describes present situation of staff, salary scales, finance, book selection and acquisition, collection, classification, suggestions to improve situation. Concludes that college libraries have been found inadequate as instruments of instruction.

027.715492 College Libraries – Maharashtra

Deccan College: Archives and libraries, *HLAICI*, v 9, Pt 1, 232-238. 1291

Deals with development of the College since early 19th century, its archives, the library as reference library. State that it has a rich collection of Sanskrit Manuscripts, Urdu Manuscripts, and has other special collections also. Gives a list of publications also.

027.715483 College Libraries – Kerala

Raman Nair, R 1292

College libraries and the process of education, *Int Lib Move* 12(3) Sept 1990 : 153-160.

States the aim of education. Mentions process of education in relation to methods to teaching. Discusses library services as heart of college. Studies the college library service in Kerala where well-trained professional staff, suitable buildings, sensible collections, etc are essential. Discusses problems and gives solutions.

027.715487 College Libraries – Karnataka

Patil, D B 1293

College libraries in Mangalore city : A study, *Ind Jl Inf Lib & Society* 3(1-2) Mar-June 1990 : 97-106.

Describes about establishment and growth of 17 out of 22 college libraries in Mangalore city. Analyses present state of these libraries, regarding their finance, book resources, furniture and equipment. Gives suggestions to improve their services.

027.72 University Libraries

Pal, S S 1294

Constitution of authority and policy formulation for management of university record resources, *ILA Bull* 26(1) Apr-June 1990 : 51-56.

Identifies the preservation role of universities in handling records as information resources. Reports on the survey for constituting an authority for launching effective programme to supplement the university information system. Provides a model policy statement for initiating an archival cell in university libraries.

Prasher, R G 1295

Converting university libraries into commonwealth, *ULI*, 106-114.

Explains the concept of resource sharing. Gives need and discuses areas of resources such as ILL, cooperative procurement, technical operations, union catalogue, cooperative storage, borrowing to members, cooperation in documentation, exchange of publications, exchange of experts. Discusses factors that retard and promote resources sharing. Details out BOSLA experiment in India.

Raina, Roshan 1296

Applying RAT to university libraries, *ULI*, 203-213.

Brings out importance of a university library and its staff. States that university libraries have failed to achieve their objectives. Suggests the application of Role Analysis Technique (RAT) to analyse and describe the roles relations of various positions of university library. Suggests that RAT should be applied for job description of various positions.

Sandhu, S S 1297

Subject specialist university librarian, *ULI*, 84-92.

States that libraries are expanding their collections and services, and appointment of subject specialist is necessary to improve the services. Deals with the selling of library services, contact with users, visit to the department by subject specialist who participates in book selection, reference service, preparation of library guides, bibliographies, etc.

Saxena, R S 1298

Periodical section of a university library and its problems, *OSUL*, 153-163.

Mentions importance of periodical section of a university library. Describes acquisition procedure through local agents, foreign agents, finance, variation in rates, ordering directly with publishers. Mentions remedy. Describes technical processing, display and storage, service to readers, personnel requirements, etc.

Sood, S P and **Sharma, C L**, *Eds* 1299

Outstanding studies in university librarianship, Jaipur : RBSA Publishers, 1991. 277 p.

Includes 18 articles contributed by experienced and knowledgeable teachers in library and information science, and librarians from all over the country and abroad on various facets of university librarianship such as finance, services, user education, personnel, building, resource sharing, periodicals, extension services, etc.

Swaroop Rani, B S 1300

University library network : A broad spectrum, *CALNE*, 220-223.

Deals with networking and their applications in university libraries leading to the development of LAN. Suggests different network alternatives and role of university librarians as intermediary. Visualises bright future.

027.72 (1) University Libraries and Computerisation

Panigrahi, Jyotirmaya 1301

University library computerisation : Manpower development, *CALNE*, 208-213.

Considers manpower as important national resources. Stresses need of manpower development. Discusses role of computer in university libraries in view of rising costs of journals and books. Emphasises need of manpower development programmes for library professionals working in university libraries in India. Suggests that library school teachers should be given training in computer application.

Pawar, S S and **Thakar, G S** 1302

Computer application in the Library of Centre of Advanced Study in Geology (Palaentology and Himalayan Geology), Panjab University, Chandigarh – a proposal, *CALNE*, 45-52.

Traces history of the Dept of Geology, Panjab University. Describes Departmental Library, its activities and services. Describes need for automation. Proposes structure of database on DBase III plus package, and its file structure design.

Satyanarayana, R 1303

Information technology and university libraries in India, *ULI*, 19-30.

Traces briefly history of IT and defines the concept. Indicates how they affect the functioning of university libraries. Emphasises need for manpower development to meet the changing structure. Points out the need for providing adequate funds for modernising libraries and formulating of library and information policy in the country.

0.27.72 (1) Departmental Libraries

Sharma, C L 1304

The problem of departmental libraries in the university set up. *OSUL*, 68-85.

Defines departmental library and its genesis and growth. Puts forward arguments in favour of decentralized collections as well as centralised collection. Gives opinion of some expert committees. Describes existing conditions of departmental libraries in some countries. Discusses modern patterns and trends towards a compromise.

027.7242 University Libraries – UK

University Grants Committee (Great Britain), Committee on Libraries (Parry Committee) (1963) 1305

Recommendations, *OSUL*, 265-273.

Includes recommendations in Appendix V of the Parry Committee (1963) of UK on such aspects as library cooperation. Collections, ILL, acquisition of library material, acquisition of foreign material, the National Library, library services, library techniques, administration and staffing and finance.

027.7244 University Libraries – France

Renoult, Daniel 1306

University libraries, *Jl Lib & Inf Sci* 16(1) June 1991 : 60-69.

Discusses growth and development of university libraries in France since 1960s. Examines impact of increase in student enrolment on library services. Discusses funding system. Emphasises need for funding for personnel, building, and documents. Brings out need for cooperation among different university libraries. Examines progress in modernization of libraries.

027.7254 University Libraries – India

First Seminar of University Librarians in India (Jaipur) (1966) 1307

Recommendations, *OSUL*, 260-264.

Includes in Appendix IV the recommendations of the First Seminar of University Librarians in India on such aspects as government of the library, library staff, acquisition, strengthening of book resources and services, ILL, loss of books, UGC, and general recommendations.

Kankachary, M 1308

New role of university librarian in the present information age, *SALP*, 92.

Suggests that activities of libraries are to be changed in the modern context; the powers and responsibilities are to be redefined. Suggests that librarians should constantly review their methods. Makes a case for in-service training courses by ILA, IASLIC.

Karisiddappa, C R and **Sangam, S L** 1309

University libraries : Problems and prospects, *LISE*, 173-180.

Describes importance of university libraries. Discusses the present position of the university libraries upto the Seventh Five Year Plan. Lists some common problems of these libraries. Gives the perspective of the 21st century and identifies such issues as book budget, resource sharing, professional staff, library buildings, library and information service, user education, etc.

Prasher, R G 1310

Information technology and Indian university libraries, *CLIS Observer* 7(1-2) Jan-June 1990 : 5-15.

Explains the concept of IT and its importance. Deals with recent developments in the realm of computer and communication technology. Presents a status report on computer applications in India in general and in university libraries in particular. Concludes that computerisation is no panacea for all ills afflicting the libraries in India.

Prasher, R G 1311

Present day university library : Its obligations, *ULI*, 5-12.

States aims of education with views of various committees. Gives functions of a modern university. Brings out importance of a university library. States that the main function of a university library is to promote higher education and support teaching, research and extension programmes of a university.

Prasher, R G, *Ed* 1312

University libraries in India; 1980s and beyond : Essays in honour of Professor T P Saxena, New Delhi: Medallion Press, 1991. viii, 290 p.

Covers 27 papers which throw light on some of the important facets of university librarianship in Indian context. Divides them in ten sections : General aspects, acquisition function, reference service, microforms, resource sharing, classification and cataloguing, library finance, personnel, library building and LIS education.

Ramaiah, L S 1313

Bibliographical control among Indian university libraries : The need for an IULNET to improve the quality of services to the academic community, *DLIS,* 59-65.

Gives status of higher education and importance of university libraries in India. Lays importance on networking for resource sharing among university libraries. Emphasises need for IULNET consisting of three units. Mentions tools and operations.

Sharma, C D 1314

Problems of university libraries in India, *OSUL,* 211-221.

Explains objectives of university library. Gives importance of university libraries in India after independence. Discusses the problems of the users, problems of collection, and problems of the personnel in university libraries in India. Also deals with professional education. Offers some remedies.

Srivastava, A P 1315

From departmental libraries to national network, *ILA Bull* 25(4) Jan-Mar 1990 : 157-178.

Describes departmental libraries and UGC Library Committee recommendation for scrapping traditional departmental libraries. Stresses the need for raising the quality of our university library services. Explains the need of library technology for utilisation of knowledge. Gives such system of knowledge utilisation of technology. Points out need for Regional Library Centres as suggested in the Report of Association of Indian Universities. States that creation of a network through modern technology like INFLIBNET. Reports India's progress in IT.

Srivastava, A P 1316

State of university libraries and learning before Independence, *Her Lib Sci* 29(1-2) Jan-Apr 1990 : 11-24.

Points out limitations in evaluating history of libraries. Discusses the establishment of Fort William College, etc, Woods Despatch, first three universities set up in 1857 and their libraries. Describes recommendations of various commissions and committees set up before Independence. Reveals lack of qualified manpower. Refers to the work of Ranganathan. Describes contribution of university libraries to the development of learning and higher education.

University Education Commission (India) (Radhakrishnan Commission) (1948) 1317

Recommendations, *OSUL*, 238-242.

Includes recommendations of Radhakrishnan Commission of 1948 on libraries etc from number 50 to 58 on staff, grants to teachers for books, grants for libraries, open access, hours of work. organisation of a library, etc in Appendix I.

027.725412 University Libraries – Bihar

027.725412 (1) Rajendra Agricultural University Library

Arjun Lal 1318

Rajendra Agricultural University Library, Bihar; at a glance, *Lib Her* 29(2-4) Oct 1990 – Jan 1991: 153-176.

Traces history and growth of this University and development of its Library since 1974 to date. Describes physical layout, collection, services, etc. Gives details of book budget, staff position, future programme, etc.

027.72542 University Libraries – UP

027.72542 (1) Aligarh Muslim University Library

Khan, Noorul Hasan 1319

Aligarh Muslim University, Maulana Azad Library; Manuscript collection, *HLAICI*, v 9, Pt 1 206-208.

Deals with the Manuscript collection of this famous library in various Indian and foreign languages. Also mentions about paintings, coins, royal edicts, etc.

Qureshi, Ishrat Ali 1320

Maulana Azad Library : A major library of the world, 1877-1988, Aligarh : Anwar Publishing House, 1989. 179 p.

Presents in 8 chapters a detailed study of the Maulana Azad Library. Highlights its invaluable treasure of Oriental collections of Mss, printed books, and its rich collections in Occidental languages. Makes a comparative study of Aligarh Muslim University with Banaras Hindu University and University of Delhi.

027.72544 University Libraries – Rajasthan

027.72544 (1) Banasthali Vidyapeeth Library

Narinder Kumar, Girish Chandra and **Gauda, Hargovind** 1321

Banasthali Vidyapeeth Library : A case study, *Lib Her* 27(3-4) Oct 1988-Jan 1989 : 120-127.

Provides history of Banasthali. Discusses collection, processing, users, services, staff strength of the library.

027.725455 University Libraries – Punjab

Bansal, G C and **Tikku, U K** 1322

University library services in Punjab, *ULI*, 31-40.

Briefly discusses Punjab, its area, population and literacy rate. Brings out genesis and growth of university libraries of Punjab. Gives collection, current journals, membership and use of these libraries. Deals with the services offered, pointing out some limitations. Offers suggestions for improvement of services.

027.725475 University Libraries – Gujarat

Tejomurty, A and **Shukla, K H** 1323

Expenditure of the university libraries in Gujarat : An analysis, *Lib Her* 29 (1-2) Apr - Sept 1990 : 9-33.

Classifies expenditure into recurring and non-recurring. Discusses university library-wise expenditure in Gujarat. Describes growth of expenditure from Plan I to VII. Discusses proportion of library expenditure university-wise to their total university expenditure. Mentions budgetary standards.

Tejomurty, A and **Shukla, K H** 1324

University library services in Gujarat, *Ind Jl Inf Lib & Society* 3(3-4) Sept-Dec 1990 : 235-251.

Gives importance of university library. Mentions working hours of university libraries in Gujarat. Explains various technical services and readers' services as provided in these university libraries.

027.725475 (1) Gujarat Vidyapith Library

Books Read by Gandhiji : List of holdings in Gandhi Adhyana Section, Gujarat Vidyapith Library, *Univ News* 28(41) Oct 8, 1990 : 35-38. 1325

Provides a list of 63 books read by Gandhiji on various subjects as biology, medicine, mysticism, fine arts, literature, religion, economics, philosophy, geography, sociology, etc available in Gujarat Vidyapith Library.

027.725492 University Libraries – Maharashtra

027.7254792 (1) SNDT Women's University Library

Deokatley, Sangeeta 1326

SNDT Women's University : Research Centre for Women Studies Documentation Centre, *HLAICI*, v 8, 75-77.

Explains the activities such as collection development, library and information services, information networking, computerisation of the Library and Documentation Centre.

027.725484 University Libraries – Andhra Pradesh

027.725484 (1) Nagarjuna University Library

Rama Rao, T 1327

Nagarjuna University Library : A retrospect with a plea for more services, *Ind Jl Inf Lib & Society* 4(3-4) Sept – Dec 1991 : 229-236.

Traces the growth of Nagarjuna University Library in terms of documents, readers, staff. Points out the amounts spent of library and documents. Discusses the importance of reference and documentation services. Pleads for their introduction to satisfy the users.

027.725484 (1) University of Hyderabad Library

Reddy, E Rama, Rao, K Nagaraja and **Burhanuddin, Mohd** 1328

Computerisation of university libraries – case study of University of Hyderabad Library, *CALNE*, 1-8.

Relates the attempts to automate library functions of University of Hyderabad. Discusses the priorities to automate library functions such as cataloguing, periodicals, union list of current periodicals, staff data, IR, etc. Describes the LIBSYS software and its features. Mention future plans.

027.725484 (1) Andhra University Library

Soma Raju, P 1329

Role of university libraries in support of research, Visakhapatnam : Andhra University Press and Publications, 1990. 144p.

Based on the Ph D thesis submitted by the author, divided into 9 chapters. Deals with place of research and role of libraries, reviving earlier user studies, growth and development of Andhra University Library, limitations of the study, projects the data and information obtained and discusses library resources, facilities, etc. Contains conclusions and suggestions.

027.725492 University Libraries – Bangladesh

Rahman, Md Zillur 1330

Growth and development of university libraries in Bangladesh, *OSUL*, 222-236

Traces history of universities in Bangladesh. Discusses in detail about Dhaka University Library, Bangladesh Agricultural University Library, Bangladesh University of Engineering and Technology Library, Chittagong University Library, Jahangirnagar University Library. Describes their organisation, physical facilities etc. Gives certain recommendations.

027.726 University Libraries – Africa

Ogundipe, O O 1331

Subject specialisation in a university library, *OSUL*, 133-145.

States that subject specialisation is becoming increasingly popular in university libraries in Africa. Defines subject specialist. Describes the development of subject specialist. Discusses need and growth of subject specialisation, its advantages and its relevance to Nigeria. Gives objectives and duties of subject specialist librarian. Deals with problems of subject specialisation also.

027.72669 University Libraries – Nigeria

Agajer, James Abayomi 1332

Nigerian University Libraries (1984-1986) and the making of Nigerian nation, *Int Lib Move* 12(4) Dec 1990 : 169-179.

Traces brief history of Nigeria. Deals with the role played by the Nigerian university libraries as quasi-national library, quasi-public library, cultural role. Discusses with the manpower development, information role, research role, ancillary role, etc.

027.72678 University Libraries – Tanzania

Nyerembe, M P 1333

The university library as a teaching library : A suggested role for the library, University of Dar Es Salaam, Tanzania, *Int Lib Move* 12(2) June 1990 : 90-98.

Describes library as a teaching-learning resource. Argues that the most efficient way to make the best use of a large library is to consider it both as a university service and a teaching department. Gives goals and objectives of user education in university library.

027.8 School Libraries

Chaturvedi, D D 1334

Standards for the school libraries, *Lib Progress (Int)* 9-10 (1-2) Jan-Dec 1989 -90 : 11-23.

Discusses importance and goals of school libraries. Defines library standards. Highlights its importance. Describes the present position of school libraries in India. Points out need to have foolproof school library standards in India. Discusses some of the standards in the foreign countries and in India formulated by the ILA and the Dept of Education, UP.

027.8 (1) School Libraries and Literacy

Woolls, Blanche

Literacy and school libraries, *Jl Lib & Inf Sci* 15(2) Dec 1990 : 162-169. 1335

Defines literacy, illiteracy and related terms. Highlights the role of school libraries which can help to solve the problem of both illiteracy and aliteracy. Provides some possible solutions to the problem.

027.809485 School Libraries – Sweden

Stenberg, Christina

Literacy and the school library: librarians and teachers together against illiteracy, *Jl Lib & Inf Sci* 15(2) Dec 1990 : 153-161. 1336

Takes a small municipality in Sweden to integrate all its libraries with the school, and the main library is located on the premises of the comprehensive school. Studies the problem involved when the school and public library are joined; a close cooperation with teachers is established.

027.80954 School Libraries – India

Kalia, D R

A plea for school library foundation, *CLIS Observer* 8(3-4) July-Dec 1991 : 1-2. 1337

In this Editorial makes out a case for a School Library Foundation in the Dept of Education of the Ministry of Human Resource Development, Government of India to promote school library development in the country in collaboration with the states with its headquarters at New Delhi, and a representative in each state.

Kaula, P N

Observations on school and public library development in India, *Granthana* 2(1) Jan 1991 : 21-30. 1338

Delivered as the Keynote address at the 2nd National Seminar on Role of Public and School Libraries in the New Education Policy and Public Library and Panchayat Raj on Nov 4, 1989 at Pune. Explains in the first part status of school libraries in the context of various reports on education. States that 37.3 per cent schools in

India do not have even a room for library, elsewhere it is only a store room. Discusses in second part the role of public library in various areas of developments in the enactment of library legislation.

Taher, Mohamed 1339

Madrasa libraries in India : a case study of Nadwat al Ulama, Lucknow, *HLAICI,* v 9, Pt 1 : 112-127.

Gives the concept of Madrasa. Describes Madrasa libraries, traditional and modern. Explains in detail the Library of Nadwat al Ulama. Gives a proposal for collection development policy. Makes a case for this library as a national centre for Madrasa libraries in India.

027.809669 School Libraries – Nigeria

Oke, N A 1340

Selection techniques for an ideal school library in Nigeria, *Int Lib Move* 12(3) Sept 1990 : 143-152.

Explains need for school libraries. Gives aims and objectives of school libraries. Describes the selection technique of library material. Discusses the selection policy. Gives some recommendations.

Onadiran, G T 1341

The school library scene in Nigeria, *Int Lib Move* 12(3) Sept 1990 : 118-124.

States that libraries are essential in the educational process. Describes school library as an integral part. Discusses practical difficulties and offers solution to them. Describes the poor condition of school libraries in Nigeria which can be improved by staff, budget and materials.

028.7 Sourses of Information. Reference Sources

Manjunatha, K K 1342

Sources of agricultural information, *Lib Sci slant Docu & Inf Std* 28(4) Dec 1991 : 150-159.

Identifies the basic concepts in literature published in agricultural sciences. Describes varieties of information sources, varieties in the subjects, conventional, primary, secondary, and tertiary literature. Analyses computer based bibliographic services.

Mishra, B N 1343

Sources of information in veterinary and animal sciences in Bihar, *NIPP*, 122-124.

Identifies services and systems available in medical and veterinary sciences at the national and international level. Describes various sources of information in veterinary and animal sciences in Bihar.

Prasad, K N 1344

What and how of standards information, *Lib Sci Slant Docu & Inf Std* 27(4) Dec 1990 : 193-212.

Discusses the usefulness of standards as information carriers. Describes different information retrieval tools offered by various national and international standards bodies. Relates the standardization activities in library, documentation and information fields.

Sachdeva, D L and **Sardana, J L** 1345

Documentary literature : Their relevance in social science (A case study of University of Delhi and Jawaharlal Nehru University), *SSI*, 194-205.

Explains forms of documentary literature. Gives scope of social sciences. Studies the degree of relevance of various forms of documentary literature to social scientists by conducting a survey on the subject of the users in the University of Delhi and Jawaharlal Nehru University.

Satija, M P 1346

Some new Indian sources of library and information science, 1985-88, *LISE*, 143-154.

Reviews various Indian sources on LIS published during 1985-88, such as bibliographies, union catalogues, biographical sources, directories, dictionaries, and state of the art works.

Sharma, Shobha 1347

Bridging the difference between information sources and literacy around the world : India's global view, *ILA Bull* 26(2) July-Sept 1990 : 73-79.

Discusses concept of literacy and information. Mentions role of information sources in making bridge to eradicate illiteracy around the world. Narrates the importance of information sources. Gives Govt of India plan to eradicate illiteracy. Describes role of libraries, library consciousness, users attitude, and willingness towards library services.

Sukhbir Singh 1348

Reference sources on Punjab : An evaluation, *Int Lib Move* 12(4) Dec 1990 : 180-190.

Defines reference book. Gives importance of reference sources in reconstructing Punjab history. Evaluates some right bibliographies on Punjab compiled by different authors in different periods to bring forth material on Punjab.

028.9 READING INTERESTS AND HABITS

Ananthakrishanan, G 1349

Inculcating the habit of reading, *Indian Express*, Nov 30, 1991, p 8.

States that reading is becoming a rare habit but in Tamil Nadu public libraries network is helping to develop it. Deals with the new eight-point programme. Stresses the need to increase library funds as cess is not enough to meet the rising needs of readers.

Choudhury, B K and **Mishra, Sanjaya** 1350

Survey of reading habits of PG students of Sambalpur University, *CLIS Observer* 7(3-4) July-Dec 1990 : 87-92.

Studies reading habits of PG students of the Sambalpur University, Orissa with special reference to their reading interests, time spent on reading and the nature of books preferred, etc. Uses questionnaire method distributed to 360 PG students of whom 288 responded.

Naik, M K 1351

The decline and fall of the well-read man, *CPT*, 6-8.

Describes how the species of well-read people is declining fast in this fast changing society. It is the time not of well-read but fast read people who swallow and not digest. Mentions three types of bad readers according to Coleridge : sponges, sand-glasses, and strain-bags.

PART-III

PUBLISHING, SOCIAL SCIENCES, LIBRARY LEGISLATION, AND OTHER RELATED SUBJECTS

039.914 Encyclopaedias in Modern Indian Languages

Padhi, P 1352

Puranic encyclopaedias in modern Indian languages : A literature survey, *CLIS Observer* 8(1-2) Jan-June 1991 : 6-13.

Highlights usefulness of Puranas in the modern age. Attempts to study the history and development of compilation of Puranic encyclopaedias from 19th century todate. Covers literature in 14 languages including English. Assesses the strength and weakness. Suggests some improved techniques and methods.

070.5 Publishing

Kumar, P S G and **Tejomurty, A** 1353

Printing and publishing: Technologies and trend-impact on library and information profession, *CPT*, 172-178.

Explains the impact of the new technology on authors, publishers and printers. Mentions two types of electronic publishing-online and ondisk. Elaborates use of PCs in database retrieval, full-text access, etc. Describes use of laser video disc in ISR. Discusses role of book and electronic publication in an information society, and both are complimentary to each other.

070.5 (1) Desktop Publishing (DTP)

Mohandas, M K, Seth, K C and **Pangannaya, N B** 1354

Cost effective Desktop publication, *IM*, 65 (Abstract only).

Analyses economies of DTP as a new documentation concept. Compares it with other conventional documentation techniques. Gives cost analysis of various documentation techniques, details capital layout and maintenance. Lists DTP manufacturers/suppliers. Concludes that in spite of little heavy investment in DTP, it is likely to become popular.

Nagi Reddy, Y 1355

Electronic publishing and its impact on libraries, *Univ News* 28(45) Nov 5, 1990 : 6-7,9.

Traces the history of technological inventions such as paper, printing press, photofilming, computers, etc. Describes the impact of electronic publishing as modern trends on information systems and services.

027.5068 Federation of Indian Publishers, Printers, etc.

Gupta, B M 1356

All India Federation of Master Printers, *HLAICI*, v 10, 1-6.

Gives aims and objectives of the Federation registered in 1985 with office in New Delhi. Discusses its activities such as conference/seminars, publications, education, etc. Lists its achievements in terms of concessions, etc.

Gupta, B M 1357

Federation of Indian Publishers (FIP), *HLAICI*, v 10, 57-65.

Gives aims and objectives, its structure and membership. Describes its international affiliation, nature of professional issues. Discusses Working Groups activities, broad activities as education and training, dissemination, fairs, seminars, publication, etc. Mentions its relation with Government. Gives future perspectives.

Gupta, B M 1358

The Federation of Publishers and Booksellers Association of India (FPBAI), *HLAICI*, v 10, 66-71.

Mentions aims and objectives, structure, membership and finance. Describes activities of FPBAI, and its publication. Discusses the nature of professional issues the Federation has been taking up.

090 MANUSCRIPTS

Collection of Oriental Manuscripts in the Federal Republic of Germany, *Her Lib Sci* 29 (1-2) Jan-Apr 1990 :67-68. 1359

Studies the availability of oriental Mss in the libraries of FRG on the basis of those catalogued in the *Catalogue of the Oriental Manuscripts in Germany* in 80 volumes of which more volumes are to be published.

Sarma, K V 1360

Manuscript collection in Tamil Nadu : A survey, *Granthana* 2(2) July 1991 : 155-162.

Presents a comprehensive survey of Mss in Tamil Nadu based on four types of collection, viz, hereditary/private collections, patronised collections, public collections and collections in private research institutions. Describes the language(s) of Mss and availability of catalogue/lists to enable scholars to identify required Mss.

Sarma, K V 1361

Variant readings and text reconstruction in Indian manuscriptology, *HLAICI* v 9, Pt 2, 466-473.

States the wealth of Mss in India. Gives condition and correctness of available Mss. Discusses textual corruption and variation in readings, involuntary and voluntary corruption. Discusses text reconstruction of the Mss.

211.6 Secularism

Gopal, S 1362

Secularism from Rammohun Roy to Jawaharlal Nehru, *Granthana* 1(1) Jan 1990 : 1-9.

Delivered as Keynote Address at the National Seminar on "Secularism in India: Rammohun to Nehru", organised by RRRLF in Calcutta on May 22, 1988. Describes the concept of secularism as a moral ethic in this context.

300 SOCIAL SCIENCES

Binwal, J C, **Chandel, A S** and **Saraf, Veena** 1363

Growth pattern of social science in a decade : A case study of sociology and economics, *SSI*, 84-94.

Attempts to study the growth pattern in different branches of sociology and economics on the basis of macro documentary output as determined by classification schedules in abstracting and indexing services as well as DDC 19.

Khan, Noorul Hasan and **Qureshi, I A** 1364

Structure and development of social science, *SSI*, 16-29.

Provides definition and nature of social sciences. Distinguishes between the social and natural sciences. Describes factors contributing to the development of social sciences. Gives an organic model as well as other models of Marx and Huxley. Discusses features of social sciences during 19th and 20th century.

Mohanrajan, P A 1365

Paradigm for social sciences in India, *SSI*, 123-130.

Defines social sciences. Traces their emergence. Mentions importance of social science study and research. Discusses social science paradigm in India as offered by the West. Describes the development of research and the social science in India in post-independent period. Provides different views of eminent social scientists.

300.72 Social Science Research

Kaula, P N 1366

Social science research in India : Pattern, development, dissemination and trend, *SSI*, 141-161.

Attempts to evaluate social science research depicting its problems in relation to India. Identifies disciplines. Discusses social science research and functions of research organization. Describes dissemination of social science research. Offers some suggestions.

Kumar, P S G 1367

Research in social science in South India : A survey and trends, *SSI*, 131-140.

Aims at knowing the state-of-affairs and stage-in-research in the major social science disciplines. Identifies structure and development of these disciplines. Gives assessment and trends.

301 SOCIOLOGY

Nikhlesh Kumar 1368

Structure and development of sociology, *SSI*, 30-52.

Describes sociology as a positive science. Traces the development of sociology from the perspective of the development of idea in the study of society. Focusses on the ideas concerning the nature of the phenomena and the method applied to understand phenomena. Provides salient features of the thinkers.

Sinha, Surajit Chandra 1369

Rammohun and Rabindranath : Their ideas on revitalisation of Indian society and civilization, *Granthana* 1(2) July 1990 : 1-13.

Delivered as the 'Raja Rammohun Roy Memorial Lecture, 1985'

in Calcutta on Oct 18, 1989. Enumerates the conceptualising of inner strength of Indian society and civilization in view of Rammohun and Rabindranath. Describes the evolution and maturing of ideas and outlook of the two personalities.

302.2 Communication

Boraiyan, R 1370

Communication of information : An instrument of research and development, *Ind Jl Inf Lib & Society* 4(3-4) Sept-Dec 1991 : 258-268.

Describes briefly the concept of information and its value in R & D activities. Delineates subtle distinction of information generation, storage, retrieval, dissemination in R & D organisation. States the process of communication, its process and channels. Outlines linkage of social groups involved in R & D with information sources through communication of information.

Tell, Bjorn 1371

Paperless communication, *INICAE* 9(2) Sept 1990 : 156-163.

Points out decline of printed information and its replacement by displayed information. Discusses the concept 'paperless communication' and status of database development stating special features of databases and their growth. Describes features of printed and displayed information. Discusses problems for future and need for professional training in information systems.

330 ECONOMICS

Misra, S K 1372

Structure and development of economics, *SSI,* 53-65.

Defines structure of economics. Discusses the main currents of economic thought before Adam Smith. Describes classical economics, neo-classical economics, Keynesian economics, and economics after 1950 giving current economic problems.

344.092 LIBRARY LEGISLATION

344.092 (1) Library Legislation – UK and India

Ramakrishnan, M N 1373

Legal provision for public library finance in UK and India, *PLSI*, 81-88.

Explains importance of library finance. Describes sources of finance for libraries in the UK as well as in India in different states with library Acts.

344.092 (1) Library Legislation – India

Abraham, Alexander 1374

Public library legislation in India, *PLSI*, 8-16.

Defines public library. Gives objectives, functions, essential requirements for library legislation. Describes the Indian scene from library law point of view. Discusses, among others, Kerala Public Libraries Act, 1989.

Barua, B P 1375

Model Public Libraries Bills – a critical review, *Granthana* 1(2) July 1990 : 15-23.

Gives a picture of library legislation in India. Makes a comparative study of Model Public Libraries Bill of Government of India, and that of the Planning Commission and Ranganathan. Discusses their impact on library legislation of different states.

Gopalakrishnan Nair, P 1376

Public library legislation in India : A national perspective, *PLSI*, 17-29.

Defines public library. Mentions need for legislation including resource sharing, financial support, economic development, etc. Describes public library development in India. Examines need for national public library legislation.

National Seminar on Model Public Libraries Act – Proceedings, *Granthana* 1(2) July 1990 : 59-61. 1377

Reports the proceedings of the National Seminar on Model Public Libraries Act organised by Indian Library Association in collaboration with RRRLF in New Delhi on 14 Feb 1990.

Ranganathan, S R 1378

Indian library manifesto, New Delhi : ABC Publishing House, 1990. 118 p.

Provides a blue-print – a dream and vision of author – for developing a National Grid of libraries for India. Contains all the papers of the author on library legislation. Includes 7 chapters with introduction by P N Kaula.

Venkatappaiah, V 1379

Indian library legislation, 2 volumes, Delhi: Daya Publishing House, 1990. 2 v.

Volume 1 : Union library bills and Acts, edited by C P Vashishth.
Volume 2 : Union library bills and Acts, edited by P S G Kumar.

Includes Act on books and libraries right from 1857. Discusses salient features, efforts for legislation, structure of the system, and working of the Act. Gives concept, need for library legislation and essential components of library legislation. Adds main features of National Policy of L & I Systems. In the Appendix gives full text of each Act.

Venkatappaiah, V 1380

Model Public Libraries Act, *ILA Bull* 26(3) Oct-Dec 1990 : 109-164.

Traces the history of library legislation and the role of the ILA in organising various conferences/seminars on the subject. Presents the final revised Model Public Libraries Act in 25 chapters which can be adopted by the states and union territories where there is no library legislation.

Venkatappaiah, V 1381

Model Public Libraries Act : Working document presented at the National Seminar, Feb 14, 1990, New Delhi, ILA, 1990, 75 p.

Discusses the detail about the public libraries act divided into 25 brief chapters. The Seminar was organised by the ILA and Raja Rammohun Roy Library Foundation on Feb 14, 1990 at New Delhi.

Venkatappaiah, V 1382

Public library acts in the states : A study, *ILA Bull* 26(4) Jan-Mar 1991 : 187-197.

Makes a study of the public libraries acts enacted in various states of India from such points as preamble, apex body, Head of the Dept, District unit chairman of the District Authority, manpower of the system, library fund, States Library Fund, position of library cess.

344.092 (1) Library Legislation – Assam

Buragohain, Alka 1383

A plea for library legislation in Assam, *CLIS Observer*. 7 (3-4) July-Dec 1990 : 99-102.

Makes a plea for library legislation in Assam. Compares the proposed legislation with other legislation in India and the UK.

344.092 (1) Library Legislation – Haryana

The Haryana Public Libraries Bill, 1989, *Granthana* 1 (2) July 1990 : 67-78. 1384

This Bill has since become an Act in Haryana to provide for the establishment, maintenance and development of public libraries in the state.

344.092 (1) Library Legislation – Kerala

Augustine, C A 1385

Kerala Public Libraries Act, 1989 : An appraisal, *PLSI*, 69-74.

Describes the special features of the Act passed in 1989 after a long wait. Discusses some aspects of prospective planning of library development in the state of Kerala.

Chandran, Manayath 1386

Kerala Granthasala Sangham Act : Background and special features, *PLSI*, 52-59.

Kerala Public Libraries Act is also called Kerala Granthasala Sangham Act, 1989. Provides background development and efforts at legislation. Examines the library organization as envisaged in the Act its salient features.

Devarajan, G 1387

Kerala Public Libraries Act 1989 : Guidelines for development plan with a perspective proposal for phased developmental programme, *PLSI*, 75-80.

States that the Act will envisage a proper development plan for establishing, maintaining, coordinating and spreading library service. Makes proposal for a phased development programme.

The Kerala Public Libraries (Kerala Granthasala Sanghom) Act, 1989, *PLSI*, 91-118. 1388

Provides the Kerala Public Libraries Act, 1989 as passed by the State Government and implemented in the state of Kerala.

Rajam, V 1389

Public library situation in Kerala and Kerala Public Libraries (Kerala Granthasala Sangham) Act 1989, *PLSI*, 64-68.

Provides public library situation in Kerala. Discusses Kerala Public Libraries (Kerala Granthasala Sangham) Act 1989, the administration under the Act, source for finance, etc.

Ramakrishnan, M N 1390

Kerala Public Libraries (Kerala Granthasala Sangham) Act, 1989 : An overview, *PLSI*, 60-63.

Explains the features and provisions as given in the Act of 1989 of Kerala. Mentions the response from library professionals.

Sunilkumar, K 1391

Library legislation in Kerala: A survey, *PLSI*, 43-51.

Traces origin of public library movement in Kerala. Describes history of library legislation in Kerala giving salient features of various draft bills till the enactment of the Act in 1989. Mentions various provisions of the Act in 1989. Mentions various provisions of the Act.

Summary of the Seminar proceedings and recommendations, *PLSI*, 89-90. 1392

Gives proceedings and recommendations of the seminar of Kerala Public Libraries Act 1989 organised in the Dept of Library and Information Science, Kerala University, Trivandrum on 25 September 1989.

Vasudevan, P 1393

Library legislation in Kerala, *PLSI*, 30-33.

Presents the thoughts about library legislation in Kerala aimed at creating a stimulus and invoking a response.

34.092(1) Library Legislation – Orissa

Shukla, B B 1394

State conference on library legislation for Orissa and UGC pay-scales for college and university librarians, Bhubaneswar, 2nd October, 1991, *Ind Jl Inf Lib & Society* 4(3-4) Sept-Dec 1991 : 305-321.

Reports about the Conference held on 2 Oct 1991 at Utkal University organised by *Ind Jl Inf Lib & Society* with Dr Shukla as convener, and attended by 147 delegates. Keynote address was given by Prof P N Kaula. Had two Technical Sessions. Mentions resolutions adopted.

344.092 (1) Library Legislation – Punjab

Narang, S P 1395

Public library legislation in Punjab : Problems and prospects, *PLSP*, 14-30.

Studies need of library legislation. States the present state of library service in Punjab. Describes role of Punjab Library Association. Discusses some problems of library legislation in Punjab and structural organisation under the proposed bill. States that Government should give required financial support from its resources.

344.092 (1) Library Legislation – West Bengal

Basak, Nanda Dulal and **Das, Binod Bihari** 1396

Library legislation and public libraries in West Bengal, *CPT*, 179-183.

Gives a brief review of public library situation prior to 1977 followed by coming of library legislation in West Bengal. Explains the developments in public libraries and their impact during the operation of the library law based on data collection upto 1987.

374.4 Distance Education

Sangam, S L 1397

Distance education to visually handicapped students : A computer assisted learning, *Int Jl Inf Lib & Society* 4(3-4) Sept-Dec 1991 : 280-284.

Mentions the blinds in India and need of distance education for these handicapped students. Explains the role of computer assisted learning. Mentions some research institution on blind.

378.54 Higher Education – India
Universities – India

Isaac, K A 1398

Should the affiliating system continue in our universities ? *Granthana* 1(2) July 1990 : 25-28.

Describes unitary and affiliating system in universities. Presents arguments in favour of unitary system as a remedy to the present maladies in higher education in India. Hints at a few action plans for implementation of the system at the national level.

384.51 Satellite Communication

Basu, Biman 1399

Satellite based communications; work of Indian satellites, *INICAE* 10(1) Mar 1991 : 84-85.

Describes the help given by the satellites in India since Aryabhatta days, in areas like broadcasting TV and radio programmes, trunk calls, forecasting the weather, surveying the natural resources, etc.

384.558 Videodiscs

Ramaiah, C K, Singh, A K and **Rajendran, V** 1400

Video discs and their applications, *IASLIC Bull* 35(2) June 1990 : 55-62.

States that video disc is one of the byproducts of optical disc family which is important tool both for business and professional applications. Reviews from origin to the present position of VDs including CD-IV and Hypermedia forms. Also gives features, advantages, disadvantages of the VDs.

418.02 Translation

Guha, B 1401

Translation services, *ISL*, 93-101.

Discusses types of translations, nature of translation work. Describes activities of some translation banks such as NTC, ITC, BLLD, etc. Discusses the need and importance of translation service to the Indian scientists.

Kaliyan, S and **Kasi Rao, V** 1402

Information dissemination; document translation – subject specialist v/s translator – who is better?, *RILISAR Bull* 7(1-4) Jan-Dec 1991 : 14-26.

Discusses concepts related to technical translation services and its role in information dissemination. Opines that translator should be a subject specialist wherever possible. Suggests recommendations in order to improve the translation activities in India.

Karisiddappa, C R, Maheswarappa, B S and **Nelogal, S B** 1403

Foreign language barrier among Indian scientists in a university environment, *INICAE*, 10(2) Sept 1991: 165-177.

Studies the foreign language knowledge, qualifications and reading ability; methods used for current awareness, missing of information published in foreign languages; the methods followed in overcoming the problem; awareness and use of existing translation tools etc. Suggests the strategy to solve the problem of foreign languages barrier among Indian scientists in a university environment.

Maheswarappa, B S and **Shashikala, K** 1404

The foreign language barrier among sericulture scientists in India, *ILA Bull* 26(1) Apr-June 1990 : 31-37.

Studies the foreign language ability, qualifications, reading ability, current awareness methods followed, action taken to overcome foreign language barrier, usefulness of translation services of INSDOC. Suggests measures to be taken to overcome the problems among sericulture scientists in India.

Maheswarappa, B S, Shashikala, K and **Nagaraj, S** 1405

The foreign language barrier among food scientists in India, *IASLIC Bull* 35(1) Mar 1990 : 35-41.

Studies foreign language knowledge, qualification and reading ability, methods used for current awareness and importance of scientific research report methods used for current awareness and importance of scientific research reported in foreign languages, measures taken to overcome the language barrier, usefulness of translation services of NICFOS and INSDOC. Suggests strategy for overcoming foreign languages problems among Indian food scientists.

Ramani, C M 1406

Indian Scientific Translators Association, *HLAICI*, v 10, 109-115.

Gives genesis of ISTA. Mentions aims and objectives, structure, membership, application. Discusses its activities as conferences and seminars, lectures, training courses, etc. Gives its publication and nature of professional issues. Reports the findings of the survey about their needs. Mentions about other activities and future programmes.

615.8516 Bibliotherapy

Joseph, Rosamma 1407

Bibliotheraphy, *Int Lib Move* 12(4) Dec 1990 : 198-200.

Defines bibliotherapy. Discusses need of bibliotheraphy. Explains its use in various countries. Describes the role of libraries in bibliotherapy. Projects also its future.

629.892 Robotics

CAD/CAM 1408

International robotics conferences, *INICAE* 10(2) Sept 1991 : 235-236.

Describes about the International Conference on CAD/CAM Robotics and Factories of the Future, December 19-22, 1989, held in IIT, New Delhi.

670 MANUFACTURING

Gupta, B M 1409

Manufacturers' Association for Information Technology (MAIT), *HLAICI*, v 10 116-121.

Gives history of MAIT. States aims and objectives. Mentions

about management, membership, reorganisation, services. Gives its representations on government forums. Discusses professional issues, interaction and representation.

808.092 Writers of Literature

Jafa, Manorama 1410

The Association of Writers and Illustrators for Children (AWIC), *HLAICI*, v 10, 31-35.

Describes the establishment, finances, activities of AWIC. States that it launched children's lending libraries scheme. Mentions about its publications. Gives some international activities.

910 GEOGRAPHY

Gopalakrishanan, R 1411

A review of structure and developments in geography, *SSI*, 66-83.

States overall definition of geography. Gives some observation about the subject. Describes the geographical approach. Discusses laws and explanations in geography. Gives the indigenous concepts. Provides the synthesis and general theory, system analysis. Outlines trends in geography.

954 Indian History
History of India

Pande, G C 1412

Reflections on the Indian renaissance, *Granthana* 2(1) Jan 1991 : 1-20.

Gives the meaning of renaissance. Explains the role of English education in influencing the new movement. Discusses concept of modernisation and Indian tradition and modern West. Explains that the model of English education adopted in India was different and it hindered the originality of thought and creativity, but also led to the adoption of a distorting of paradigm of historiography.

PART-IV

INDEXES

SUBJECT INDEX

AUTHOR INDEX

CICIL LIST

CONCEPTS IN COMMUNICATION, INFORMATICS & LIBRARIANSHIP

(CICIL)

General Editor: **S.P. AGRAWAL**

CICIL-1 Development of Library Services in India: Social Science Information
S.P. Agrawal Rs. 150

CICIL-2 Development of Documentation in India: Social Science Information
S.P. Agrawal Rs. 250

CICIL-3 UNESCO and Social Sciences: Retrospect and Prospect
S.P. Agrawal and **J.C. Aggarwal** Rs. 250

CICIL-4 INDIANA : A Bibliography of Bibliographical Sources
M.K. Jain Rs. 200

CICIL-5 Dimensions of Library and Information Science: Kaula Festschrift
V. Venkatappaiah (Eds.) Rs. 600

CICIL-6 Book Numbers: Some Indian Methods
M.P. Satija and **S.P. Agrawal** Rs. 100

CICIL-7 National Policy for University Libraries in India: Problems and Perspectives
N.B. Inamdar and **L.S. Ramaiah** (Ed.) Rs. 250

CICIL-8 Media Utilisation for the Development of Women and Children
B.S. Thakur and **Binod C. Agrawal** Rs. 150

CICIL-9 Terrorism: An Annotated Bibliography
Susheela Bhan (Ed.) Rs. 275

CICIL-10 Transnational Library Relations: The Indo-American Experience
M.B. Konnur Rs. 175

CICIL-11 Geography of Marketing and Commercial Activities in India (Documentation on Research Information)
R.S. Dixit Rs. 130

CICIL-12 Information India 1988: Global View
S.P. Agrawal and **J.C. Aggarwal** Rs. 200

CICIL-13 Women's Education in India: Historical Review, Present Status and Perspective Plan
S.P. Agrawal and **J.C. Aggarwal** Rs. 360

CICIL-14 Cultural Communication in India: Role and Impact of Phonograms
J.M. Ojha Rs. 220

CICIL-15 Second Historical Survey of Educational Development in India: Select Documents 1985-1989
S.P. Agrawal and **J.C. Aggarwal** Rs. 490

CICIL-16 Documentation Encyclopaedia of UNESCO and Education
J.C. Aggarwal and **S.P. Agrawal** Rs. 800 (set of 2 parts)

CICIL-17 Attitude Towards Information: A Study of Post-Graduate Teachers and Researchers in Social Sciences
N.G. Satish (in press)

CICIL-18 Librarianship and Bureaucratic Organisation: A Study in the Sociology of Library Profession in India
P.K. Jayaswal Rs. 175

CICIL-19 Literature Search
K.A. Isaac Rs. 150

CICIL-20 Child Education in India: Index to Scholarly Writings in Indian Educational Journals and Newspapers since independence
S.P. Agrawal and **Naresh Kanta** Rs. 100

CICIL-21 Lok Sabha and Vidhan Sabha Elections in India 1989 & 1990: Process and Results with Comparative Study of Manifestos
S.P. Agrawal and **J.C. Aggarwal** Rs. 250

CICIL-22 Islamic Studies in India: A Survey of Human, Institutional and Documentary Sources
Mohamed Taher Rs. 180

CICIL-23 Panchayati Raj: An Annotated Bibliography
N.B. Inamdar, N.G. Satish and **Anil Takalkar** 290

CICIL-24 Information India 1989-90: Global View
S.P. Agrawal and **J.C. Aggarwal** Rs. 500

CICIL-25 First Handbook of Psychological and Social Instruments
Udai Pareek and **T. Venkateswara Rao** Rs. 500

CICIL-26 Educational and Social Uplift of Backward Classes: At What Cost and How? Mandal Commission and After
S.P. Agrawal and **J.C. Aggarwal** Rs. 275

CICIL-27 Mass Media and New Horizons: Impact of TV & Video an Urban Milieu
H.R. Trivedi Rs. 180

CICIL-28 Indian Writings on Education : An Indicator to Indian Educational Journals Grouped by Subject Deseriptors 1979 to 1986 (in two parts)
S.P. Agarwal Rs. 900 (per set)

CICIL-29 Nation in Crisis
S.P. Agrawal and **J.C. Aggarwal** Rs. 200

CICIL-30 Information India 1990-91: Global View
S.P. Agrawal and **J.C. Aggarwal** Rs. 500

CICIL-31 Development of University Libraries in India after Independence
O.P. Gupta Rs. 270

CICIL-32 Handbook on Child : With Historical Background
Pramila Pandit Barooah Rs. 320

CICIL-33 Weaker Section in Indian Society : Undiscovered Past, Uncertain Present and Unpredictable Future : Index to Writings in Indian Scholarly Journals and 10 National Newspapers Classified under 1500 Descriptors 1886-1990
S.P. Agrawal and **Rajeev Kumar Sharma** Rs. 600

CICIL-34 Communication Informatics and Librarianship in India : An Introductory Guide to Publications Based on a Survey of Libraries in Capital City of India
S.P. Agrawal and **Pushpa Rani Sharma** Rs. 720

CICIL-35 Problems of Collection Development in Special Libraries
M.S. Sridhar Rs. 225

CICIL-36 National Information Resources for Social Sciences in India : Mobilisation, Dispersal and International Enhancement
S.P. Agrawal Rs. 225

CICIL-37 Modern History of Punjab : A Look Back into Ancient Peaceful Punjab Focusing Confrontation and Failures Leading to Present Punjab Problem, and a Peep Ahead : Relevant Select Documents
J.C. Aggarwal and **S.P. Agrawal** Rs. 400

CICIL-38 India Information Sources : Economics and Business
Kyllikki Ruokonen and **Manohar Lal** Rs.

CICIL-39 Educational Planning in India : With a Slant to Educational Financing and Administration, Vol. 1, Reports of Committees and Commissions, Five Year Plans, Statistical Tables
J.C. Aggarwal and **S.P. Agrawal** Rs. 650

CICIL-40 Integrated Library System : Two Case Studies : Latin America and India
Maria Luiza Rigo Pasquarelli, Rosaly Favero Krzyanowski, Ines Maria M. Imperatriz and S.P. Agrawal Rs. 160

CICIL-41 Social Science Information in India: Effort towards Bibliographical Control
S.D. Vyas Rs. 300

CICIL-42 Higher Education in India Since Independence: U.G.C. and Its Approach
O.P. Gupta Rs. 360

CICIL-43 Government and Politics in India: A Bibliographical Study of Contemporary Scenario Chronicling Rajiv Gandhi Era
S.P. Agrawal and **Rajeev Kumar Sharma** Rs. 500

CICIL-44 Second Handbook of Psychological and Social Instruments
D.M. Pestonjee Rs. 300

CICIL-45 Development/Digression Diary of India; 3D Companion Volume to Information India: 1990-91
S.P. Agrawal Rs. 200

CICIL-46 Development/Digression Diary of India; 3D Companion Volume to Information India: 1991-92
S.P. Agrawal Rs. 300

CICIL-47 Information India 1991-92: Global View
S.P. Agrawal and **J.C. Aggarwal** Rs. 500

CICIL-48 Committees and Commissions in India 1974, A Concept's Project, Compiled by a team of professionals guided by **Virender Kumar** (Vol. 12) Rs. 450

CICIL-49 Committees and Commissions in India 1975, A Concept's Project, Compiled by a team of professionals guided by **Virender Kumar** (Vol. 13) Rs. 450

CICIL-50 Committees and Commissions in India 1976, A Concept's Project, Compiled by a team of professionals guided **Virender Kumar** (Vol. 14) Rs. 450

CICIL-51 Committees and Commissions in India 1977, A Concept's Project, Compiled by a team of professionals guided by **Virender Kumar** (Vol. 15) (in four parts) Rs. 450 each

CICIL-52 Committees and Commissions in India 1978, A Concept's Project, Compiled by a team of professionals guided by **Virender Kumar** (Vol. 16) (in two parts) Rs. 450 each

CICIL-53 Subject Guide to Communication, Informatics and Librarianship in India (Based on a Survey of Library Holdings in Capital City of India)
S.P. Agrawal and **Pushpa Rani Sharma** Rs. 400

CICIL-54 Restructurring of Library and Information Science Curriculum
A. Tejomurty Rs. 250

CICIL-55 Committees and Commissions in India 1979, A Concept's Project, Compiled by a team of professionals guided by **Virender Kumar** (Vol. 17) (in two parts) Rs. 450 each

CICIL-56 Committees and Commissions in India 1980, A Concept's Project, Compiled by a team of professionals guided by **Virender Kumar** (Vol. 18) (in two parts) Rs. 450 each

CICIL-57 Third Historical Survey of Educational Development in India
S.P. Agrawal and **J.C. Aggarwal** Rs. 700

CICIL-58 Model Library Legislation
Velaga Venkatappaiah Rs. 400

CICIL-59 Indian Library and Information Science Literature (1990-91)
Sewa Singh Rs. 525